ARGUMENTATION
AND DEBATE

·The M Co·

ARGUMENTATION AND DEBATE

BY

CRAVEN LAYCOCK

ASSISTANT PROFESSOR OF ORATORY IN DARTMOUTH COLLEGE

AND

ROBERT LEIGHTON SCALES

INSTRUCTOR IN ENGLISH IN DARTMOUTH COLLEGE

New York

THE MACMILLAN COMPANY

LONDON: MACMILLAN & CO., LTD.

1905

Norwood Press
J. S. Cushing & Co. — Berwick & Smith Co.
Norwood, Mass., U.S.A.

TO

CHARLES FRANCIS RICHARDSON

TEACHER, COLLEAGUE

AND

FRIEND

PREFACE

THE growing recognition of the importance of Argumentation as a separate subject of study in American colleges, and the increasing emphasis which is put upon the necessity for a proper method of presenting it, are probably due to the appreciation of two facts. In the first place, it is coming to be acknowledged that Argumentation is a peculiar art, distinct from all others. Many of its principles are derived from the fundamental elements of other arts and sciences. Formal logic, rhetoric, oratory, and the rules of court procedure all contribute to it of their precepts; but though it is thus composite in nature, it is essentially a unified art, demanding investigation for its own sake. Furthermore, it is realized that argumentative skill does not belong exclusively to any one profession or class of men. To know how to argue is necessary not alone for the lawyer or the publicist, but equally for the preacher, the scientist, the business man, or, indeed, for any one who may wish to influence the opinions or actions of his fellows; it is a power which every educated man should have an opportunity to acquire. With these requisites in mind, the authors have made it their purpose, taking these component elements from their various sources, to develop from them a body of principles, by the study and practice of which the student may gain, so far as possible, the ability to create or control the beliefs of others.

Any one seeking by argumentation to influence the thoughts or acts of another must employ either the written symbol or the spoken word. In this day of the newspaper, the magazine, and the essay much of the most potent argumentation comes from the pen or the public press, so that the needs of the hour call for training in the written form. On the other hand, there is a large class of students who are in search of training for the court room, the deliberative assembly, or the platform. Consequently, the requisites of both these kinds of presentation must be recognized in any treatment of the art as a whole. Accordingly, with a view to these requirements, the following plan has been adopted in presenting the subject. The work is divided into two parts : the first contains a discussion of the general principles of argumentation, applicable alike to written and to spoken discourse ; the second part is devoted to the setting forth of certain additional precepts peculiar to oral debate. Finally, realizing that a thorough mastery of the subject can come only from continued practice, the authors have given, in the Appendix, a brief outline of the methods of instruction which they have found to be most serviceable, and have ventured a few suggestions which may prove helpful in supplementing the study of the text.

HANOVER, N.H.,
    May 30, 1904.

CONTENTS

BOOK IV

PRESENTATION

PART II

DEBATE

ARGUMENTATION
AND DEBATE

INTRODUCTION

ARGUMENTATION is the art of producing in others a belief in the ideas which we wish them to accept.

Belief is an element which is most truly fundamental in the ability of man to grow and in his power to create. It is the beliefs of the individual about religion, about politics, and about society, which determine his attitude toward men and events, and which govern his actions in the affairs of life. Moreover, a man's belief is rarely, if ever, entirely original: his creed is wrought out of the ideas of priests and prophets; his political principles are made up of materials taken from economists and statesmen; his social tendencies are influenced by the theories of philosophers and reformers; and in all his conceptions, far more than he can realize, he is influenced by the opinions of his daily companions. So that the revelation of truth and the establishment of justice in human affairs must depend largely upon the power of those who stand at any time for what is true and just, to control the convictions of their fellows and so to make them see the best and seek after it. What, then, of the art whose work it is "to produce beliefs in the minds of others"? Must it not be respected and cultivated as the embodiment of much that is worthiest in human thought and action?

But argumentation is worthy of respect and study, not simply because it is one of the noblest and most truly creative of the arts, but also because it is so nearly universal and indispensable. We find its uses made manifest in nearly every branch of affairs: in the legislative assembly the struggles of parties are settled and policies worked out from them by argument; in the court room it is argument which decides the conflicting claims of individuals, determines their rights and privileges, and regulates the duties of the citizen to the State; if churchmen meet to formulate their beliefs, they must argue in order to reconcile their varied ideas and tenets and harmonize them in a single creed; in the meeting room of the directors of a corporation it is by argument that its members determine what is honorable and what is expedient; and, wherever in the home or on the street men differ about their private concerns, they argue to adjust their differences and find the truth. Indeed, wherever active-minded men with opinions meet, there is sure to be argumentation.

The nature of argumentation, concerned as it is with the forces that control the thoughts and acts of men, discloses the first and most elementary of all its principles. There are two more or less distinct elements in human beliefs, viz., reason and emotion. Of these two elements it is sufficiently accurate to say that reason is the guiding power and emotion the moving power. Consequently, in order to make another individual think or act as we desire, we must, with rare exceptions, affect both these elements. Successful argumentation, therefore, must almost always be of a twofold nature : it must contain an appeal to the intellect and an appeal to the will; or, in other words, it must contain both conviction and persuasion.

By the force of pure reasoning a man may make others see that this or that statement is justified, that this or that argument is logical, or even that the whole idea he is contending for is true ; but it does not follow that he has made them believe in the propositions he advances. In order to make them fully accept his views of the matter or agree to act as he wishes, the arguer must also affect their wills by appealing to their emotions. The weakness of any argumentative effort which consists only of conviction, *i.e.* an appeal to the reason, is this : that, though the person addressed may *understand*, he may not really *believe*, because the impulses which give force to his inmost convictions, and which stimulate him to action, may not have been reached.

The purely emotional appeal is no more effective than the simple intellectual demonstration. It is of no advantage for a speaker or a writer to stimulate the moving impulses of his audience unless he can hold them in control; for he may find he has set free a force that is as likely to act to his detriment as to his benefit. Then, too, he will probably find that the effect of his appeal is but fleeting and unreliable ; he will find his hearers are only stirred to shallow and passing excitement, and that calm deliberation will reveal the unsubstantial nature of the argument and so leave their permanent beliefs unaffected.

Consequently, argumentation, "whatever be its form, proposes to itself two objects : (1) to convince the hearer that the contemplated act is his duty, or will promote his virtue or his happiness; and (2) to urge upon him the ideas which are embodied in the act with such force as to arouse in him a controlling impulse to perform it." [1]   The proportion of conviction and persuasion in any particular case must, of course, depend upon the circumstances : in a college debate little persuasion is needed; the campaign orator uses but little conviction.   Both, however, are necessary in all effective argumentation.

Whatever the relative amounts or importance of conviction and persuasion, in every piece of argumentative work there are four processes indispensable in the execution : (1) to find out just what you want to establish; (2) to gather the materials needed for the proofs ; (3) to arrange these materials ; (4) to present them in good rhetorical or oratorical form. For convenience we may name these four processes respectively (I) Invention, (II) Selection, (III) Arrangement, and (IV) Presentation.

I. *Invention* consists in determining upon those ideas in the truth of which the speaker or writer wishes to make his hearer or reader believe.   No man can hope to influence the beliefs of others unless he first

---

[1] Robinson, "Forensic Oratory."

has in his own mind an exact idea of the convictions he wishes to inculcate, and a clear conception of the points of fact he must establish to convince his readers or hearers, and the kinds of emotional appeal he must use to persuade them.

II. *Selection* consists in choosing from all the sources of human knowledge those facts and inferences that will serve to establish the ideas determined upon. Of all the evidence and arguments that may be found on any question, the arguer can use and wishes to use a comparatively small amount, and his success must depend in great degree upon his tact and good judgment in choosing for his use those materials that will appeal strongly to the minds and hearts of those he seeks to influence.

III. *Arrangement* consists in ordering these selected materials in such a way as to secure the maximum effect upon the beliefs of the persons addressed. However valuable the facts or appeals chosen for use may be, their efficiency will depend upon the plan in accordance with which they are utilized, for they cannot be presented clearly or forcibly except as they are brought into proper relations with each other and with the whole proof.

IV. *Presentation* consists in putting the materials into good rhetorical or oratorical form. To convey to another the ideas invented, selected, and arranged, demands a many-sided skill. In written argument it calls for the application of the principles of rhetoric; in spoken argument it calls for oratorical ability; in

debate it calls for the peculiar powers of resource
and adaptability which the circumstances of this form
of controversy demand.

In view, then, of the nature and relations of these
steps mentioned above, the First Part of the following text, which consists of a discussion of the general
principles of argumentation, will be divided into four
Books, corresponding to these four processes.   It
should, however, be clearly understood that this division of the Part is simply for convenience.   It does
not mean that there are any distinct lines of demar-
cation between these various processes : in any piece
of argumentation the progress is continuous, from
the first conception of the ideas to be considered to
the final presentation, and any separation of it into
parts must be more or less arbitrary, and is here
attempted only because it may help in presenting
some of the fundamental principles with greater
clearness.

The dividing of the text into two Parts is more
significant.   Debate, by which in this connection we
mean oral controversy between two opposing sides
on some definite question at some definite time, is but
one of the many forms of argumentative effort ; but
the conditions surrounding this particular kind of discussion are unique, and consequently require adaptations of the general principles of the art and make
necessary the supplementing of these general principles with a few special rules and precepts.   Consequently the Second Part, which is devoted to a

consideration of Debate, though closely connected with the preceding chapters and dependent upon the principles therein enunciated, is parallel with the discussion in the First Part rather than one with it.

It must, however, not be assumed, because particular consideration is given to oral controversy, that this is the most important branch of the art. Quite the contrary is true. In the first place, to-day the printed symbol exerts quite as potent a mastery over the beliefs of men as does the spoken word. Then again, reliable strength in debate can only be developed by thorough study of the written form of presentation; for constant and careful practice with pen and ink is the only sure source of many of the qualities of mind and temper that are most truly indispensable in a good debater. The ability to analyze keenly, skill in making accurate definitions, the habit of logical and forcible arrangement of ideas, are powers that can be acquired only by the close application and self-study that can be found to the best advantage in writing. The spoken form of argumentation calls for special treatment because some of its circumstances and attributes are distinctive, but the general principles of the art as a whole are best presented and studied in the written forms.

Bearing in mind the necessity for resolute practice in writing, the student should remember that in the effort to become master of any art there will always be a time when matters of detail and the careful study of methods will seem irksome. The musician and the

painter find little that is inspiring in those days spent
in running the scales or learning to hold the brush;
but they must realize that these are the rudiments
from which at length are made the noble symphony
and the beautiful landscape.   So with the beginner
in argumentation : he is likely to feel that many of
the lesser rules and precepts are but fetters that only
chafe him and hold him back.   This suspicion may
well seem to be confirmed by his experiences; he
may see his former spontaneity and self-assurance
gone, and find himself tripping and stumbling over
laws and borne down by criticism.   But he must be
patient and have faith that at length these troublesome technicalities will be forgotten, slowly growing
into those unconscious habits of mind which always
constitute the real strength of the master.

PART I
ARGUMENTATION

BOOK I. INVENTION

CHAPTER I

THE PROPOSITION

ARGUMENTATION differs, at the very outset, from any of the other kinds of rhetorical composition in one important particular. In any of the three other forms, we may have for our subject a simple word or phrase, denoting merely some general concept existing in the mind, which we wish to portray for our reader. If we wish to write a narrative, we may choose some such subject as " The Battle of Manila," or " An Ascent of the Jungfrau." For an exposition we might well select such a topic as " The New York Clearing House," or " Forest Fires ; Their Cause and Their Prevention," — these phrases would make excellent titles for compositions of this nature ; but in argumentation such terms would be wholly valueless.

To take an example : suppose a student desiring to write an expository discourse should determine on the title, " Bimetallism." This would be a worthy subject ; he could, in his composition, treat of the history of the movement in favor of this plan, explain the economic principles involved, portray the operation of these principles and their effect upon political and industrial conditions, and so forth, thus making of the whole an exposition of the nature and workings of bimetallism.   But as the subject of an argumentative effort this term would be useless, for it does not suggest anything definite to be proved or disproved; it does not state any belief which the writer wishes his reader to accept.   The author might discuss any one of a dozen ideas or beliefs; he might argue that the United States should adopt a bimetallic standard at the ratio of sixteen to one; that the bimetallic standard was a benefit to industrial conditions in Mexico; that international bimetallism is impracticable.   If this argument took the form of a discussion between two opposing sides, the opponents would probably turn out to be arguing two entirely different questions, never meeting each other on any one definite issue.   The result might be an interesting discussion, but it would not be a debate.

The reason is obvious why such a phrase as that suggested is not adapted to argumentation.   Argumentation deals with "beliefs."   But a belief or an opinion cannot be accurately expressed in a word or a phrase.   It demands a complete statement, a full sentence.   To return to our illustration, in order to express any definite belief about "bimetallism," we must expand this word into a complete sentence, such as: The adoption of the bimetallic standard in the ratio of sixteen to one would be detrimental to American industry.   With the subject in such form as this, the writer has a single idea to establish or destroy, the reader has a single definite belief to accept or reject, and if two opposing parties take up this subject they must meet on a distinct and unavoidable issue, and one must overthrow the other.

Perhaps the difference explained above, between the kind of subject required in argumentation and the kind required in the other forms of composition, may be made clearer by adopting the distinction, made by the older writers in rhetoric, between a *term* and a *proposition*. A term is any word, or phrase, or combination of words other than a sentence. A proposition we may define as a statement that something is or is not. To illustrate: in the case cited above, " bimetallism," " international bimetallism," " bimetallism at the ratio of sixteen to one," are all terms; " The adoption of the bimetallic standard would be detrimental to American industry " is a proposition. Bearing this distinction in mind, we may say that a term may be properly used as the subject of any other form of composition, but in argumentation a proposition is necessary.

This necessity of having a proposition is not always realized. In a certain historical club there was assigned as the topic of an evening's debate, " William Pitt's Place in English History." A few of the disputants spoke of his parliamentary abilities, of his power as an orator and political leader; others gave their attention to a consideration of his statesmanship, commending his foreign policy or criticising his selfishness and unscrupulousness; others com-

mented on his personality and his private life; and
so on, each speaker looking at the subject from his
own point of view, and no one endeavoring to prove
or disprove any particular proposition. The discussion was in many ways interesting, but as a
debate the evening's work was a failure; no one had
been induced to accept any definite belief about the
subject, and no conclusion had been established.
In order to turn the discussion into a debate which
should have some certain result, the subject should
have taken some such form as: *Resolved*, that William Pitt was the greatest parliamentary leader of the
eighteenth century; or, William Pitt's conduct of
Irish affairs was detrimental to the interests of the
Irish people. The disputants made the mistake of
trying to argue a term.

In contrast with the method of this historical club,
call to mind the court of law. Here it is necessary
that the deliberations accomplish definite results.
There must be no waste of time or energy, and the
end of it all must be a final settlement of the question presented for consideration. With these purposes
in mind, the court of law demands that whenever any
question is brought before it, "pleadings" be made
and that these pleadings "shall set forth with cer-
tainty and with truth the matters of fact or of law,
the truth or falsity of which must be decided to
decide the case." In other words, the court demands
that any man who would argue before it must, before
he begins his demonstration, make a clear and un-

mistakable proposition, stating the things that he intends to prove true or false.

The making of a proposition is of great advantage to the reader or hearer in enabling him to understand the discussion and get some real fruit from it. But it is no less an advantage to the writer or speaker. In the first place, if he does not know the exact proposition in issue, he is almost sure to waste time and effort in arguing about matters that are wholly outside the real question and in proving things that are "beside the point." Then again, he must know the proposition in order to understand the position taken by his opponent, and so be enabled to refute him. The proposition is simply a statement of the things the writer or speaker must establish or destroy, and he cannot expect to be successful, either in positive proof or in refutation, unless he understands just what is the work necessary for him to do.

The proposition may be expressed or not as circumstances seem to require. In a deliberative assembly, such as the House of Representatives, it would be found expressed in the form of some bill or resolution. In the court of law it is put into the shape of pleadings, as explained above. In an intercollegiate debate it would take the guise of a question mutually agreed upon beforehand. Indeed, it should always be expressed unless there is some particular reason for not doing so. The formulating of it always makes the proof clearer to the reader or the audience, and so makes the proof of more lasting impression upon their minds. To state the proposition in words is also often an effective method of exposing the weakness or sophistry of an opponent who is "begging the question," arguing "beside the point," or evading the issue. Sometimes circumstances render such a statement undesirable or impossible. A speaker in a political campaign, or a man who happens to be drawn into some newspaper controversy, might well find it awkward to put his case into the form of a cut-and-dried statement. But, even then, and indeed under all circumstances whatever, it is advisable to have clearly in mind a definitely formulated proposition.

In brief, then: As the first step in any work of argumentation, always formulate a proposition. A proposition is a statement that something is or is not.

Methods of formulating the Proposition

Now that we have seen the necessity of having a proposition either in the mind or on paper, the question arises: How can we best find and formulate this proposition? The formulating of the proposition is not always an easy matter. To begin with, it is not always easy to determine just what is the question really in issue; it may be obscured by the words of the discussion; it may become confused with other kindred but different questions; it may be separated with difficulty from the general problem that embraces it. Then again it is often difficult to put the question into words after it is found. Looseness in expression, ambiguity, the failure to know the true acceptations of the words in the proposition, are mistakes fruitful in possibilities of serious error. The writer must know how to find out what it is he wants to prove and how to express himself in such a way that there can be no question as to his exact meaning.

The process of formulating the proposition naturally divides itself into three parts : (*A*) Finding out what is the real question at issue, *i.e.* the facts and ideas, the truth or falsity of which must be decided to decide the question. (*B*) Formulating the question in words. After the facts in issue have been determined on, they must be expressed in the form of a complete statement. Then the statement must be tested by a definition of its terms to find out just what the statement means as it stands. (*C*) Comparing the meaning of the statement so expressed with the meaning of the real question in issue, *i.e.* comparing the results of the first and second processes. If the statement thus formulated does not express just what is intended, it must be modified until it does. Whatever the circumstances, these three steps, though they are usually so intermingled as not to seem like separate operations, must always be taken in order to find the true proposition.

A. Finding out what is the question really in discussion, *i.e.* the facts or ideas the truth or falsity of which must be decided to decide the question.

The student starting out in his search after the proposition will usually find that it exists originally

c

in his mind in the shape of some problem of a general nature. This problem, we have already seen, is of too vague and indefinite a character to be a fit topic for an argumentative effort. In order to develop from it a suitable proposition, it must be narrowed down and restricted within the bounds of some concrete and particular issue. The work, then, of determining on the exact question to be discussed is largely the work of selecting out of a broad and general problem some single, concrete, and limited issue.

In performing the work of this first step there is no exact rule or method for all cases. Sometimes it may be necessary for the disputant-to-be to examine the contents of his own mind. More often it becomes desirable to do a considerable amount of preliminary reading and investigation in connection with the search. But, whatever the circumstances, the "narrowing down" process is essentially the same, and there are certain steps that are always serviceable.

In the first place, it is generally helpful to consider the conditions under which the question arose. If the writer will understand just how he came to be interested in the problem he has in his mind, he will be able to see more clearly just what is the phase of it with which he is most concerned and which he desires to discuss ; or, if he is investigating the problem by the reading of books or current magazines, the matters really in issue will take more definite form in proportion as he understands the circumstances that generated them and brought them into discussion. Secondly, after gaining a comprehension of the origin of the question, it remains for him to *analyze*, according to his own natural methods, the ideas embraced within the general problem as it exists in his own mind or in the minds of others, in this way selecting the parts he wishes to consider and classifying them in such a manner that the result shall be a single, distinct, and concrete question.

To take an example: Let us suppose that a student in want of a debatable proposition finds himself interested in "the labor problem." He cannot argue "the labor problem"; it is merely a term, and is too vague and indefinite an idea. He must "narrow it down." To do this, he first considers the origin of the question; he finds, perhaps, that his interest has been aroused by some magazine article discussing compulsory arbitration as a cure for strikes, or by some comment among his friends on the incorporation of labor unions. Having gone thus far, it remains for him to analyze his ideas and so reduce the question still farther. Is it in the United States that he thinks labor unions should be incorporated? Further, does he believe they ought to be incorporated under State laws or under Federal laws? Does he want to consider only the incorporation of the unions, or does he wish to discuss the kindred issue of the desirability of a compulsory arbitration law? And so he goes on, interrogating his own mind, till perhaps he phrases his question as follows:

Resolved, that in the United States labor unions should be compelled to incorporate under Federal laws.

If this work of analysis is done properly, the result is a proposition. But this is only the first step; the question still remains: Is this the proposition? Does it contain the ideas the student has in mind? The statement thus made must be tested to see if it expresses just what the writer intends.

This testing of the proposition as first formulated is very important. A carelessly constructed sentence may result in the making of a proposition which is very far from the embodiment of the writer's ideas. And this carelessness may have very serious results. In an intercollegiate debate, a false grammatical construction or the choice of a wrong word may mean the difference between victory and defeat. To avoid these dangers, care must be taken that each word of the statement, and the statement as a whole, shall be capable of but one interpretation.

The failure to understand the exact meaning of a given proposition is often evidenced in the class room. Take, for illustration, a discussion of the question: *Resolved*, that labor unions in the United States are detrimental to the industrial interests of the country. In a debate on this proposition, the affirmative admitted that the principle of the organization of labor was right, and that labor unions ought to exist in some form; "but," they said, "labor unions to-day are detrimental because they inflict certain injuries on the consumer and the employer, by such means as strikes, the limitation of output, the uniform wage scale," etc. The negative said, in substance, "We admit that labor unions declare strikes, and that strikes are bad; we admit that the unions sometimes limit output; but we contend that on the whole the unions are not detrimental, because the industrial conditions would become worse if they did not exist at all." Clearly the two sides did not meet at all in the discussion. They were arguing two different questions. The affirmative was arguing whether or not the policies and principles of the unions at that time were such as to do greater injury than good to industry; the negative was arguing the question whether or not labor ought to be organized at all. The confusion arose from a failure to find out what the proposition really meant. It meant either the one thing or the other, but, in the same debate, it could not mean both. The discussion could not bring about any result till it had been settled what was the true interpretation of the question. The disputants had found *a* proposition, but not *the* proposition.

B. Clearly, then, the next step is that of testing the statement that has been formulated, to find out just what it means as it stands. Each word that may be at all ambiguous must be examined and its true intent discovered, and the grammatical structure of the sentence and the relation of the words to each other must be investigated, in order to be sure of the

rightful interpretation to be put upon the statement
as a whole. This work of testing the meaning of the
proposition may be called *definition*.

The word "definition" suggests a simple and easy
task. "Look in Webster or the Standard Dictionary,
and the work is done." But this is a mistake.
Sometimes the statement is so simple that very little
effort is necessary to be sure of its meaning. But
often to test properly a proposition is a long and
complicated process.

To take an example : Suppose a student is trying
to prepare some question for an intercollegiate
debate. He finds himself vaguely interested in some
of the problems of the Far East, perhaps in the so-
called "Chinese Question." By a careful scrutiny of
his own ideas, or by reading in books and magazines,
he finds that it is the political aspect of the problem
that most interests him. He further analyzes the
political conditions in the Far East and selects what
seem to him the fundamental facts in the situation
and the most vital issues that have arisen from them.
He soon finds that there are two really important
questions embraced within this Chinese problem : the
first is the question as to the possibility or the desirability of preserving China's territorial integrity ; the
second, the question as to what rights and privileges
China should be allowed to hold as a nation among
the nations, the question as to whether her powers as
a sovereign nation should be in any way destroyed or
curtailed. The student finally decides that it is the

latter of these two issues in which he is most interested ; the question he wants to discuss is the question
whether or not China shall be allowed to conduct all
her internal affairs with the perfect freedom of a
sovereign state, without interference from other
states. He finds that the writers whom he has been
reading have frequently used, in this connection, the
word "independence," so he adopts the word and
makes the following statement : *Resolved*, that the
independence of the Chinese Empire should be preserved. He has taken the first necessary step ; he
has reduced the general problem to a specific question
and has put it into the shape of a proposition. But
is this statement *the* proposition ? Does it accurately
express what he intends ? Clearly the word that may
be ambiguous is the word "independence." He
starts out to define that word. He first consults
Webster's Dictionary, and he finds there this definition : "Exemption from reliance on others or control
by them." This definition seems to fit his idea ; but
if he is wise he will not accept it. The definition is
valueless. The dictionary merely gives the acceptation
of the word in its general usage. This question of
Chinese independence is a question of international
relations, and the term "independence" is a technical
term in the code of the law of nations. "Independence," then, must have the special meaning given it
in international law.

The student must seek this special meaning. He
may look in some larger dictionary, which will ex-

plain the term in its technical interpretation; if he is wise, he will directly consult the international law authorities themselves. In Lawrence's " Principles of International Law," p. 111, he would find the following: " Independence may be defined as the right of a state to manage all its affairs, whether external or internal, without interference from other states, as long as it respects the corresponding right possessed by each fully sovereign member of the family of nations."

This would surely seem to be a final definition. But if the student should go into a debate with that as his understanding of the word, he would probably meet with an unpleasant surprise. If he should carry his investigation farther, he would find that there are exceptions to the rule laid down in the definition, exceptions that are really a part of the rule of law. He will find that one nation or a group of nations may directly interfere in the external or internal affairs of another nation without violating that nation's rights of independence, provided the intervening nations are interfering in order to protect their own rights of sovereignty. He would find further that the theory of independence permits a nation, even when its own sovereign rights are not endangered, to interfere in the affairs of another nation and restrict the exercise of some of its natural rights of sovereignty, provided the restrictions imposed are of a certain limited nature as to their extent and duration. These exceptions are as important as the so-called " definition " itself. In fact, the debate, if well argued, would probably turn on the truth of these exceptions and their application to the question.

An understanding of the true meaning of this word "independence" could only be found by this painstaking investigation. No less careful or less thorough definition could have disclosed the import of the word ; and this accurate knowledge was indispensable in order to make the proposition of any real value.

In the case of nearly every such definition, the same method has to be pursued. First, find its ordinary acceptation. Second, determine whether it may have any meaning that is technical or in any way peculiar. If it does have such a peculiar meaning, the definition must be sought in the exposition of some writer who will explain this special interpretation. If it is a term in science, go to the specialist in that science ; if a political phrase, go to the statesman or historian ; if a legal term, go to the jurist. Third, even after the definition is obtained from a good authority, consider the questions : Are the terms of this definition that I have found exact ? Are there any exceptions to the general statement ? The exceptions sometimes *destroy* the rule.

These, then, are the first two processes in formulating the proposition : *A*, finding out just what the ideas are that make up the question, and stating these ideas as accurately as possible ; and *B*, testing this statement by a definition of its terms in such a way as to find out just what the proposition means as it stands, to see if it is the true expression of these ideas.

C. For the third and last step, it only remains to compare the results of the first two processes. If the work of definition shows the statement as originally formulated to be inaccurate or ambiguous, if it is found that the tentative proposition does not express the ideas that the author intended it to express, then the statement must be changed till it finally does put into words, clearly and accurately, the real question.

In choosing a proposition there is one precaution that needs especially to be observed : the error must be avoided of combining two separate ideas in a single proposition ; two questions, closely akin to one another but really distinct from each other, may easily become confused and be carelessly joined together in a single statement. For example, students often devise such propositions as, *Resolved*, that a high protective tariff is hostile to the economic interests of the United States, and reciprocal trade relations should be established with the Dominion of Canada ; or, *Resolved*, that labor unions are detrimental to industry, and they should be compelled to incorporate. Now in each of these propositions there are two problems presented ; these problems are similar in the nature of the ideas contained in them, but the issues to be determined are very different.   The proofs necessary to establish the fact that labor unions are detrimental to industry are not at all the same proofs required to show that they should be compelled to incorporate; so that the attempt to combine in one demonstration what are really two distinct proofs must result in confusion.   We may handle each of these questions separately, but we cannot hope to treat them successfully at the same time.   Consequently, in formulating our ideas, we must be sure not only to have the form of a proposition, but to have a single proposition.

CHAPTER II

THE ISSUES

THE issues are the ideas or matters of fact upon the establishment of which depends the establishment of the proposition.

We have seen, in the preceding chapter, that, in order to have intelligent argumentation, we must first have a proposition. The formulating of the proposition insures that we have one single question that can be argued directly and so brought to a definite conclusion. This proposition thus makes clear the general position which the disputant must maintain.

But the disputant is not yet ready to select the evidence or the arguments with which to support his proof. He has merely found the field of battle. Before he can open the fight, or even arrange his forces, he must examine the ground he has chosen, find out its points of vantage and of weakness; he must decide just where to make his intrenchments and what plan of operations to adopt. The proposition discloses the task that must in the end be accomplished, but it does not show what are the steps necessary in the accomplishment, or just what method may be most effective.

The proposition gives a single question for discussion; but even in any such single question there are innumerable arguments and great masses of evidence that may be brought forward. All these arguments and all this evidence cannot be used; it is not all of equal value; some of it will have such a direct and obvious bearing on the question that it must have great significance; but much of it will have such an indefinite and remote bearing that to use it at all would be a waste of time. Clearly, then, the next thing for the disputant to do is to get some standards by reference to which he can determine the value of these materials. In order to know what proofs to use, he must first find out just what are the points he needs to establish by the proofs.

In any question, among the endless array of facts and arguments, there are always certain facts that are critical. These few facts are so vital that the whole question must hinge on them. A century and a half ago, John Ward, in his "System of Oratory," said: "But in all disputes it is of the greatest consequence to observe where the stress of the controversy lies. For, without attending to this, persons may cavil about different matters, without understanding each other or deciding anything." In any discussion the "stress of the controversy" inevitably falls upon the proving or disproving of a few points, which are the centre and soul of the question; whichever side wins in the struggle over these

points wins the whole contest. These points are
always the same in the same question : they exist
independently of the wills of the disputants; they
are to be *discovered*, not *invented*. These facts are
the issues.

To use the terms employed by Professor Robinson
in his book on " Forensic Oratory," there are both
" primary issues " and " subordinate issues."   " Every
cause, civil or criminal, consists of one or more propositions either of fact or of law, affirmed upon the
one side and denied upon the other. . . .   Each of
these primary issues may in its turn contain other
issues either simple or complex, whose determination
is essential to the determination of the issues which
include them. . . .   Thus in the charge of burglary,
the defendant may deny the breaking, on the ground
that the door by which he entered was ajar." [1]
These primary and secondary issues are found in all
argumentation.   The use of them in the law courts differs slightly from their use in argumentation elsewhere
in this : in a court the primary issues are declared and
set forth in the pleadings, before the real argument
begins ; whereas in ordinary argumentation the finding and explaining of these primary issues is part of
the proof itself.   But under all circumstances these
issues and the method of finding them are essentially
the same.

The primary issues in both cases must be sought
first.   The outcome of the argument may depend

[1] Robinson, " Forensic Oratory," p. 62.

almost entirely on the establishment of some one or more of the subordinate issues; as, in the instance cited from Professor Robinson, the question of the guilt of a man charged with breaking and entering hangs on the seemingly small fact that the door was slightly ajar. "A thing insignificant in itself may be very significant in its consequences." But the significance of any such *subordinate* issue is derived from the fact that it affirms or denies one of the *primary* issues, so that its bearing and importance cannot be understood until one knows the primary issue which it serves to establish. The primary issues, then, must be found first.

Hereafter, in this book, the term "the issues" will be used to designate the primary issues. When any other issue is referred to, it will be specifically called a "subordinate issue."

The necessity of knowing the issues is obvious. Without an understanding of them the proposition is nothing more than a name. Argument on any question implies some difference of opinion; it means that there are certain ideas affirmed by one side and denied by the other. The proposition is merely an expression of this clash of opinion, and an understanding of its meaning depends entirely upon a comprehension of the points of conflict. If the writer would prove his proposition, he must prove these critical points. Moreover, the value of his materials depends upon their relation to these points: any evidence that gives a direct and substantial support to these vital facts is valuable; whatever does not bear directly on these facts is, at best, of secondary importance.

If a disputant makes a mistake in finding these critical points on which the discussion must turn, he may well spend his time in proving some fact that will not help him after it is proved. This danger is realized and guarded against in the courts of law. They demand that the issues shall be clearly stated in the beginning, and that every piece of evidence, whether of fact or of law, shall have a direct and evident bearing on some one of these issues, anything that cannot conform to this test being declared irrelevant and being excluded from consideration. Then again, a speaker or writer who does not know the issues will probably confuse his readers or hearers by giving them a false, distorted view of his case. If a disputant does not comprehend just what are the few vital points of his case, around which all the lesser facts must be grouped, his proof will almost certainly lack the unity and coherence that are indispensable for clearness and force in presentation. The issues serve to gather and bind together the materials of the proof, making them a single, manifest whole.

The Method of finding the Issues

(1) In any question there are a great many facts that clearly cannot be the critical points that make up the issues. There are many ideas and facts that

are commonly associated with the proposition which do not really have any important bearing on it. These should be carefully put aside at the outset. Then again, there are many other facts which are properly embraced within the meaning of the question which may be very valuable as evidence to prove other facts, but which manifestly are not important in themselves. For illustration, in a civil suit for damages in a court of law the honesty or the intelligence of a witness might, under some circumstances, become very significant, the establishment of some vital point depending upon his reliability. Yet the character of this witness would not be mentioned in the pleadings as one of the issues, for his credibility is not important in itself, but only because of its effect upon some other and larger point in the case. In seeking the issues, the first step should be to exclude such facts as these, which are manifestly of only secondary importance.

The following, taken from Mr. Jeremiah S. Black's speech " In Defence of the Right of Trial by Jury," illustrates the effective use of this method. Here the speaker found his issues by the exclusion of irrelevant matter.

" The case before you presents but a single point and that an exceedingly plain one. It is not encumbered with any of those vexed questions that might be expected to arise out of a great war. You are not called upon to decide what kind of rule a military commander may impose

upon the inhabitants of a hostile country which he occu-
pies as a conqueror, or what punishment he may inflict
upon the soldiers of his own army or the followers of
his camp; or yet how he may deal with civilians in a
beleaguered city or other place in a state of actual siege
which he is required to defend against a public enemy.
The contest covers no such ground as that. The men
whose acts we complain of erected themselves into a
tribunal for the trial and punishment of citizens who were
connected in no way whatever with the army or navy.
And this they did in the midst of a community whose
social and legal organization had never been disturbed
by any war or insurrection, where the courts were wide
open, where judicial process was executed every day
without interruption, and where all the civil authorities,
both State and National, were in the full exercise of their
functions. . . .

" Keeping the character of the charges in mind, let us
come at once to the simple question upon which the court
below divided in opinion : Had the commissioners jurisdiction, were they invested with legal authority to try the
relators and put them to death for the offence of which
they were accused ? "[1]

(2) But the fault of taking too many facts under
consideration in fixing upon the issues is probably not
so common as the fault of considering too few facts.
The issues cannot be found without a complete understanding of the proposition in all its phases. The
phase that is, on hasty judgment, passed over as
seemingly insignificant often develops with careful
scrutiny into some new line of thought and discloses

---

[1] " Great Speeches by Great Lawyers," pp. 484, 485.

a new and vital issue. "In science, the residual phenomenon will sometimes pull down the hypothesis that has explained everything else. . . . The older naturalists had framed a complete theory of genera and species, but neglected variation; and yet these despised variations became, in the hands of Mr. Darwin, the key to the history of creation." Nothing that is relevant can safely be ignored, however much it may seem a matter of detail. The question must be thoroughly investigated in all its phases before any attempt is made to find issues.

(3) Akin to this study of all the phases and points of view is the necessity of knowing both sides of the question. With a knowledge of only his own side, a disputant may invent some points that he decides he will prove; but he cannot know the real issues. The issues are always the points on which there is a conflict of opinion. To determine where this conflict is, he must obviously know what his opponents maintain, what they are willing to admit, and what they deny. Consequently there is nothing that will help more to reveal the critical points in any discussion than to compare the arguments advanced by the conflicting sides.

(4) When we have gained the proper knowledge of all the facts, the process is then a process of selection.

The first step of selection that may be taken is *the exclusion of admitted matter*. Clearly, if both sides admit the truth of a certain idea, that idea cannot be a critical point. The clash of opinion cannot arise from such a point, so that it is practically irrelevant in the question. By excluding such facts as these, we can narrow the material down to the significant facts, which only are valuable.

This is a method often used by great lawyers and deliberative orators. Mr. William Wirt, in the case of Gibbons *vs.* Ogden, finds the issues of the case by first excluding the matters that may be admitted by either side. The legislature of New York had granted to Robert Fulton and others certain exclusive rights of navigation on the waters of the state. Mr. Wirt, in his speech, was endeavoring to prove the grant to be unconstitutional. He began : —

" In discussing this question, the general principles assumed as postulates on the other side may be, for the most part, admitted. Thus it may be admitted, that by force of the Declaration of Independence each state became sovereign ; that they were, then, independent of each other ; that by virtue of their separate sovereignty they had each full power to levy war, to make peace, to establish and regulate commerce, to encourage the arts, and generally to perform all other acts of sovereignty. I shall also concede that the government of the United States is one of delegated powers, and that it is one of enumerated powers, as contended for by the counsel for the correspondent. . . .

" The peculiar rule of construction demanded for those powers may also be conceded. But the express powers are to be strictly construed ; the implied powers are to be construed liberally. By this it is understood to be meant, that Congress can do no more than they are *expressly* authorized to do; though the means of doing it are left to their discretion, under no other limit than that they shall be necessary and proper to the end."[1]

(5) Having excluded from consideration all admitted matter, the remaining facts are many and of varied importance; but somewhere among them are the sought-for issues. In analyzing these facts it is important to notice what are the points on which there is a direct and earnest "clash of opinion." If the opponents in any discussion affirm and deny some particular matter in direct contradiction of each other, this particular matter of fact is sure to be significant. One of two things is true: either (1) the difference of opinion on the whole question depends in some degree on a difference of opinion concerning this fact, or (2) this is a fact that neither side can afford to admit.

It is often a help to ask this very question: *Can the other side afford to admit this fact?* Certainly, if they cannot afford to admit it, we have accomplished something if we succeed in establishing it against them, and it must be one of the most important points in the case. It was in this way that Webster, in the famous White murder trial, established one of his issues in the face of the contradictions of the opposing counsel.

" The counsel say that they might safely admit that Richard Crowninshield, Jr., was the perpetrator of this murder. But how could they safely admit that? If that were

[1] 9 Wheaton, 160.

admitted, everything else would follow. For why should
Richard Crowninshield, Jr., kill Mr. White? He was not
his heir, nor his devisee; nor was he his enemy. What
could be his motive? If Richard Crowninshield, Jr., killed
Mr. White, he did it at some one's procurement who himself had a motive. And who, having a motive, is shown
to have had any intercourse with Richard Crowninshield,
Jr., but Joseph Knapp, and this principally through the
agency of the prisoner at the bar? . . . He who
believes, on this evidence, that Richard Crowninshield, Jr.,
was the immediate murderer cannot doubt that both the
Knapps were conspirators in that murder. . . . The
admission of so important and so connected a fact would
render it impossible to contend further against the proof
of the entire conspiracy as we state it."

In either case — if either the fact is denied by the
other side, or the other side cannot afford to admit it
— the fact is one of the critical points among which
the issues are to be found.

(6) It must not, however, be assumed that every
fact that is denied or that cannot safely be admitted
is one of the issues. It may be a subordinate issue,
important only because the proof of it establishes or
helps to establish some larger fact. In that case the
larger fact, that the subordinate fact serves to prove,
is one of the issues.

Usually this discrimination between the issues and
the subordinate issues is not difficult. The issues are
the points the proving of which directly proves the
proposition itself; the proving of the subordinate
issues, on the other hand, helps to prove some larger

fact, which larger fact in turn serves to prove the proposition. The issues are related *directly* to the proposition; the subordinate issues, *indirectly*. For an example, take the question: *Resolved*, that labor unions should be compelled to incorporate. In the consideration of this question the fact would be emphasized that labor unions had very rarely broken their contracts with their employers in the past. This would clearly be only a subordinate issue. It would not serve to establish the proposition directly; it would be significant only because it would help to establish the larger fact, that there was no necessity for compelling the unions to incorporate. This last-mentioned point, on the other hand, would be one of the issues; it would be a critical fact not admitted by the opposing side, on which there was a clash of opinion, and it would stand in direct and immediate connection with the proposition.

It is often a help in making this discrimination between primary and subordinate issues to bear in mind the nature of this relation between the issues and the lesser materials of the proof. The issues are always few in number, rarely more than four points in any one question; and these points should be, as nearly as possible, of coequal value. They are centres around which all the lesser facts are gathered, thus serving to bring all the materials of the proof into connection with the proposition. In selecting the issues, then, points should be chosen which are nearly equal in value to one another, and which are of such a nature that all the evidence and arguments that it is desirable to use in the case can be logically grouped around them.

(7) In finding the issues it is often profitable to study the history of the question. We have seen the desirability of this investigation in the work of formulating the proposition. It is of equal service in finding the issues, and is one of the most common devices used in the court room or the assembly. The nature of any controversy must depend largely upon the circumstances of its birth. If to-day in America we discuss the question whether it is desirable to enact " anti-trust laws," the whole question turns on the history of the so-called "trusts" and their effect in the past on the economic and political conditions of the country. If we consider the question whether free trade would be preferable to protection, we find that it is the past history of the question in other countries that shows what are the points of conflict between the opposing systems.

The following is an excellent illustration of finding the issues, taken from the argument by Daniel Webster before the Supreme Court in the case of Luther *vs*. Borden. The events that gave rise to this case occurred in Rhode Island in 1841–42 and were what was popularly known as the Dorr Rebellion. Mr. Webster began : —

" It is well known that in the years 1841 and 1842 political agitation existed in Rhode Island. Some of the citizens of that State undertook to form a new constitution of government, beginning their proceedings toward that end by meetings of the people, held without authority of law, and conducting those proceedings through such forms as led them, in 1842, to say that they had established a new constitution and form of government, and placed Mr. Thomas W. Dorr at its head. . . . All will remember that the state of things approached if not actual con- flict between men in arms, at least the ' perilous edge of battle.' In June, 1842, this agitation subsided. The new government, as it called itself, disappeared from the scene of action. The former government, the Charter govern- ment, as it was sometimes styled, resumed undisputed control, went on in its ordinary course, and the peace of the State was restored.

"But the past had been too serious to be forgotten. The legislature of the State had, at an early stage of the troubles, found it necessary to enact special laws for the punishment of the persons concerned in these proceedings. It defined the crime of treason, as well as smaller offences, and authorized the declaration of martial law. . . . This having been done, and the ephemeral govern- ment of Mr. Dorr having disappeared, the grand juries of the State found indictments against several persons for having disturbed the peace of the State, and one against Dorr himself for treason. This indictment came on in the Supreme Court of Rhode Island in 1844, before a tribunal admitted on all hands to be the legal judicature of the State. He was tried by a jury of Rhode Island, above all objection, and after all challenge. By that jury, under the instructions of the court, he was convicted of treason, and sentenced to imprisonment for life.

"Now that an action is brought in the courts of the United States, and before your honors, by appeal, in which . . . it is alleged that Mr. Dorr, instead of being a traitor or an insurrectionist, was the real governor of the State at the time; that the force used by him was exercised in defence of the constitution and laws, and not against them; that he who opposed the constituted authorities was not Mr. Dorr but Governor King; and that it was *he* who should have been indicted, and tried, and sentenced." [1]

To summarize, in finding the issues: (1) put aside all matters that are not related directly to the proposition; (2) but be sure to understand the question in all its phases and all its details; (3) know both sides of the question thoroughly; (4) exclude all irrelevant matter and all matter that each side can admit without damaging its cause; (5) select the points on which there is a direct clash of opinion between the opposing sides or which cannot be admitted by the one side or the other; (6) discriminate between the issues and the subordinate issues; (7) study the origin and history of the question.

Finally, there is one error which is responsible more than all others, especially with beginners, for failures in finding the issues. It is all too easy to confuse the issues with what is commonly known as a partition, which consists in a mere statement of points to be proved in the discussion. It is a simple matter in any question to select arbitrarily a few important facts which it seems desirable to establish; but this is not by any means the same thing as de-

---

[1] The Works of Daniel Webster, Vol. VI, pp. 217-219. Little, Brown and Co., Boston, 1851.

termining upon the issues. To make the distinction clear : suppose two armies are contending for the possession of a given territory, the control of which both understand must depend upon the holding of two particular points, a pass and a certain height of ground. Now there are various positions which the two opposing forces may seize and hold, and various lines of attack which they may adopt, depending upon the peculiar habits and methods of the respective generals ; but these positions and this strategy are valuable only as they serve to give the command of these two critical points. In a like manner, let us suppose two disputants are arguing the question : *Resolved*, that the army canteen should be reëstablished. Now the settlement of this question will depend upon the decision of two issues; namely, (1) whether the canteen is beneficial to the individual soldier, and (2) whether it is beneficial to the army as a whole. A speaker on the affirmative might in his argument state his intention of proving three points as follows : (1) that the opinions of reliable army officers are favorable to the canteen; (2) that the number of arrests for drunkenness increased when the canteen was abolished; (3) that the canteen is beneficial in other countries. These three points may be well chosen, but their importance must be derived from their efficiency in establishing the affirmative side of the two issues mentioned above. A partition, then, is a statement of the points the arguer intends to prove ; the issues are the points he must prove in order to prove his case. If the points of the partition are well chosen, they will usually correspond closely with the issues; but they may be entirely different, and they are not in any case necessarily identical.

BOOK II. SELECTION

CHAPTER I

PRELIMINARY READING

In the discussion of the chapters under the head of Invention we have seen how a question must be analyzed in order (1) to understand what is the real proposition to be established, and (2) to find out the vital ideas or matters of fact which must be demonstrated to establish this proposition.

We next come to the consideration of the means and methods to be employed in the work of demonstrating these vital points, or issues, which have been determined upon. As we shall see later, much depends on the methods by which we arrange our material and present it to the reader or hearer. But before we can arrange our proofs or present them, we must, obviously, get the material to be used. This getting of material naturally divides itself into two parts : first, the gathering of material by preliminary reading and investigation ; and second, the selecting from all this material of those parts that will best serve our purpose in the given case.

All argumentation which involves preparation of any kind involves a considerable amount of preliminary reading. The amount varies ; but in most serious argumentative work the time thus spent is probably greater than that spent in all the other work of preparation taken together. The lawyer spends by far the greatest part of his time in examining witnesses and documents. The able senator or representative preparing for debate works longest and hardest in the collection of facts and figures. The intercollegiate debater labors for weeks in every library and on every document he can reach to gather the materials for a twelve-minute speech.

In the case of the beginner in argumentation, it must also be admitted that more time is wasted here than elsewhere. To a man who has had no practical experience, there does not seem to be any particular need of method in reading. Newspapers, magazines, and encyclopædias all seem alike as long as he can find in them anything bearing on the question. His method commonly is to start in anywhere and read as long as he can. Inevitably he wastes many hours at the start on worthless material, and later, to make up the time, he rushes along over the best authorities with careless haste. Again, such a reader does not really comprehend or assimilate what he reads. He reaps a harvest of quotations from here and there, picks out a few points from this writer and that, and he thinks his preparation is complete.

This inability to gather material intelligently is a serious weakness. To have a rational method is nowhere more necessary than here. There must, of course, be individuality in all work of this kind; personality should everywhere be cultivated rather than repressed. But there are some principles that have been engendered by common experience and that have a universal application.

I. The Use of a Note-book

It is a not uncommon mistake for a student to trust the safe-keeping of the ideas that he finds to his memory, with the almost inevitable result that, when called for, the ideas are not available. They either vanish and contribute nothing to the cause, or they must be sought anew at some future time at the cost of reduplicated work. Often it becomes necessary to verify some idea that has been suggested by some magazine article or to reënforce it with some good authority, and the chances are strongly against the probability that the original article can be found again. It is an extraordinary memory that can recall such a reference. Again, it is not always possible to tell at the beginning just what evidence will finally be valuable. Facts that seem trivial at the moment when we read them may turn out in the end to be important. But if no note is taken of them, they are almost surely lost. Against these and many other evils there is but one safeguard. A note-book should be always at hand, in which to take down ideas, arguments, and quotations when they are discovered.

II. Reading from the General to the Specific

A lawyer preparing his case for court begins his examination of witnesses with the examination of his client. With his story as a foundation he then goes on to seek the lesser details that he needs to " fill in " his case. He knows that to begin with the testimony of his lesser witnesses would result in confusion and waste of time. He might find that the testimony he had spent hours in seeking was more easily found elsewhere, or that, after all, it was of no service to the cause of his client.

The principle applies with equal force in the search for evidence by preliminary reading. For example, the American newspaper is a valuable source of material. Few are the discussions where it cannot be used with effect, if it is used properly. But in most cases it should be handled as the lawyer would handle the witness who testified that the defendant, on a certain day and hour, came to a certain livery stable and hired a certain horse and carriage. Such evidence might hang a man ; the whole question of the guilt of a murderer might depend on the identification of that particular horse and carriage. But that witness is not the first to be examined ; it might happen that his testimony had no bearing on the case. The newspaper should be used in a similar way. It is valuable as a means of corroboration ; it may be valuable as a source of facts for the support of some vital argument. But it should rarely be read first.

Various dangers arise from such premature reading of the newspaper. In the first place, it would often mean a waste of time. A writer of acknowledged authority on a particular problem will put

into a few lines the substance of the whole of a
popular newspaper editorial. Again, the student
who seeks such a lesser source first will find that
he has spent time in gathering arguments and facts
that better writers easily refute. More serious
still, an investigator will often get from such a
doubtful source false impressions that later reading
cannot entirely efface. The work of preliminary
reading, in this respect, is an exact analogy to the
work of the architect or the constructor. What kind
of judgment would it be on his part to plan his roof
and windows before he knew the size of the house or
the general style of its architecture? The writer who
goes in search of newspaper facts before he knows
the fundamental conditions of the problem in hand
and the broad outlines of his case shows no better
judgment.

The effective method is : —

A. Begin the investigation with the reading of
books and magazine articles that give an understanding of the general conditions on which the question
is founded. The understanding so gained is a touch-
stone by which all else may be tested.

B. Next, take up magazine articles or pamphlets
bearing on the particular question in dispute. By
this time the main ideas on which the proof must
be founded gradually appear, and the case as a
whole begins to assume a definite form.

C. Finally, make a discriminating use of such
sources as the newspaper, to get the details of evidence.

E

To take an example: Suppose that in the year 1898 a student had been preparing to debate the question, *Resolved*, that the United States should permanently retain the Philippine Islands. He would first have taken up books and magazine articles by such writers as Mr. John Foreman, Professor Dean C. Worcester, or Mr. R. R. Lala — men who had lived in the Islands and were acquainted with the conditions there. From them he would have found out the character of the people, their social and economic conditions, the nature of the country, climate, etc. Also he would have taken a general survey of the territorial history of the United States, her past acquisitions, and her success in " colonial " administration; this from such sources as selected chapters from Hildreth's " History of the United States," Winsor's " Narrative and Critical History of America," or Hinsdale's " The Old Northwest." Then, too, the constitutional question would have demanded early investigation. He would have read such authors as Thomas M. Cooley on the powers of the Federal government to acquire and permanently hold territory as colonies; he would have consulted the decisions of the Supreme Court affecting the question of the constitutionality of such action.

The opinions of public men and the many pamphleteers of the day, concerning the political potentialities of the Filipinos and the economic prospects of the archipelago, concerning the powers and duties of Congress, were innumerable; and most of them were as visionary and worthless as they were high-sounding and pretentious. Any man, not acquainted with the real conditions of the problem, would have accepted the statements of these men at their face value. He would have wasted time by giving them serious attention, and — far more detrimental — he might well have founded a large part of his case upon this worthless evidence, to find, when confronted with a better informed opponent, that his argument was "builded upon the sand." So, in the end, the reading of these authorities on the fundamental conditions of the question would have saved him time and perhaps the misfortune of defeat.

Next, he would have turned to magazine articles and pamphlets bearing on the particular question of the future policy of the United States with respect to the retention of the Islands. Here he would have availed himself of the writings of such men as Senator Cushman K. Davis, Colonel Charles Denby, and President J. G. Schurman. From such sources he would have gathered ideas about the rights and duties of this country in the situation and the commercial interests of the American people. By this time he would have been able to discern just where there were conflicts of opinion in the question. These points of conflict, in the light of his knowledge of the general problem, would have gradually taken form as the issues. His case as a whole would have been established on a firm foundation and wrought into fairly definite form.

Finally, he would have secured from the Congressional Record and the reliable newspapers of this country and other countries the details of the political movements of the day, such as resolutions of Congress bearing on the question, the conduct of the army and navy in the Islands, the attitude of other governments toward the United States, etc.

It is only by following such a plan of reading as this that there can be secured the three things most to be sought in the work of reading preliminary to arrangement and final presentation, *viz.:* (1) a grasp of the question as a whole; (2) an understanding of the vitally important points in the case; and (3) the getting of evidence that is relevant and reliable.

III. Reading on Both Sides of the Question

To know both sides of the question thoroughly is indispensable in all stages of argumentation. In the first place, without such knowledge a disputant cannot have that understanding of his case as a whole which must precede the intelligent use of evidence and arguments. We have already seen that the first step in preparation, and one of the most important steps, is always the finding of the issues. But these issues cannot be found except by knowing both sides. The issues are always the points on which there is a direct clash of opinion, and clearly these points can only be picked out by comparing the assertions of the opposing parties and ascertaining just where these assertions are contradictory.

Again, a disputant who knows only the arguments on his own side of the case may find himself helpless when confronted with some unexpected argument of his opponent. This inability to meet and repel an opponent is fatal to success in a war of words, and it must be guarded against in preparation. Such arguments are rarely to be answered by inspiration. Inspiration is not always reliable. The necessary knowledge must be gained before the actual crisis comes; and it can only be gained by studying the other side of the question and considering how any attack may best be met.

IV. What to look for in Reading

In reading any book or article, two things are generally to be sought. First, the reader should find the point of view which the writer takes of his subject as a whole and the points which he seems to regard as the critical facts in the case. Second, the reader should look for any new points of evidence, or any quotable matter. These points and quotations should be noted *as they arise.* It is a common experience of a beginner that he passes over some idea or some apt quotation without taking note of it, to find that later if he only had it at hand it would be a valuable piece of evidence or a strong argument from authority.

New evidence is valuable wherever it is found,

and some note should always be taken of it. Quotations, on the other hand, are valuable only as they
come from some writer who is a generally recognized
authority on the subject. And it should be borne
in mind that as to who is an authority the audience
is always the final judge. No matter how great the
knowledge of any writer, if he is unknown to the
audience or doubted by them, the quotation ceases
to have value as evidence or as an "argument from
authority." But in reading the words of a writer
of acknowledged standing, the note-book should be
freely used. The quotation may be taken down in
full, or some reference may be noted to the place
where it is found; but it must not be suffered to
escape entirely.

V. Assimilation

"Assimilation is the process by which plants and
animals convert food into the various tissues of their
own proper substance." When a man eats, if the
food he takes is properly assimilated, it ceases to
exist as food and becomes part of the man himself.
So in argumentation, assimilation is the process by
which the student converts the materials gathered
from all sources into the fibres of his own finished
argument.

We have stated in the preceding section that the
first thing to be sought in the reading of any book
or article is the point or points which the writer
regards as vital in the case. Merely to seize upon

these ideas and force them bodily into the proof without change of form, would inevitably produce the same disastrous effects that would ensue if a man should eat without digestion. The proof would be weak and ill formed. It would be a mere jumble of facts and figures. The varied and conflicting ideas of different men would be mixed together in confusion. The force of evidence that might be made convincing would be spent with no effect. To beget strength and vitality in proof, the ideas and arguments of other writers and thinkers must be so fused with one another and with the ideas of the student himself, that the final product bears little if any resemblance to any one of the parts of which it is made; it is not the idea of this book or that, nor the idea of the reader, but an indivisible composite of all. Like the body, the proof is made of all kinds of substances, but it must itself be new and a distinctive unit.

There is but one way in which material can be so assimilated. It must be done by the careful and constant thought of the reader as he progresses, step by step. When one starts out to read on any subject, he nearly always has in his own mind some original conceptions of the question. In the first place, then, he should understand just what these conceptions are. Then, when in the course of his reading he finds some new idea, some new argument, he should compare it carefully with the contents of his own mind, and modify his own conceptions ac-

cordingly. The ideas that result will not be those
he has read, nor will they be those he had originally :
they will be new. This process must be kept up un-
remittingly. The material cannot be stored up for
future assimilation any more safely than a man
could postpone the digestion of his food. Each bit
of material must be understood, compared, and assimilated when it first comes to the eye. The evidence gathered in this way ceases to exist in its
various foreign forms. The ideas no longer overlap
or conflict with one another. They fall into their
proper places as parts of one working body.

Such a method also gives to the proof the invaluable quality of personality. Complete originality
in argumentation is very rare. The most effective
speech or essay often contains ideas and evidence
that have become time-honored by their frequent
usage. But the ideas are so altered by the personality of the author that they are made new. They
take on fresh forms and colors and gather an original force. No quality is more valuable to charm or
interest an audience than this quality of personality ;
and the personality that is forceful in argumentation is always attributable largely to the power of
assimilation.

The power of assimilation is gained only by practice. It may well grow into an unconscious habit
of mind ; but the creation and development of it
must always come from conscious self-training. The
ability to assimilate is, of course, engendered and

strengthened by other means than preliminary reading in argumentation. But nowhere is the application of the power more practical or more important. And a student who is entering upon the serious pursuit of argumentation, however truly he may possess this quality of mind in general, will do well to watch himself for a time, lest he fall into other habits.

CHAPTER II

EVIDENCE

WE now come to the consideration of the second of the two parts in the process of Selection, viz., the choosing from whatever materials we have been able to gather, of those facts, arguments, or appeals that will best serve our purpose in the case in hand. Here, as everywhere, we must remember the dual nature of all argumentation : our materials must be judged and chosen in accordance with the standards both of conviction and of persuasion. Persuasion requires that we consider the character, intelligence, and personal interests of our audience or readers, and the circumstances in which we are arguing, so that we may make use of the ideas and methods that will strike most directly and forcibly upon the imagination and peculiar emotions of those we address. Conviction requires that we understand what it is that constitutes the inherent strength of the various kinds of proofs, so that we may employ evidence and arguments that will seem to the minds of others to be logically strong and accurate. Leaving the standards of persuasion to be discussed at a later time, let us now turn to the question : What are the elements of strength and of weakness in the various kinds of proof ?

I. Proof, Evidence, and Arguments

A. Proof is the name used to designate "all the means which serve to convince the mind of the truth or falsity of any fact or proposition." Proof may be divided into two parts: (1) evidence, and (2) arguments.

(1) Evidence consists of all the *matters of fact* that may be used in the generating of proof. It is the raw material from which the finished product, proof, is to be manufactured.

(2) Argument, in its restricted meaning, is the name used to designate the process by which, from knowing the existence of one fact, or a certain number of facts, we infer the existence of other facts. This meaning of the word "argument" must not be confused with other meanings. The word may be used to refer to a finished discourse as a whole; it may refer to an entire debate or discussion; or, as here, it may mean simply a single process of reasoning. There is, perhaps, no better definition of an argument, in this sense, than Cardinal Newman's definition of reason, as "any process or act of the mind by which, from knowing one thing, it advances on to know another!" To continue the analogy of manufacturing, an argument is the machinery by which the raw material, evidence, is turned into the finished product, proof.

For an example, take the following extract from a chapter in "Jonathan Swift," by John Churton Collins, in which the author endeavors to prove that

Swift was not married to Esther Johnson : " What, again, could be more improbable than that Esther Johnson, a woman of distinguished piety, nay, a woman whose detestation of falsehood formed, as Swift himself told us, one of her chief attractions, would, when on the point of death, preface her will with a wholly gratuitous lie ? For not only is that will signed with her maiden name, but in the first clause she describes herself as an unmarried woman." This whole selection is proof. The facts that Esther Johnson was a truth-loving woman, that she signed her will with her maiden name, and that she described herself in the first clause as an unmarried woman, are evidence. The process of reasoning by which we infer from these facts that in her will she told the truth and was, therefore, unmarried, — the inference that these proved facts establish the truthfulness of her assertion that she was unmarried, — that process is an argument.

II. Evidence consists of All the Matters of Fact that may be used in the Generating of Proof

Evidence is commonly divided into two classes : (A) direct, and (B) indirect or circumstantial evidence. This is sometimes a clarifying distinction to have in mind, although for the practical purposes of argumentation it is not very significant. (A.) Direct evidence consists of the testimony of persons who declare the existence of the fact in issue, speaking from their own personal knowledge. " A man testifies that he actually saw A inflict a mortal wound on B, of which B instantly died ; this is a case of direct evidence." [1] (B.) Indirect or circumstantial is the name applied to all other kinds of evidence. It consists of testimony to the existence of other collateral facts, from the existence of which the existence of the fact in question is to be inferred by a process of reasoning. " If a witness testifies that a deceased person was shot with a pistol, and the wadding (used in this pistol) is found to be part of a letter addressed to the prisoner, the residue of which is discovered in his pocket," [2] that is indirect or circumstantial evidence. From the existence of these facts the jury may infer the guilt of the prisoner.

Without entering into any full discussion of these kinds, it is sufficient to know that the most effective proof is gained by the use of the two kinds in combination. Direct evidence may be untrustworthy because of mistakes in the observation of the witness or because of prejudice. Circumstantial evidence may be inconclusive because of a possible ambiguity in the inferences to be drawn from it. But when the two kinds are used together, each confirming the other, the evidence becomes of the highest possible efficiency.

With respect to its form, we may classify evidence as : (A) written, and (B) unwritten. In the court of law a considerable part of the evidence is unwritten. It is obtained largely from the spoken testimony

[1] Greenleaf, " Evidence," p. 24.   [2] *Ibid.*

of witnesses, present before the judge or jury. In argumentation elsewhere, however, the evidence is largely written. It is often akin in its nature to the spoken testimony of the courts, in that it expresses the beliefs of different persons as to the existence of certain facts. But the persons themselves are rarely present to express their beliefs orally. Their opinions are gathered from books, magazines, newspapers, and documents.

III. Tests of Evidence

Most important for our purposes are the tests to be applied to determine the value of evidence. To know whether a piece of evidence is strong or weak is essential to the intelligent making of a case. We can use only limited amounts from all we gather, and we must have the power to discriminate. Then, too, we must know what is strong enough to be put in the forefront of the proof, and what is so weak as to be valuable only for the purpose of " filling in " and re-enforcing the more important parts.

There are two vital tests of evidence : (A), the test of the quality of the evidence itself, and (B), the test of the sources from whence it comes. For convenience in our discussion, the sources of evidence will be referred to as " witnesses."

A. Tests of the quality of the evidence itself.

(1) *Burden of proof.*

It should always be kept in mind that the burden of establishing the truth of any statement rests

upon the person who originally makes the assertion. "The burden of proof as to any particular
fact lies on that person who wishes the court to
believe in its existence, unless it is provided by law
that the burden of proving that fact shall lie on
any particular person." [1] Even if the statement
is negative in nature — if it is a denial of the existence of some other fact — the denial itself is an assertion and must be supported by evidence. No
disputant has a right to demand that his opponent
prove the falsity of any statement until he — the
original maker of the statement — has demonstrated
or tried to demonstrate its truth. Simple denial is
answer enough to simple assertion.

This burden is of added weight if the fact whose
existence is asserted is of an extraordinary nature.
Witnesses who would be sufficient by their testimony
to establish the facts of a robbery would not be sufficient to establish the existence of a sea-serpent at
a New England summer resort. So, too, of propositions that suggest innovations or departure from the
present order of things. The presumption is with
him who upholds the present or the natural conditions. In the question " *Resolved*, that in the United
States private ownership of railroads is preferable
to national ownership," the negative advocates a
radical change in the present economic and political
conditions of the country. Contrary to the rule of
debate that the burden of proof is on the affirmative,

[1] Stephens, "Digest of Evidence," p. 146.

in such a case as this the presumption is with the affirmative, and that presumption the negative must meet and overthrow.

These considerations lead naturally to the mention of the most desirable qualities of evidence.

(2) *Evidence should be consistent with human nature and human experience.*

Any man properly hesitates to accept as a fact anything that runs contrary to his own past experience or the experience of his fellow-men. To make him believe in any evidence that contradicts the beliefs of his life and his habits of thinking requires explanation, enforcement, and substantiation that soon become an argument in themselves, and even then the unqualified acceptance of the proof may be a matter of doubt.

If the evidence is in this way contrary to ordinary human experience, one must never neglect to maintain its truthfulness by explaining just why it is credible and valuable. Campbell, in his " Philosophy of Rhetoric," expresses the situation, when he says : " From experience we learn to confine our belief in human testimony within the proper bounds. Hence we are taught to consider many attendant circumstances which serve . . . to corroborate . . . its evidence. The reputation of the attester, his manner of address, the nature of the fact attested, the occasion of giving the testimony, the possible or probable design in giving it and several other circumstances have considerable influence in fixing the degree of credibility." Evidence, then, should as far as possible be consistent with ordinary human experience and the natural course of affairs. If it is of any extraordinary nature, its credibility must be shown before it will be of value or effect.

The weakness of evidence that is of an extraordinary nature and contrary to common experience, is exposed in the following selection from the speech by John Henry North in the case of Rex *vs.* Forbes and others. Mr. North's client was charged with committing criminal assault upon the Lord-lieutenant of Ireland. Testimony was given by a certain Dr. M'Namara, who said that he actually saw the defendant hurl a bottle at the Lord-lieutenant in a public theatre. Mr. North attacks the testimony as follows : —

" The Doctor in the middle gallery sees Handwich in the third row of the upper one, though between them there were two benches covered with people, and the boarded parapet in front of the upper gallery besides ! Through all these obstacles he sees him in that dark corner of the gallery where he represents him to be placed ; sees him fling the bottle, and is now able, at this distance of time, to identify his person. The bottle itself he saw in what he learnedly calls its *transit*. A word or two on that same transit. I hold it physically impossible that a bottle could have taken the course described by Farrell and M'Namara, from the upper gallery to the stage, without being observed by four or five hundred spectators. Just think what the theatre is : a wide, illuminated area, whose bounding surfaces are studded with eyes as numerous as

F

those of Argus. Not a square inch in that field of view which was not painted on the retina of some one eye or other in that vast assembly. Consider, too, the time — the interval between the play and farce — when the attention of the audience was not fixed upon the stage, when people were all looking about them, recognizing and greeting their friends and acquaintances. Was there no one to mark this bottle but Farrell, M'Namara, and the young medical student? What, not one giggling girl in the boxes, glancing round for admiration! not an opera-glass pointed! no fortunate observer of the transit but the astronomer from Ballinakill! Is all this credible? But this is not all — voonders upon voonders, as the Dutchman said when he got to London — the greatest miracle is to come. Down comes the bottle, thundering from the upper gallery to the stage, and falls unbroken!" [1]

(3) *Evidence should be derived from witnesses who can testify to the fact from their own personal knowledge.*

This is the rule from which arises the rule of the law courts which is known as the rule of "hearsay evidence." Hearsay evidence is defined by Greenleaf as "that kind of evidence which does not derive its value solely from the credit to be given to the witness himself, but rests also, in part, on the veracity and competency of some other person. . . . Its extrinsic weakness, its incompetency to satisfy the mind as to the existence of the fact, and the frauds that may be practised under its cover combine to support the rule, that hearsay evidence is totally inadmissible." Hear-

[1] "Great Speeches by Great Lawyers," p. 659.

say evidence, in brief, is the evidence of persons who testify to the existence of some fact, on the ground that they have been informed of its existence by some third person.

What the courts exclude, argumentation elsewhere should treat with suspicion. Second-hand evidence is unconvincing. The testimony is too many stages removed from the fact itself. An audience will almost invariably suspect that the arguer cannot or dare not produce the original authority. Again, it is too easily overthrown. If any witness who has a first-hand knowledge can be brought to testify to any fact of a contradictory nature, the hearsay testimony is immediately brought to the ground. For example, in endeavoring to prove that labor unions would not seek to evade compulsory incorporation, it would be weak evidence to give the testimony of a government official, an economist, or even a commissioner of labor. The willingness of the unions to be incorporated must be proved from the words and actions of the labor leaders themselves, the presidents and counsel of the workingmen's organizations. Theirs are the only reliable first-hand statements.

There are a few exceptions to this rule excluding hearsay testimony: such as evidence of general reputation, public rumor, and reputed ownership or holding of office. Of this class are such matters as a general belief in a community that a man and woman are married, or that a man is secretly controlling the political officers of the city or the state.

But even then the evidence is really first-hand, because it is the very fact of public rumor and conviction that is the basis and material of the argument.   And even in such a case, the burden is on the user of the evidence to show that it is trustworthy.   He must prove that his witnesses are honest and unprejudiced, that they were in a position to know the prevailing public sentiment, and he must show that their opinion is widespread and has some rational foundation of truthfulness.

(4) *Evidence must be consistent with all the known facts of the case.*

The necessity is evident of avoiding contradiction between different pieces of evidence presented in the proof.   Inconsistency in the disputant himself is unpardonable.   Its discovery by an opponent or by the audience will ruin all confidence in the guilty person.   So, when Oppius was charged with defrauding the soldiers of their pensions, Cicero refuted the charge by proving that the same persons charged Oppius with a design to corrupt the army with his extravagant gifts and liberality.

A more common mistake is to adduce evidence that is contradicted by the commonly known or easily proved facts of the question.   A few years ago in a trial of a civil suit the defendant was on the witness stand.   He was seeking to establish an alibi.   In the course of his testimony he was asked to tell of all his movements and doings on a particular day.   He told of several purchases he had made in the stores

of the city, of his visit to a barber's shop, and of
various other incidents. When his testimony was
finished, the examining lawyer stated the simple fact
that the day in question had been the day of the
observance of President William McKinley's burial.
Every shop and store had been closed. The testimony was not to be reconciled with the facts well
known to the judge and the jury, and was dis-
credited.

Webster used this test effectively in the White
murder trial to overthrow the testimony of one of
the witnesses of the defence.

" Balch says, that on the evening, whenever it was, he
saw the prisoner; the prisoner told him he was going out
of town on horseback, for a distance of about twenty
minutes' drive, and that he was going to get a horse
at Osborn's. This was about seven o'clock. At about
nine, Balch says he saw the prisoner again, and was then
told by him that he had had his ride, and had returned.
Now it appears by Osborn's books, that the prisoner had a
saddle-horse from his stable, not on Tuesday evening, the
night of the murder, but on the Saturday evening previous.
This fixes the time about which these young men testify,
and is a complete answer and refutation of the attempted
alibi on Tuesday evening." [1]

(5) *There are certain kinds of evidence that are
exceptionally valuable.*

(a) *Admissions and declarations against interest.*
These are the terms given in the courts to the

[1] The Works of Daniel Webster, Vol. VI, p. 83. Little, Brown
and Co., Boston, 1851.

testimony of persons contrary to what their own concern in the cause would require. It is there regarded as of such importance that second-hand evidence of such statements is made admissible, contrary to the general rule excluding all hearsay evidence. Sometimes the admission or declaration is made when the person is aware of its damaging nature; sometimes, when unaware. The value of it needs no explanation.

Such testimony is ordinarily reliable; but there are exceptions. If the statement is made by a person unconscious of its effect on his own interests, we must be sure that it was not made carelessly or under the influence of an intent to gain some other end. If it is a deliberate admission or confession, there may have been some hope of reward elsewhere that led the witness to suffer a lesser evil for a greater gain; or the statement may have been given under compulsion. In either case its value is gone. But the presumption is always in favor of the trustworthiness of this kind of evidence. To take an example: a statement by any "protected" manufacturer that the tariff duties were too high — if such a thing were possible — would be a worthy bit of evidence. But if it could be proved that he was about to embark in some new enterprise where the tariff could not help him, that his purpose was the destruction of some greater rival, or that he was in the hire of a political manager, its force would be destroyed.

(b) *Undesigned evidence.*

Undesigned evidence consists of testimony given

by persons who, when they gave it, had no thought
that it would ever be used as evidence in the case in
question.   Speaking for another purpose, a person
often lets fall a statement that is merely incidental.
The value of any such evidence lies in its freedom
from the suspicion of any hidden motive.   It is in-
genuous and presumably honest.   But it has a very
serious weakness.   The testimony may well have
been careless.   The witness, thinking the assertion
of slight importance, may have been indifferent as to
its accuracy.

Mr. Webster, in the following selection from his
argument in the White murder trial, enforced the
value of some of his evidence by showing that it
was undesigned : —

"Mr. Southwick swears all that a man can swear.   He
has the best means of judging that could be had at the
time.   He tells you that he left his father's house at half-
past ten o'clock, and as he passed to his own house in Brown
Street, he saw a man sitting on the steps of the ropewalk ;
that he passed him three times, and each time he held
down his head, so that he did not see his face.   That the
man had on a cloak, which was not wrapped around him,
and a glazed cap.   That he took the man to be Frank
Knapp at the time ; that, when he went into his house, he
told his wife that he thought it was Frank Knapp ; that he
knew him well, having known him from a boy.   And his
wife swears that he did so tell her when he came home.
What could mislead this witness at the time ?   He was
not then suspecting Frank Knapp of anything.   He could
not then be influenced by any prejudice.   If you believe

that the witness saw Frank Knapp in this position at this time, it proves the case." [1]

B. Tests of the sources of the evidence.

Evidence which seems on its face to be credible, consistent, and convincing may be rendered of no account by an exposure of weakness in the source from whence it comes. If it can be shown that the statements, however plausible, are mere careless assertions of unreliable persons, or that the testimony was given with some dishonest motive, its value is gone. So it is always necessary in selecting one's own proof or in attacking the proof of an opponent to know what kinds of witnesses make good evidence, and what kinds, bad evidence.

(1) *The kinds of evidence with respect to the sources.*

Looked at from the viewpoint of the sources from whence the evidence is derived, there are two kinds of evidence; (*a*) ordinary evidence, and (*b*) expert evidence. There are certain tests that may be applied to all witnesses; these are the tests of the sources of ordinary evidence. Then the examination of the class of witnesses known as " experts "demands the application of certain other peculiar tests.

(2) *Tests of the sources of ordinary evidence.*

(a) *Physical powers.*

Most human knowledge comes through the avenues of the five senses, and it is from the information so

---

[1] The Works of Daniel Webster, Vol. VI, p. 90. Little, Brown and Co., Boston, 1851.

received that we get evidence. Clearly, then, the physical powers of a witness may have great influence upon his reliability. If a witness is color-blind, his testimony that green signal lights were displayed at the time and place of a railroad accident must be ignored. However, this test is not very common outside of the court room. The writers that furnish the materials of student debate and of ordinary disputation everywhere are usually beyond the reach of such examination, and their testimony is not commonly of such a nature that it makes much difference whether they are blind, or deaf, or otherwise unfortunate physically. But whenever physical weakness may have any possible effect on the testimony, the test should be rigorously applied. It is one of the most effective of all possible tests, for such a defect in a witness is conclusive against his testimony.

(b) *Mental powers.*

More important for the purposes of general argumentation than the test of physical endowment is the test of mental powers.

(1) *Memory.* The test of the memory of a witness is applicable everywhere. In the courts, it is a part of the "stock in trade" of a cross-examiner. In ordinary disputation it is less common, but not less significant. A defective memory is damaging, because it raises a strong presumption of error in the statement of testimony. If the witness cannot remember things in general, it is probable that he cannot clearly remember about the particular fact in

question. His impressions will probably be vague
and indistinct, and so his statements will be unreliable.

In the White murder trial, Webster used this test
in attacking a witness of the defence : —

" Mr. Burchmore says, to the best of his belief, it was
the evening of the murder. Afterwards he attempts to
speak positively, from recollecting that he mentioned the
circumstance to William Peirce as he went to Mineral
Spring on Fast-day. Last Monday morning he told
Colonel Putnam he could not fix the time. This witness
stands in a much worse plight than either of the others.
It is difficult to reconcile all he has said with any belief
in the accuracy of his recollections." [1]

(2) *Accuracy of statement.* The accurate use of
words and phrases is not by any means universal.
We shall treat later of the different kinds of " liars " ;
but many mistakes of verbal expression are wholly
undesigned. Provincial phrases, personal peculiarities in speech, a tendency toward exaggeration, may
often lead a witness to say in a sentence or a paragraph what he does not really mean. In getting
written evidence, to avoid the mistake of misunder-
standing the witness, the real import of the testimony
should be gathered from the evidence as a whole
rather than from the exact words of any particular
sentences. The phrases must be interpreted in the
light of the context, and if there be any question as
to their rightful meaning, the proper interpretation
should be explained to the audience.

[1] The Works of Daniel Webster, Vol. VI, p. 83. Little, Brown
and Co., Boston, 1851.

Witnesses who are habitually inaccurate must, of course, be treated with suspicion. There are many writers whose practice it is to deal in generalities and bold over-statements. If they have a reputation for that style of writing, their testimony is of almost no value ; and, in any case, their credibility is liable to question.

c. Opportunity for the observation of the facts.

This is an obvious but not unimportant test. If the situation or experience of the witness has been such that he has not had a chance to observe the existence of the facts to which he testifies, and to observe them closely and carefully, his statements are clearly untrustworthy. In the courts it is a common method of impeaching testimony to show that a witness was too far distant from the scene to see clearly, that he did not have time to observe carefully, that he did not arrive in season, etc.

This test is no less important in other kinds of argumentation. Innumerable are the writers who are ready to venture the most positive statements on the foundation of a few weeks' investigation, or who carelessly make bold assertions of some general truth, when they have observed only a few phenomena, and when those they have observed are as likely as not to have been exceptional or sporadic in nature. It is not uncommon that an author or a traveller visits such a country as Russia for a few months or a year, and, on his return, writes articles or a book on Russian society, Russia's political

methods, and her economic prospects. Now, such a
man is not to be criticised for writing in the magazines
or publishing a book; his narrative may well be
interesting. But, as evidence, his statements and
prophecies generally amount to nothing; Russian
society and politics cannot be analyzed in a month.
Again, how often we find newspaper writers and
pamphleteers giving the most emphatic testimony to
defects in methods of colonial administration by their
own government, when they have never ventured
beyond the borders of their home states. Their
earnestness may be good and their patriotism com-
mendable, but their testimony is worthless. In all
such cases as these the opportunities for observation
are insufficient to make good evidence.

   d. Veracity of witnesses.

The two common defects in the truthfulness of a
witness are: (1) exaggeration, and (2) deliberate perversion of the truth.

   (1) *Exaggeration may be accidental or intentional.*

Accidental exaggeration arises from habits of mind
in the witness. Some men have an irresistible impulse to "make things big," like Falstaff, with his
"eleven men in buckram." Intentional exaggeration
is simply one kind of deliberate lying.

A witness who exaggerates can best be exposed by
investigating his accuracy in other instances. Collins
uses this test in his argument to prove that Swift
was not married to Esther Johnson, when, in speaking of one of the witnesses, a certain Dr. Madden,

he says : " Of Madden it is sufficient to say that in temper and in blood he was half French, half Irish ; and that as a writer he is chiefly known as the author of a work wilder and more absurd than the wildest and most absurd of Whiston's prophecies and Asgill's paradoxes." If a witness habitually exaggerates, none of his statements can be accepted at their face value.

(2) *Deliberate perversion of the truth implies some motive.*

(a) With an expert the motive is most often that of pride. One expert is opposed to another in some court trial or perhaps on some economic question. Each feels that his reputation depends on the overthrow of his rival. Consequently, though they may begin with the most honest intentions, they yield to the demands of the occasion, their testimony degenerates into a spirited argument, and exaggeration and misrepresentation are bred. (b) With other witnesses the motive is some interest in the question at issue. They feel some sympathy with the parties most deeply involved in the outcome, or they themselves have some interest of " office, place, and power."

A witness must be tested with these possible weaknesses in view, in two respects : (1) Is he interested in the outcome ? and (2) What is his general moral character ? This second test is significant, because it tells us to what extent the witness would permit unworthy motives to influence his words. A reputation for low moral character in a witness makes his testimony of little or no value.

This test is one of the most common in the courts. Rufus Choate gave a good illustration of its effectiveness in his speech in the Dalton divorce case. While attacking one of the leading witnesses of the plaintiff, he said : —

" I begin, therefore, with the foundation witness in this case, John H. Coburn, and I respectfully submit to you, that tried by every test of credibility which the law recognizes, on your oaths you are bound to disbelieve him.   It is not that a laugh can be raised against Coburn or his testimony — that is nothing ; it is that, according to those tests which are founded on the longest and widest experience the law deems satisfactory to show whether a jury can safely believe or not, he is not to be believed.   I submit, then, that John H. Coburn is not an honest man, and is not, therefore, entitled to be heard in so delicate a work as bringing every word my client spoke on that evening to her husband ; he is not an honest man, and I put it on your solemn oath to you, that there is not a man on that jury who, on the exhibition of John H. Coburn, would intrust him to carry a bundle worth five dollars from this courthouse to the depot." [1]

(3) *Tests of the sources of expert evidence.*

Expert evidence is the testimony of a witness who is valuable not simply because he can testify to the existence of certain facts of his own experience, but because he possesses the peculiar knowledge of a specialist, which enables him to interpret the facts

[1] "Great Speeches by Great Lawyers," p. 307.

that are presented to him. The ordinary witness testifies that a certain alleged fact is true because he actually observed it to be so; the expert testifies that the same alleged fact is true because certain other facts exist, and his peculiar and exceptional knowledge justifies him in inferring the existence of the fact in question.

To take a simple illustration. The question is whether a certain man who was shot and killed wore a certain coat on the day of the murder. The ordinary witness may testify that he saw him near the place of the murder a short time before the deed, and that he was wearing the coat in question. The expert finds certain stains on the body and sleeve of the coat, and from this fact, by the use of his exceptional knowledge of chemistry, he infers that the stains are blood stains and freshly made. Clearly in this case the value of the testimony of the expert depends upon his skill in chemical analysis. This is always the primary test of expert evidence : Is the witness possessed of such knowledge that he will draw the correct conclusions from the facts presented to him ?

In general argumentation this kind of evidence is what is known as the " argument from authority." This is a false name, for it is not properly an argument, — *i.e.* a process of reasoning, — but evidence. This so-called " argument from authority " consists in establishing a fact by quoting the opinion of some person whose knowledge is such as to justify the acceptance of his inferences as truthful. In theological questions, the Bible is the standard source of authority; in politics, the writings of statesmen; in science, the conclusions of specialists in its various departments. In discussing the question whether the independence of China should be preserved, the affirmative might well quote such a man as Sir Robert Hart, to show that the Chinese were capable of developing a righteous and effective governmental system. His long experience in dealing with the Oriental races and his connection with the administration of Chinese political affairs had given him an understanding of the political qualities and potentialities of the race that justified him in voicing his prophecies with confidence. His statement would be good "authority."

The following is an example of argument from authority from the speech by Patrick Henry on "The Right of a State during the Revolution to confiscate British Debts." In seeking to prove that the confiscation of British debts is warranted by necessity, he says: —

"The necessity being great and dreadful, you are warranted to lay hold of every atom of money within your reach, especially if it be the money of your *enemies*. It is prudent and necessary to strengthen yourselves and weaken your enemies. Vattel, Book 3d, ch. 8, sec. 138, says: 'The business of a just war being to suppress violence and injustice, it gives a right to compel by force him who is deaf to the voice of justice. It gives a right of doing against the enemy whatever is necessary for weaken-

ing him, for disabling him from making any further resistance in support of his injustice, and the most effectual,
the most proper methods may be chosen, provided they
have nothing odious, be not unlawful in themselves, or
exploded by the law of nature.' Here let me pause for
a moment and ask whether it be odious in itself or
exploded by the law of nature to seize those debts ? "[1]

The "authority" used for the purposes of such
expert evidence as this must bear two special tests :
(*a*) Is the witness possessed of the knowledge
necessary to justify his acceptance as an expert in
the matter in question ? (*b*) Is his authority recognized by the audience ? However great the knowledge or skill of an expert, if his greatness is unknown
to the hearer or reader, the effect of quoting him
will be a mere "flash in the pan." The audience or
reader will see in the pretended "authority" nothing
more than a meaningless name, and so will ignore his
statement. The disputant must always be sure that
the worth of his expert is accepted; and if there may
be any doubt, his first duty is to establish for him
a satisfactory reputation.

To summarize : —
I. Proof is composed of (*A*) evidence and (*B*) argu-
    ments.
    A. Proof is the name used to designate all the
        means which serve to convince the mind
        of the truth or falsity of any fact or
        proposition.

[1] "Great Speeches by Great Lawyers," p. 13.

G

  B. Evidence consists of all the matters of fact that may be used in the generating of proof.

  C. An argument is the process by which from knowing one fact or a certain number of facts we infer the existence of other facts.

II. Evidence may be divided into : —

  A. Direct evidence and indirect or circumstantial evidence.

  B. Written evidence and unwritten evidence.

III. The tests of evidence.

  A. Tests of the nature of the evidence itself.

   1. The burden of proof rests on the person who originally asserts the existence of the fact.

   2. Evidence should be consistent with human nature and human experience.

   3. Evidence should be derived from witnesses who can testify to the fact from their own personal knowledge.

   4. Evidence should be consistent with all the known facts of the case.

   5. Certain kinds of evidence are especially valuable.

    a. Admissions and declarations against interest.

    b. Undesigned evidence.

  B. Tests of the sources of evidence.

   1. There are two kinds of evidence classified with respect to their sources : —

    a. Ordinary evidence.

    b. Expert evidence.

2. Tests of the sources of ordinary evidence.

    a. Physical powers of witnesses.

    b. Mental powers of witnesses.

        (1) Memory.

        (2) Accuracy of statement.

    c. Opportunity for observation of the facts.

    d. Veracity of witnesses.

        (1) Exaggeration.

        (2) Deliberate perversion of the truth is due to: —

            (*a*) Interest in the outcome of the controversy.

            (*b*) Defective moral character.

3. Tests of sources of expert evidence.

    a. Is the witness possessed of the special knowledge necessary to justify his acceptance as an expert?

    b. Is his authority recognized by the audience or reader?

CHAPTER III

KINDS OF ARGUMENTS

THERE is a distinct difference in purpose and method between argumentation and formal logic. It is near the truth to say that formal logic is the science of which argumentation is the corresponding art. Logic aims merely to investigate and explain "the operations and processes of thought." "Its first business must be to investigate the nature of thought," as it is actually carried on in the human mind; but it makes no attempt to prescribe any practical rules for correct thinking. Argumentation, on the other hand, finds only a secondary interest in scientific logic, its purpose being to make practical rules and suggestions which will facilitate correct reasoning and the producing of beliefs in the minds of others.

This difference is strongly marked in the methods employed by each in the treatment of the kinds of arguments, or, as the term is in logic, of "inferences." Logic explains the different ways in which the mind *may* work in making an inference or reasoning. In argumentation the purpose in discussing the methods of inference, or "the kinds of arguments," is to make clear the rules that must be followed in order to make arguments that will be valuable for the purpose of convincing and persuading others. For this purpose the necessity of knowing the various kinds of arguments that may be used is twofold: it is necessary (1) in order to be able to select the arguments that will be valuable in constructing one's own proof, and (2) in order to be able to attack the proofs of an opponent.

Since these are our only two purposes, little attention need be given to the questions of what kinds of arguments are most naturally used, or in what forms these arguments are generally stated or explained. For example, the causal connection in many arguments is often not understood by the person making the argument, and hence inferences from cause to effect or from effect to cause may seem to be comparatively few in number. Again, in many instances where the causal connection is understood, it is not explained in the statement of the proof. But these facts are not of any real significance for our purposes. In order to be able to select good arguments for our own use, and in order to be able to attack the weak arguments of others, however others may understand them and however they may be stated, we must know *what it is in the arguments that makes them strong or weak*.

Nearly all writers on the subject of rhetoric have divided the kinds of arguments into three classes, and have given to these classes the names, antecedent probability, sign, and example. The meanings given to these titles and the classifications made under them have been various and confused, so that there is practically no definite and accepted division. Any division which shall be of service in argumentation must have for its purpose the establishment of standards by which we may determine whether any particular arguments are good or bad, strong or weak, as the materials of proof. Consequently, in order to give a practical insight into the proper selection and use of arguments in argumentation, and a practical power to detect the most serious fallacies, the kinds of arguments should be classified and explained in such a way as to make clear, as far as possible, *on what the strength of the various kinds of arguments depends*.

We have seen that an argument is a process by which, from knowing the existence of a fact or a certain number of facts, we infer the existence of some other fact or facts.

In the first place, then, it should be stated that in nearly every argument the validity of the inference depends upon a connection of cause and effect between the facts from which we infer and the facts to which we infer. This causal connection is not always actually understood by the person making the argument, and is often not stated. But this connection is, nevertheless, in most cases, the source of strength or weakness in the reasoning. It must be understood in order to know the real force of the argument and detect the fallacies of opponents. "Whether the given inference be right or wrong, whether it be express and deliberate, or rapid and free, whether it take the form of a cut-and-dried syllogism, an argument from analogy, or from circumstantial evidence, in all cases equally it is our belief about the way things hang together in nature that provides alike the sole motive power of inference and the sole foundation on which we rest our proof." [1]   However, there are many valid arguments in which this causal connection is not evident, and in these cases it must also be determined what is the element of their strength.

The lines of division between the classes of arguments cannot always be drawn with absolute distinctness.   Many arguments with slight changes in phrase pass from one class to another.   But this is wholly immaterial : the classes and names are nothing in themselves.   It is the understanding of the structure and substance of the arguments that is essential.

I. Antecedent Probability

The argument from antecedent probability is an argument from cause to effect.

It is sometimes said that the argument from antecedent probability requires a preliminary assumption ; it is said that the argument consists in assuming the existence of some fact and then producing evidence to show that the assumption is

[1] Sidgwick, "The Process of Argument," p. 46.

justified. This is not true. Very often it is convenient in presenting or explaining the argument to
make such an assumption. As, for instance, in a
criminal trial, a lawyer, when he is arguing before
the jury, may assume for the time that A murdered
B, and then go on to show that A had a motive.
This is an argument from antecedent probability,
but the assumption made by the lawyer is not an
essential part of the argument. For the sake of
clearness he may first show that A's pistol was found
beside the body, and present various other kinds of
evidence, to create a presumption of guilt against A,
before he discusses his motives. Such a method is
obviously more sensible than examining the possible
motives of all the persons who might possibly have
committed the crime, especially since the lawyer is
hired to prosecute this particular man, A. Moreover,
the effect on the jury is helped by the corroboration
of other kinds of arguments, the arguments from
sign in this case. But this assumption is not essential. The strength of the argument itself depends
entirely upon the connection of cause and effect
between the motive and the deed. The argument
is conclusive if it can be shown that these motives
of A were the cause that would produce the
effect in question, viz., the murder of B; and its
validity will vary with the strength of this causal
connection.

The argument from antecedent probability, then,
is an inference from a known cause to an unknown

effect; it consists in showing that a certain known fact or combination of facts is of such a nature as to bring to pass the existence of another fact, whose existence is in dispute.

For example, in the famous White murder trial, Daniel Webster showed that the Knapps believed they could get Captain White's fortune by murdering him and stealing his last will, and then argued that this motive was the cause that produced the effect in question, viz., their murder of Captain White. Again, if one of the larger universities of the country is known and acknowledged to have a very strong foot-ball team, it is an argument from antecedent probability to infer that this team will defeat a team from some small college of two or three hundred students. It is inferred that the known cause — the strength of the university team — will produce the effect of a victory over a weaker rival. A good illustration of this kind of argument is found in the following selection from a speech given at a National Democratic Convention to account for hard times under a Democratic administration : —

"When the Democracy came into power in 1893 it inherited from its Republican predecessor a tax system and currency, a system of which the McKinley and Sherman laws were the culminating atrocities. It came into power amidst a panic which followed upon their enactment with strikes, lockouts, riots, civil commotions, while scenes of peaceful industry in Pennsylvania had become military camps. Besides its manifest features, the McKinley law had thrown away fifty millions of revenue

derived from sugar under a special plea of a free breakfast table, and substituted bounties to sugar planters, thus
increasing expenditure, thus burning the candle at both
ends and making the people pay at last for their alleged
free breakfast.

"From the joint operation of the McKinley law and
the Sherman law, an adverse balance of trade was forced
against us in 1893, a surplus of $100,000,000 in the
treasury was converted into a deficit of $70,000,000 in
1894; and engraved bonds prepared by a Republican
secretary to borrow money to support the Government
were ill omens of preorganized ruin that awaited the coming Democracy and depleted treasury."

The orator argues that these acts of Republican
maladministration were the causes that produced the
effect of hard times.

It may be noticed that in many such instances the
argument from cause to effect is preceded by a sort of
preliminary argument from effect to cause. Before
we argue that the strength of the foot-ball team will
be the cause of victory, we may prove that the team
is strong by showing that it has won victories over
other teams in the past. This is an inference from
effect — the past victories — to cause — the strength
of the team. But this is not the important part of
the inference. The strength of the team is not really
the question; it is in this case generally admitted. If,
however, the abilities of the team are questioned and
must first be proved by showing past evidences of
their achievements, the argument thus becomes more
truly an argument from certain known effects of a

given cause to other effects of the same cause, *i.e.* an argument from sign. As has already been remarked, the lines of division between the classes are not definite.

An argument from antecedent probability may be attacked in several ways, but they are all the same in that they are all directed toward the destruction of the connection between cause and effect. In order to be conclusive, the argument must show that the known or proved fact would necessarily act as a cause to produce the effect; and it is here that the argument is best attacked.

The following are the most effective methods of refuting this argument.

(1) *Is the connection of cause and effect complete?*

The two facts, one of which is called the cause and the other, the effect, are rarely in immediate connection with each other. There are almost always several intermediate steps between the two. " Intermediate links in a chain of causation are so many opportunities for counteraction, in the same way as a length of railway provides opportunities for an accident. They are intermediate conditions. The pull on the trigger will fire the shot if, and only if, the catch, the spring, the hammer, the cap, and so on, all act in the expected manner. Therefore our forgetfulness of intermediate links takes effect just in the same way as our forgetfulness of conditions generally ; it may give us a false security."

It follows, then, that the closer the causal connection, the surer is the argument, and that any argument may be destroyed by showing that some of the necessary intermediate links are lacking. It might be proved that A was inspired with a most malevolent hatred of B, that he would welcome any favorable opportunity of attacking him, even that he had actually sought to do him injury; but in order to connect this motive with the murder of B, it must be shown that none of the necessary intermediate steps were lacking. It must be proved that A was present at the time, that he had the necessary weapon, that he was physically strong enough to do the deed. The destruction of one of these links destroys the argument.

(2) *Is the cause adequate to produce the effect in question?*

It is not difficult to imagine any number of facts that might possibly follow from the existence of some other fact. But such connections are not always sufficient to make a valid argument. It is not sufficient that a fact might have a general tendency to produce a certain effect. It must be shown that the assumed cause is in itself *adequate* to account for the existence of the effect in question.

Ex-Governor Black of New York, in the trial of Roland B. Molineux for the murder of Mrs. Adams, used this test when, in speaking of the motives assigned by the prosecution as the cause of the murder, he said: "They have failed utterly to supply a motive. It is absurd to suggest that out of a mere quarrel such as Cornish and Molineux had, should grow a hatred so profound as to inspire a man twelve months later to commit murder."

In 1893 the so-called "hard times" from 1892 to 1896 were said by some people to have been caused solely by the unexpected failure of a prominent English banking house. The failure in question might have been a startling incident of the day, it might perhaps have precipitated failures and misfortune elsewhere ; but it was clearly no adequate cause for such a widespread and prolonged misfortune.

(3) *The operation of other causes in the case in question may prevent the action of the assumed cause.*

The chain of connection between the cause and the effect is most often impaired by the intervention of some other cause which destroys some of the connecting links. If a man takes a dose of deadly poison, the chances are that it will cause his death ; but it may be shown that this effect will not actually follow in this case, by showing that the man took an antidote. The antidote causes the expulsion of the poison from the system and prevents the occurrence of the natural effect.

One may argue that the Chinese race are very numerous, that as a people they are physically formidable, that they are peculiarly fortunate in climate and in economic resources, and, consequently, that there is great danger of a commercial "Yellow Peril." This is a clear inference from cause to effect. But his argument may be attacked, by showing that certain racial peculiarities of the Chinese prevent them from being aggressive competitors, and make them thus incapable of the powers of initiative and self-advancement necessary for independent commercial progress as a race. The operation of this second cause will destroy the connection of cause and effect on which the argument depends.

(4) *Might not the fact in question be accounted for by the action of some other cause?*

Very often the argument from antecedent probability is used to account for the existence of some particular phenomenon. It is human nature to wish to know the cause of any alleged fact. If you say something is true, somebody immediately wants to know why it is natural that it should be true. To recur to the example of the criminal, if a lawyer tries to account for a robbery, he must show that his explanation of it is natural and reasonable. So he tries to show that the man he is prosecuting had a motive for committing the crime.

In attempting to overthrow such an argument, it may not be sufficient to show that the connection of cause and effect is weak. A weak cause is better than no cause at all. Consequently, it is necessary to substitute some other argument from cause to effect for the argument that has been attacked. The causal connection that seems the more reasonable will be accepted to the exclusion of the other.

For example, in the Molineux trial the defence attacked the argument of the prosecution to show that the defendant had a motive that caused him to commit the murder in question, by producing evidence to show that another man concerned in the case had stronger motives and consequently that it was no more rational to accuse the defendant than it was to accuse this man.

In refuting arguments from antecedent probability the rhetorical treatment may take various forms, but the analysis of the argument is always the same ; the attack is always directed toward one point, — the connection between cause and effect.

II. Arguments from Sign

The argument from sign is, in general, what the name implies. It rests upon the assumption that two certain facts will always or usually accompany each other, and that consequently the presence of one will be a sign of the presence of the other. As in the argument from antecedent probability, most arguments from sign depend for their validity upon a causal connection ; but we shall also find that there is a class of arguments from sign in which this causal connection is not fully understood, or, at least, is hard to trace. Arguments of this last-mentioned class depend for their strength upon the fact of an invariable association in the past between the facts in question.

For convenience, the arguments from sign may be divided into three classes :—

A. Arguments from effect to cause.

B. Arguments from one effect to another effect of the same cause.

C. Arguments from the association of phenomena in the past.

A. Arguments from effect to cause.

The most necessary and inevitable accompaniment of any fact is its cause. Consequently if it can be shown that any alleged fact whose existence we wish to prove is or was the cause of any known fact, the proof of this alleged fact is indisputable. When we see ice, we safely conclude that the temperature has been below a certain point; and the argument is beyond dispute, because it is only a certain degree of coldness that will freeze water.

William Seward argued from effect to cause in the following part of his defence of William Freeman. Freeman was on trial for murder, and Seward's defence was that of insanity on the part of the prisoner : —

"There is proof, gentlemen, stronger than all this. It is silent, yet speaking. It is that *idiotic smile* which plays continually on the face of the maniac. It took its seat there while he was in the State prison. In his solitary cell, under the pressure of his severe tasks and trials in the workshop, and during the solemnities of public worship in the chapel, it appealed, although in vain, to his task-masters and his teachers. It is a smile, never rising into laughter — without motive or cause — the smile of vacuity. . . .

"That chaotic smile is the external derangement which signifies that the strings of the harp are disordered and broken, the superficial mark which God has set upon the tabernacle to signify that its immortal tenant is disturbed by a divine and mysterious commandment. If you cannot see it, take heed that the obstruction of your vision be not produced by the mote in your own eye, which you are commanded to remove before you consider the beam in your brother's eye. If you are bent on rejecting the testimony of those who know, by experience and by science, the deep afflictions of the prisoner, beware how you misinterpret the handwriting of the Almighty."[1]

A number of years ago, in Yorkshire, England, a traveller, having in his pocket certain marked coins, was attacked in the early evening, murdered, and robbed. The following day coins of this peculiar stamp were found on the person of a certain manservant at an inn in the vicinity. This servant was unable to account for his possession of the money, and on this evidence he was tried, convicted, and hanged. This was a clear argument from sign — from effect to cause. It was argued that his possession of the coins was the effect of his taking them from the body of the murdered man on the evening before.

But several years after it was found that the conviction was a mistake. The keeper of the inn confessed that he himself committed the murder and, in order to transfer the guilt, got his servant intoxicated and put the coins into his pocket. The argument from sign was fallacious, because the effect in question was the result of another cause than that assumed.

[1] Works of William H. Seward, Vol. I, p. 468.

H

This example of the robbery illustrates the most common weakness of the argument from effect to cause and suggests the way in which it may best be refuted.

(1) *May not the known effect be due to some other cause than the one alleged?*

A mariner at night seeing lights ahead infers that a ship or a lighthouse is at hand. But his inference may be sadly false. The lights may be set or manipulated on shore with the purpose to mislead him and profit by the wreck of his ship. Again it is argued that Shakespeare must have written the works attributed to him, because he was credited with their authorship all through his life. It is said that this effect must have been due to the cause, that he did actually write the works. But those who oppose this view attack the argument by showing that the popular belief may be attributed to other good causes, — to the comparative lack of interest in the authorship at the time, or the desire of the real author to conceal his identity, — and so, that the reputation is no sure sign of authorship.

(2) *Is the alleged cause capable of being the real cause of the effect in question?*

We may also attack the argument directly, in much the same way that we would attack the argument from antecedent probability, by showing that the cause which it is alleged produced the known effect was really not adequate to produce it. But it must be observed that this alone is not sufficient to destroy the argument. Although this phenomenon might not in itself have been a sufficient cause, other causes might have coöperated with it in producing the effect, and so the known effect may still be a sign of this alleged cause. To make the refutation complete, it must be shown that these other causes, whose coöperation was necessary, did not exist.

There are many other devices that may be invented and employed in different cases, which are too numerous or complicated to be explained here. The foregoing are the most common and effective tests; and of the other tests it may be remarked that they are all directed to destroy the causal connection, and that they may be readily invented if the nature of this inference from effect to cause is understood.

B. Arguments from one effect to another effect of the same cause.

The second class of the arguments from sign involves a process of inference that is, in a sense, a combination of the argument from cause to effect and the argument from effect to cause. This second class consists of arguments that are an inference from a known effect of some unknown cause to the existence of another effect of the same cause.

A certain fact or combination of facts is known to exist. From the existence of this known fact the existence is inferred of another fact which is alleged to be its cause — the argument from effect to cause. Then a second step is taken; it is inferred that this cause produces another effect, this second unknown effect being the fact which it is the aim of the argument to prove.

To illustrate by a diagram : —

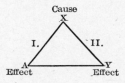

The effect *A* is known, *i.e.* it is admitted or it has been established by evidence; but it is not known what was or is its cause. From this known effect is inferred by process number I (argument from effect to cause) the existence of *X*, which is alleged to be its cause. Then by process number II (argument from cause to effect) is inferred the existence of *Y*, which is alleged to be another effect of the cause *X*. The argument seeks to prove *Y* as an inference from *A*, and in doing so it passes through the connecting cause *X*.

In the evening we observe a redness of the sky, and we argue that there will be fair weather the next day. It is an argument from effect to effect. The redness is due to certain atmospheric conditions, and these conditions are such that they will produce fair weather. We argue that a certain man will succeed as the president of a corporation. We first point to his success in other enterprises requiring executive skill and creative power; from them we infer their cause, his abilities, and then reason that these abili-

ties will produce their effect, viz., success in his new
undertaking.

The following illustration is taken from the speech
of David Paul Brown in defence of Alexander William Holmes (before the Circuit Court in Philadelphia,
in 1832). A vessel was wrecked, and, in order to
save as many as possible of the passengers, orders
were given to throw overboard a part of them. The
defendant obeyed the order and threw certain men
over the side of the ship into the water. He was
tried for murder, and Mr. Brown is here arguing to
show that the defendant acted in good faith and with
right motives. He said : —

" I am strengthened in this position by the indisputable
fact that Holmes, the prisoner, during the whole voyage,
was upon the kindest and most harmonious terms with all
the passengers ; that he preserved the same friendly relation to them after the loss of the ship ; that he had perilled
his life more than once to preserve them ; that he has
literally stripped himself of his apparel for their comfort ;
in short, his desire to save them seemed to absorb all consideration of mere personal or individual safety. In these
circumstances, to suppose anything cruel or wanton upon
his part is to run counter to everything that is possible or
natural. I infer, therefore, that he supposed the peril to
be imminent and instantaneous, or he never would have
complied with the orders of the mate. . . . I maintain,
therefore, that the most favorable construction is to be
placed upon his motives ; and it is justly to be inferred
that he acted upon the impression that the danger was
imminent, and that death was inevitable to all, except by
resorting to those means which he actually adopted. . . .

But even taking all the statements of the witnesses for the prosecution, highly colored — I will not say discolored — as they are, and torture them as you may, it is impossible for you to arrive at any other conclusion than that Holmes was actuated by the kindest and most generous influences ; and certainly I need not say that kindness and generosity are opposed to wantonness and barbarity." [1]

He argues that the former actions of Holmes were the evidences of their cause, viz., his sincere interest for the welfare of the passengers, and then argues that this cause produced the effect in question, his honesty of motive in this particular instance.

In a great part of the arguments of this class it is noticeable that more than one effect is usually adduced to prove the existence of the cause, each effect giving added evidence of the single cause alleged.

The points of weakness in this kind of argument are evident. It is a combination of the two foregoing arguments, — from sign and from antecedent probability ; and if either one of these component inferences is defective or can be attacked, the whole argument is destroyed. Referring to the diagram given above, the argument can be attacked in either leg of the triangle. The tests are, therefore, the tests already given for the arguments from cause to effect and from effect to cause.

For example, the argument of Mr. Brown might be attacked at two points. It might be shown that the effects he mentioned — his relations with the pas-

[1] " Great Speeches by Great Lawyers," pp. 143–144.

sengers and his apparent solicitude in their behalf, etc. — might not really be due to the alleged cause, viz., his interest for their welfare, but to another cause — perhaps his desire to win favor or pecuniary gain. Again it might be attacked (test number 3, of arguments from antecedent probability) by granting the sincerity of his motives in general, but showing that certain circumstances peculiar to this particular case prevented the natural operation of the cause. Perhaps the defendant was so fearful for his own life that his usual honesty was put aside and he acted selfishly or maliciously.

The argument from effect to effect is, perhaps, not so common as the arguments from cause to effect, or from effect to cause. These two arguments are more commonly used separately, than in combination as the argument from effect to effect.

C. Arguments from the association of phenomena in the past.

The third class of arguments from sign is composed of arguments based upon the past association of facts or phenomena. Two phenomena have been observed to happen together so many times in the past as to seem to justify the belief that they will accompany one another in the future. So when one of the facts or phenomena is observed to be present in any particular case, it is inferred that the other also is present. In such arguments the causal relation is not readily understood or explained, although it undoubtedly exists.

We may infer that any ruminating animal has cloven hoofs; conversely, we may infer that any animal with cloven hoofs is a ruminant. These inferences are reasonably safe because in most cases the two characteristics have been found to exist together, although scientists do not understand the exact nature of the connection. The argument about ruminant animals depends on the fact that the concurrence of the two phenomena seldom fails. In some cases the rule has been broken; the pig and the tapir, for illustration, have cloven hoofs, but are not ruminants: consequently, the convincingness of the argument is weakened, and any considerable number of exceptions would make it valueless.

It is, then, clear where the argument may be open to attack. The habit of hasty, unreasoning generalization is very common. In many debates this very fallacy is predominant. A speaker or writer cites a few instances of the concurrence of two facts in the past and argues that because they have happened together in the past, they must happen together in the present instance. Really, what he has established is, that they *may* happen together; he has *proved* nothing, and his attempts may be rendered null either by (1) pointing out that the cases are too few to establish a law of concurrence, or, better, (2) by producing definite examples where the one phenomenon has occurred without the other.

Arguments of this kind are rare, and clearly they must from their nature be of doubtful value. The co-

existence of the two facts in past instances is not
shown to be anything more than mere accident, and
chance is at best a weak foundation on which to base
an inference. The argument gathers its force wholly
from the frequency of the past concurrence of the
phenomena. In order to approach conclusiveness we
must have: (1) a very large number of cases of the
observed concurrence of the facts or phenomena, and
(2) complete uniformity in the operation of the rule,
that when one occurs the other accompanies it.

III. The Argument from Example

The third and last division of the kinds of arguments is composed of those which depend for their
strength upon the resemblance between the case in
question and some other case or cases, which are adduced either as analogous in nature to this particular
case, or as establishing some general law that is applicable to it.

There are two classes of arguments from example,
which may be called, respectively, (A) the argument
by generalization, and (B) the argument from analogy.

A. The argument by generalization.

In arguments of this kind we "consider one or
more known individual objects or instances of a
certain class as fair specimens, in respect of some
point or other, of that class; and consequently draw
an inference from them respecting either the whole
class or other less known individuals of it." [1]

---

[1] Whately, " Elements of Rhetoric," p. 52.

The following from Burke's "Speech on Conciliation" is an illustration of an inference from individual instances to a truth respecting the whole class
to which they belong : —

"In large bodies, the circulation of power must be less
vigorous at the extremities. Nature has said it. The
Turk cannot govern Egypt, and Arabia, and Curdistan,
as he governs Thrace ; nor has he the same dominion in
Crimea and Algiers, which he has at Brusa and Smyrna.
Despotism itself is obliged to truck and huckster. The
Sultan gets such obedience as he can. He governs with a
loose rein, that he may govern at all ; and the whole of the
force and vigor of his authority in his centre is derived
from a prudent relaxation in all his borders. Spain, in
her provinces, is, perhaps, not so well obeyed as you in
yours. She complies too, she submits, she watches times.
This is the immutable condition, the eternal law, of ex-
tensive and detached empire."

Chief Justice Marshall, in his opinion delivered in
the case of McCulloch *vs*. Maryland, used the argument by generalization as follows : —

"The power of creating a corporation, though apper-
taining to sovereignty, is not, like the power of making
war or levying taxes or of regulating commerce, a great
substantive and independent power, which cannot be
implied as incidental to other powers, or used as a means
of executing them. It is never the end for which other
powers are exercised, but a means by which other objects
are accomplished. No contributions are made to charity
for the sake of an incorporation, but a corporation is created to administer the charity ; no seminary of learning is

2 Burke's Speeches, p. 87.   James Duffy, London, 1871.

instituted in order to be incorporated, but the corporate character is conferred to subserve the purposes of education. No city was ever built with the sole object of being incorporated, but is incorporated as affording the best means of being well governed. The power of creating a corporation is never used for its own sake, but for the purpose of effecting something else."

In the following, Channing, arguing that the sufferings of the slaves are evils and should be done away with, infers from individual instances of a class to "another less known individual of it " : —

" Allow that the sufferings of the slave are less than those of the free laborer. But the sufferings are Wrongs, and this changes their nature. Pain as pain is nothing compared with pain when it is wrong. A blow, given me by accident, may fell me to the earth ; but, after all, it is a trifle. A slight blow, inflicted in scorn or with injurious intent, is an evil, which, without aid from my principles, I could not bear. Let God's providence confine me to my room by disease, and I more than submit, for in his dispensations I see parental goodness seeking my purity and peace. But let man imprison me, without inflicting disease, and how intolerable my narrow bounds. So if the elements take away our property, we resign it without a murmur ; but if a man rob us of our fortune, poverty weighs on us as a mountain. Anything can be borne but the will and the power of the selfish, unrighteous man. . . .

" My hostility to the system does not rest primarily on the physical agonies it inflicts, but on a deeper foundation : on its flagrant injustice, and on the misery necessarily involved in a system of wrong." [1]

[1] Channing's Works, Vol. V, pp. 37–39. G. G. Channing, Boston, 1849.

He adduces examples to prove the general truth
that, regardless of the pain it inflicts, injustice or
wrong always creates an evil, and then applies this
general truth to the instance of slavery, so proving
that slavery is an evil.

B. The argument from analogy.

In arguments from analogy we compare two or
more objects or instances which are *not* alike *in
themselves*, but which *are* alike in the *relations they
bear to other facts or circumstances*, and infer that
something true of the objects in the one class is true
of the object or objects in the other.

"Thus an egg and a seed," says Whately, "are
not in themselves alike, but bear a like relation to the
parent bird and to her future nestling, on the one
hand, and to the old and young plant on the other,
respectively, this *relation* being the genus which both
fall under : and many arguments might be drawn
from this analogy."

Lincoln argued from analogy when, in reply to
politicians advising him to change generals at a certain time during the Civil War, he said he didn't
think it wise to "swap horses while crossing a
stream." He did not imply that the horse and general had similar qualities of body or of mind. They
were not alike in themselves ; but they bore the same
relations, respectively, to the crossing of the stream
and to the prosecution of the war, and in so far as
this similarity of relation applied the argument was
valid.

The following is an illustration from Reid's " Intellectual Powers " : —

" We may observe a very great similitude between this earth which we inhabit and the other planets, — Saturn, Jupiter, Mars, Venus, and Mercury. They all revolve round the sun, as the earth does, although at different distances and in different periods. They borrow all their light from the sun, as the earth does. Several of them are known to revolve round their axis like the earth, and by that means have like succession of day and night. Some of them have moons that serve to give them light in the absence of the sun, as our moon does to us. They are all, in their motions, subject to the same law of gravitation as the earth is. From all this similitude it is not unreasonable to think that these planets may, like our earth, be the habitation of various orders of living creatures. There is some probability in this conclusion from analogy."

The distinction between these two kinds of arguments from example, viz., the argument by generalization and the argument from analogy, is a distinction that may easily become distorted, unless it be kept clearly in mind that generalization involves a direct comparison of the objects compared, whereas analogy involves a comparison of *the relations* the objects bear to other objects or circumstances. The word "analogy" has so many different meanings given to it in ordinary conversation that it is not strange that the term is often misused in this connection.

We see a round, yellow ball; it has a certain peculiar feeling as we pick it up. We conclude it is an orange and will have a certain flavor. This is not an

argument from analogy, but an argument by generalization.   In a number of other instances in our past
experience we have found that objects that look and
feel as this one does have had a certain flavor and
have been called by this certain name.   By a direct
comparison of these attributes we have formed the
generalization that all objects of this feeling and
appearance are oranges; we apply the generalization
to this "unknown individual" of the class and argue
that it is an orange.

In the argument from example, as in the other two
classes of arguments, the connection of cause and
effect is present.   The difference is, that in the other
classes the inference is directly from cause to effect,
or effect to cause, whereas in this class the inference
depends upon a comparison of causes and effects.
In the argument from antecedent probability we
argue that certain known facts are of such a kind
that they must *from their very nature* produce a certain effect.   In the argument from example we
argue that certain known facts will be the cause of a
certain effect because they are similar to certain other
facts which have been the cause of a similar effect in
the past.   If the facts that we pronounce as "examples" have happened to follow one another in the
past merely by accident, then no amount of comparison can prove anything more than that similar facts
may happen together in the future by accident; the
comparison cannot give valid grounds for a belief
that they certainly *will* follow one another.   The

causal connection must be present in order to make
the argument true.

There are, then, clearly two points of possible
weakness in the argument from example: —

(1) *The causal connection in the " examples " may be
defective, or —*

(2) *The resemblance between the "examples" and the
instance in dispute may not be a true resemblance.*

(1) The tests of the causal connections have been
given in the treatment of the other classes of arguments.

(2) In order to give grounds for a valid argument,
it is important, not that the resemblances are many,
but that they are such as to bear directly upon the
argument. Horses and generals are not alike in their
relations, in many ways; but Lincoln's argument de-
rives its force from the fact that the two are similar
in the relation that is important to the argument.

"Cæsar had his Brutus, Charles I his Cromwell,
and George III may profit by their example."
Cæsar was very unlike Charles I in most of his
personal qualities; he ruled a different country,
in a different age. George III was the very opposite of the Roman in temper and character; his
people, his advisers, his century, were not similar
to those of either of the men cited as "examples."
But the three cases were similar in the essential
element: Cæsar, Charles I, and George III all repre-
sented the pressure of tyranny upon a spirited, liberty-
loving people. In each case oppression was the

cause of the effect, rebellion; and whatever other differences there may be in the circumstances, the *causes* are similar in nature. Such an argument only emphasizes the fact that the causal connection is essential in this class of arguments, and that the similitude between the instances is a similitude of causes and effects.

We often hear it argued that men and nations are alike in certain particulars, and that consequently nations must have youth, manhood, old age, and decay. The argument is not valid, because the resemblance is not a resemblance that has any bearing on the argument. Men and nations are alike in their moral responsibilities; for both, self-indulgence or misjudged action brings its punishment; for both, the same intellectual qualities may bring success. But they are not alike in the one essential point, viz., physical organization.

In discussions about institutions of government this fallacy is common. For instance, advocates of the election of the President of France by direct vote of the people urge that, since this method has given us an efficient executive in this Republic, it would produce like good results in the French Republic. In many respects the circumstances in the two countries are parallel; but how great are the differences! The peoples of the two nations are unlike in race and temperament. The American people are substantially of English stock, conservative, long trained in the practices of popular government, appreciative of the value of republican institutions, and firm in their defence of the principles of democracy. The French people, on the other hand, are emotional and impulsive, prone to change and revolution, and their political ideals are impregnated with traditions of monarchy and empire. Then again, the success of this method of election in the United States depends largely upon the system of "checks and balances," which is so finely organized in our written Constitution; whereas France has no stable constitution, no Supreme Court capable of preserving the balance of power between the legislature and the executive, and indeed, the whole government seems to be parliamentary in principle. So that such a popular election in France would involve various dangers and complications impossible, or at least improbable, in the United States, and would undoubtedly lead to seriously different consequences. The analogy, therefore, is not a true one, and the argument has little, if any, validity.

In arguing by generalization, (1) the resemblance between the cases given as examples must be such as to justify the making of a general law concerning them, and (2) the case in question must be such that the general law is applicable to it.

In the argument by analogy, the case or cases given as examples must resemble the case in question, in the relations which they respectively bear to surrounding facts or circumstances.

And finally, in both arguments, the *resemblances must be such as to have a direct bearing on the argument.*

CHAPTER IV

FALLACIES

A COMPLETE classification of all the possible fallacies of inference is hardly practicable. The human
mind is capable of too much error to allow even a
mention of all the logical sins it may perpetrate. But
in the development of the science of formal logic the
more common and flagrant breaches of valid reasoning have been searched out and exposed. Those fallacies which are said to exist "not in the *form* but in
the *matter* — those which have their source in equivo-
cation and presumption — are called material fallacies." Of these so-called "material fallacies" the
more important for purposes of argumentation are as
follows : —

I. False cause.

II. Ambiguous terms.

III. Composition and division.

IV. Ignoring the question, or arguing beside the
point.

V. Begging the question.

I. False Cause

Fallacies of this class are all fallacies of defective
causal connection between the things from which

and to which we argue, and the various methods that may be used in exposing them have been fully discussed in the preceding chapter. One kind of fallacies, however, belonging to this class, deserves special mention,—*post hoc ergo propter hoc*, usually called simply *post hoc*. Of all forms of fallacies arising from false cause, this is probably the most common and the most insidious. The fallacy consists in assuming that because one occurrence precedes another in time, the one is the cause of the other. Many of the common superstitions of ancient and of modern times illustrate this fallacy. For instance, thirteen people sit at table together, and within a few months one of the number is accidentally drowned; immediately some one argues that the death is the effect of the thirteen sitting at meat together.

Again, it has recently been argued that, because the number of crimes perpetrated by negroes in the Southern states has increased since educational opportunities were first offered to the negro, therefore the growth of crime is directly due to the growth of education. It certainly is not sufficient for the arguer to base his contention simply on the fact that the one thing has followed the other, and few thoughtful men will be inclined to accept the conclusion thus drawn. Until something more is done to show a definite causal connection, we may safely call this a *post hoc* fallacy.

The most common form of this fallacy, perhaps, is that used by the political arguer. It runs something

like this : Such and such a political party came into
power at such a time, and for a number of years
thereafter the country suffered from financial depres-
sion ; therefore the policies and administration of this
political party are the cause of the unfortunate state
of affairs. Now, the statement may or may not be
true, but the argument in the above form certainly
contains a fallacy. To show that this fallacy does
exist, and that the conclusion is not worthy of acceptance, it is necessary only to point out the fact that
any one of a half dozen other causes might, at least
as readily, have produced the same result.

An illustration from a current periodical will
make clear the commonness of this class of fallacies, and will also suggest the care that is necessary
to guard against them. In *Harper's Weekly* for
March 5, 1904, the editors noted the fact that various
college presidents had estimated that "the college
graduate has one chance in forty of 'succeeding in
life,' whereas the man who hasn't been to college has
only one chance in ten thousand." The inference
naturally drawn from this statement is that the mere
fact that a man secures a college education multi-
plies many times his chances for success. To this
inference and to the possible fallacy that may lurk
therein the editorial in question addresses itself as
follows : —

"Not many persons doubt any longer that an American
college education is an advantage to most youths who can
get it, but in these attempts to estimate statistically what

college education does for men there is a good deal of confusing of *post hoc* and *propter hoc*. Define success as you
will, a much larger proportion of American college men
win it than of men who don't go to college, but how much
college training does for those successful men is still debatable. Remember they are a picked lot, the likeliest
children of parents whose ability or desire to send their
children to college is evidence of better fortune, or at least
of higher aspirations than the average. And because their
parents are, as a rule, more or less prosperous and well
educated, they get and would get, whether they went to
college or not, a better than average start in life. In
order to make an estimate that would be really fair of
what college does for boys, it would be necessary to compare the fortunes of two groups of boys from something
like the same rank of life and of something like equal
ability, one a college-taught group and the other not. But
that cannot well be done. The colleges get the likeliest
boys. If one boy out of a family of four goes to college, it is the clever one. The boys who might go to
college and don't are commonly the lazy ones who won't
study. The colleges get nowadays a large proportion of
the best boys of the strongest families. The best boys
of the strongest families would win far more than their
proportionate share of success even if there were no
colleges."

The surest ways of determining what constitutes a
valid causal connection have been given in the preceding chapter. The principles there enunciated are
set forth by Mill in categorical form in his so-called
" Five Canons." These rules are slightly modified by
Professor Jevons, and are quoted from his " Lessons
in Logic " as follows : —

" 1. **Method of agreement.**

" If two or more instances of the phenomenon under investigation have only one circumstance in common, the circumstance in which alone all the instances agree is the cause (or effect) of the given phenomenon, *i.e. the sole invariable antecedent of a phenomenon is probably its cause*.

" 2. **Method of difference.**

" If an instance in which the phenomenon under investigation occurs, and an instance in which it does not occur, have every circumstance in common save one, that one occurring only in the former, the circumstance in which alone the two instances differ is the effect, or the cause, or an indispensable part of the cause, of the phenomenon.

" 3. **Joint method.**

" If two or more instances in which the phenomenon occurs have only one circumstance in common, while two or more instances in which it does not occur have nothing in common save the absence of that circumstance, the circumstance in which alone the two sets of instances (always or invariably) differ is the effect or the cause, or an indispensable part of the cause, of the phenomenon.

" 4. **Method of residues.**

" Subduct from any phenomenon such part as is known by previous inductions to be the effect of certain antecedents, and the residue of the phenomenon is the effect of the remaining antecedents.

" 5. **Method of concomitant variations.**

" Whatever phenomenon varies in any manner whenever another phenomenon varies in some particular manner, is either a cause or an effect of that phenomenon, or is connected with it through some fact of causation."

II. Ambiguous Terms

This fallacy consists in confusing the meaning of words or phrases in such a way as to lead to unsound reasoning. Such fallacies may arise in many ways.

(*a*) We may confuse the etymological meaning and the common meaning of a word; as, for instance, the sophistical argument often founded on the word "representative."

" Perhaps no example of this can be found that is more extensively and mischievously employed than in the case of the word ' representative.' Assuming that its right meaning must correspond exactly with the strict and original sense of the verb ' represent,' the sophist persuades the multitude that a member of the House of Commons is bound to be guided in all points by the opinion of his constituents; and, in short, to be merely *spokesman:* whereas law and custom, which in this case may be considered as fixing the meaning of the term, require no such thing, but enjoin the representative to act according to the best of his *own* judgment, and on his own responsibility." [1]

(*b*) We may confuse two or more common meanings of the same word, where the word has different meanings in different circumstances. The word "democratic" in one connection is the name of a political party; in another it designates a body of political and social ideas and principles. So we argue falsely: all Americans should be democratic; consequently vote the Democratic ticket. The word "church" may mean the whole body of believers, or

[1] Mill, "System of Logic," p. 503.

it may mean the officers of this body, viz., the clergy; and many false arguments and beliefs are based on the confusion.

There are many other sources of confusion from ambiguity in terms. Their variety and frequency only emphasizes the necessity of careful definition. Definition is the weapon before which all ambiguity must fall.

III. Composition and Division

The fallacy of composition arises "when we affirm something to be true of a whole, which holds true only of one or more of its parts when taken separately or distributively." It is sometimes argued, for instance, that because a large number of those composing a given race are ignorant, immoral, and contemptuous of the law, therefore no member of that race is worthy of the respect of honorable men. But the argument, when stated in this bald form, hardly calls for refutation : the fallacy is evident on its very face. When, however, the argument is clothed in a garment of words and phrases, the falsity of the inference is not so easily detected. This fallacy of composition usually arises from a too great readiness to draw unwarranted generalizations.

The fallacy of division is the converse of the fallacy of composition. "It consists in assuming that what is true of the whole is also true of the parts taken separately." To illustrate : In a recent college debate it was argued that a treaty providing for reciprocal trade relations between Canada and the United States would not be beneficial to the United States taken collectively, and then the inference was drawn that it would not be beneficial to the state of Massachusetts. Now, as a matter of fact, the economic conditions and economic needs of Massachusetts are different in many ways from those of the United States in general, so that a tariff policy that injured the country as a whole might, nevertheless, help her as a state. When, therefore, the arguer assumed that the arguments which applied to the states, taken collectively, would necessarily apply to any one of the states, taken separately, he was guilty of the fallacy of division.

IV. Ignoring the Question, or arguing beside the Point

This fallacy consists in mistaking the conclusion to be proved, or endeavoring to prove something which has no important bearing on the point at issue. One is liable to fall into this fallacy either in positive proof or in refutation. In one's own proof one may waste effort in the attempt to establish what is not worth establishing, or one may attempt to deceive by proving something so near like the real conclusion that it seems the same. In refutation, this error lies in mistaking the point to be answered, or in deliberately misrepresenting an opponent's position in order to make reply easier.

Mill cites the example of the refutation made against Malthus's theory of population: —

" The attempts, for instance, to disprove the population doctrines of Malthus have been mostly cases of *ignoratio elenchi* — ignoring the point. Malthus has been supposed to be refuted if it could be shown that in some countries or ages population has been nearly stationary ; as if he had asserted that population always increases in a given ratio, or had not expressly declared that it increases only in so far as it is not restrained by prudence, or kept down by poverty and disease. Or, perhaps, a great collection of facts is produced to prove that in some one country the people are better off with a dense population than they are in another country with a thin one ; or that the people have become more numerous and better off at the same time. As if the assertion were that a dense population could not possibly be well off : as if it were not part of the very doctrine, and essential to it, that where there is a more abundant capital there may be a greater population without any increase of poverty, or even with a diminution of it." [1]

Webster, arguing for the prosecution in the White murder trial, exposed in an opponent the fallacy of ignoring the point, as follows : —

" The prisoner's counsel catch at supposed flaws of evidence, or bad character of witnesses without meeting the case. Do they mean to deny conspiracy? Do they mean to deny that the two Crowninshields and the two Knapps were conspirators ? Why do they rail against Palmer, while they do not disprove, and hardly dispute, the truth of any fact sworn to by him ? Instead of this, it is made a mere matter of sentimentality that Palmer had been prevailed upon to betray his bosom companions and to violate the sanctity of friendship. Again I ask, Why do they not meet the case ? If the fact is out, why not meet it ? Do they mean to deny that Captain White is

[1] Mill, " System of Logic," p. 517.

dead? One would almost have supposed even that, from some remarks that have been made. Do they mean to deny the conspiracy? Or, admitting a conspiracy, do they mean to deny only that Frank Knapp, the prisoner at the bar, was abetting in the murder, being present, and so deny that he was a principal? If a conspiracy is proved, it bears closely upon every subsequent subject of inquiry. Why do they not come to the fact? Here the defence is wholly indistinct. The counsel neither take the ground nor abandon it. They neither fly nor light. They hover. But they must come to a closer mode of contest. They must meet the facts and either deny or admit them." [1]

In addition to these forms we often encounter the same fallacy in the shape of the argument *ad hominem* or the argument *ad ignorantiam.*

The *ad hominem* is an appeal or attack directed at the character, principles, or former beliefs and statements of some person, rather than at the subject-matter in controversy. It is often heard in law courts where one attorney aims to win his case by attacking the character of his opponent or by placing himself personally in a better light before the jury. It is more common in popular harangues and political campaigns, where men and not principles are attacked. This appeal to personal popularity has often been a great power in American politics, even to the extent of making and unmaking Presidents. It is often useful in persuasion, but it is clearly a fallacy of reasoning.

[1] The Works of Daniel Webster, Vol. VI, p. 59. Little, Brown and Co., Boston, 1857.

The argument *ad ignorantiam* consists in attempting or claiming to prove some proposition by arguing that the opposite cannot be proved. The fallacy is essentially a confusion of positive proof and refutation. To show that an opponent's case cannot be established is a proper kind of attack in argumentation; but it is only negative and destructive in nature. It proves nothing positive, and the fallacy consists in maintaining that the lack of proof that a proposition *is not* true, establishes that it *is* true. "Thus," says Creighton, "we cannot prove affirmatively that spirits do not revisit the earth or send messages to former friends through mediums." But this does not prove that spirits do walk the earth.

The fallacy may take various forms, all consisting essentially in this confusion of positive proof and refutation. Every day we hear men argue against some measure, merely supporting their positions by raising objections to this detail and that, and proclaiming the act therefore to be essentially bad. Large combinations of capital "stifle the small producer," they place the responsibility for industrial leadership in the hands of a comparative few, and often make these few men very rich; but it does not necessarily follow that "trusts" are bad. There are objections that may be raised against any proposition, but the objections are not conclusive against it unless it can be shown that they overbalance all that may be said in its favor.

V. Begging the Question

This fallacy consists in assuming the truth of some proposition which is the same as, or equivalent to, the conclusion to be proved, and thence inferring the truth of the conclusion. This fallacy may take any one of several forms. The most common are: (1) assuming the truth of a proposition which is the same as, or equivalent to, the conclusion that is to be proved; (2) assuming the truth of some general proposition which includes the truth of the conclusion to be proved; (3) arguing in a circle.

(1) It seems at first sight that no man would be so foolish or so bold as to assume the truth of his conclusion as one of the means of proving it. But names and phrases often cloak the error, and in the course of the intervening discussion the assumption may be forgotten before the conclusion is reached; so it is not always an easy fallacy to run to earth.

(2) Assuming the truth of some general proposition from which the particular conclusion in question must follow, is but another form of the same mistake. To take an example cited by John Ward, Vol. I, p. 159, of his "System of Oratory":—

"So when the Clodian party contended that Milo ought to suffer death for this reason, because he had confessed that he had killed Clodius, that argument reduced to a syllogism would stand thus:

"*He who confesses he has killed another ought not to be allowed to see the light.*

"*But Milo confesses this.*

" *Therefore he ought not to live.*

"Now the force of this argument lies in the major or first proposition, which Cicero refutes by proving that the Roman people had already determined contrary to what is there asserted : ' *In what city,*' says he, ' *do these men dispute after this weak manner ?   In that wherein the first capital trial was in the case of the brave Horatius, who, before the city enjoyed perfect freedom, was saved by the suffrages of the Roman people, tho' he confessed that he killed his sister with his own hand.*' "

In this case the advocate who was prosecuting Milo assumed the truth of a general proposition, which included the particular proposition he sought to establish. He assumed that every man who has killed another ought to die, when it was admitted that Milo had killed Clodius. Cicero refuted the argument by pointing out the fallacy and showing that the general assumption was false, because the Roman people had in the past pardoned a man who had killed another.

(3) More common than either of the two foregoing is the fallacy called "arguing in a circle." It is one of the frequent errors of careless arguers and a common trick for confusing a sluggish thinker. The fallacy consists in taking two propositions and using them each in turn to prove the other.

For instance, the counsel for the plaintiff in the case of Ogden *vs.* Saunders argued in a circle, and was exposed by Mr. Webster : —

" The plaintiff in error argues in a complete circle. He supposes the parties (in the making of a contract) to have had reference to it (the statute law) because it was a binding law, and yet he proves it to be a binding law only upon the ground that such reference was made to it."

Sir James Fitzjames Stephen, in his " Introduction to the Indian Evidence Act," Ch. II, gives the following illustration : —

" A ship is cast away under such circumstances that her loss may be accounted for either by fraud or by accident. The captain is tried for making away with her.   A variety of circumstances exist which would indicate preparation and expectation on his part if the ship really was made away with, but which would justify no suspicion at all if she was not.   It is manifestly illogical, first, to regard the antecedent circumstances as suspicious, because the loss of the ship is assumed to be fraudulent, and, next, to infer that the ship was fraudulently destroyed from the suspicious character of the antecedent circumstances."

These are not, by any means, all the fallacies men commit in their reasonings, but they are the ones most frequently encountered in public writing and speaking. The ability to detect such mistakes as these explained above, either in the proof of an opponent or in his own proof, is a power which the arguer can hardly overestimate.   In testing his own work it will, at least, guard against drawing inferences that will not bear even superficial scrutiny ; and in testing the arguments of an opponent, though he may not be able entirely to discredit them, he may, unless the inferences are logically drawn, be able to raise a serious question as to their accuracy.

BOOK III.   ARRANGEMENT

CHAPTER I

GENERAL PRINCIPLES OF ARRANGEMENT

WE have now analyzed our question, found out what
we want to prove, and chosen the materials to use in
making the proof.   We have chosen our recruits and
gathered them together; but that is all.   Our army is
only half made; it is but a confused and straggling
mob.   To tempt the fortunes of battle with such an
array would mean defeat.   The forces must be organized into companies, regiments, divisions; they must
be officered with captains, colonels, and generals, and
at their head must be placed a commander, the
master spirit of all; they must be drilled and disci-
plined and taught to know their rights and their
duties.   Organization is no more necessary in an
army than is arrangement in an argument: every
master of the art of war knows how to organize his
forces; every master of the art of debate knows how
to arrange his proofs.   The results from lack of
organization are the same in both, — discord, wasted
strength, and weakness.   It is only by careful arrangement that ideas and evidence can be kept from
self-contradiction and confusion, that their strength
can be saved and directed to accomplish anything.

To secure an effective arrangement of materials in argumentation, the qualities to be sought are three in number : —

      I. Unity.
     II. Coherence.
   III. Emphasis.

I. Unity

It is essential to the success of any piece of argumentation that the ultimate effect produced by it upon the audience shall be a single impression. The judges in a college debate may accept many of the ideas of the affirmative and appreciate much of its evidence; but the affirmative will not win unless the judges are dominated by the single impression that their whole case is stronger than that of the negative. A jury may accept much of the testimony and argument of a plaintiff, yet give the case to the defendant, having greater confidence in the defendant's case *as a whole ;* for to them it may seem that the defendant's testimony " hangs together " better, his arguments may seem more cumulative and coöperative. In any deliberative body it is the measure that seems wisest from the greatest number of viewpoints that is made into law.

To achieve an impression that will bring belief or action, our materials must be so arranged as to be a single unit of force. Little facts and great ideas must work together, each enforcing the other. Each fact must corroborate its fellows, and inconsistency must

K

never appear.   Everything must work for the single ultimate purpose of proving, not this idea or that, but the proposition.   Such unity as this can be obtained only by the most painstaking efforts and the most careful tact.

In any piece of argumentation the most vital force is obviously the proof itself, — the evidence and the arguments.   It would, however, be a very defective effort which contained nothing else besides the giving of testimony and the manufacture of it into proof. These materials must be introduced in such a manner as will clear the way before them and place them in the field advantageously for action.   This is the work of the divisions of the oration called variously by different writers the introduction, the narration, the partition.   By whatever name we call it, some preparation is needed before the work of the discussion can be well done.   The audience must know what the dispute is about, what are the issues to be decided, and what are the points of fact that decide them.   Then, too, our work is never complete till we have gathered together evidence and arguments at the end of the discussion, to show how we have made good the fair promises and claims of the beginning; no work of composition is finished without a conclusion, or peroration.   From the viewpoint of unity the introduction and conclusion are indispensable.   It is practically impossible to bind together evidence, arguments, and ideas of all kinds and degrees of importance, and make them work in

harmony, simply by means of logical internal arrangement.   There must be some other external force to
weld them together and establish them in their true
relations to one another and to the whole.

The work of the introduction is to make clear the
real nature of the question in controversy, why it
is in dispute, how it is related to other problems, what
the really significant facts are.   Such an explanation
presents the question to the audience as a single complete problem, distinguished from other problems; it
fixes the proofs that are to follow in their true relations to the proposition and to each other by explaining what facts are vital in the case, how these facts
may be proved, and how the disputant intends to
create the proof.

The work of the conclusion is to bind finally together the many and varied elements of the proof.
However perfect the introductory precautions, as evidence and arguments are marshalled in rapid succession, and as each fact and each idea is emphasized in
its importance, the reader or hearer loses his grasp
on the case as a whole.   He may believe this testimony or accept that idea, but his beliefs are vague or
hesitating about the conclusiveness of the proof as
a whole.   He is not yet brought to that place where
he can be trusted to render a favoring decision or to
carry out his approval into action.   It still remains
to show that the proof of this point and that, though
insufficient in themselves, when added together prove
the proposition.   The *cumulative* force of the whole

must be displayed ; proof, evidence, and arguments must be gathered together and at length delivered as one blow. This is the work of the conclusion, and if it is well done, the end is but a restatement — though in very different manner — of the beginning. The conclusion should usually be so related to the introduction that the proof seems to lead around in a circle, so that in the end we arrive again at the point from which we started.

In addition to the work of the introduction and the conclusion, in giving unity to the composition, care must be taken in the arrangement of the matter in the body of the discussion itself. The proposition is the chief element that works for coherence in the whole composition ; by relation to it all must be bound together in one. Consequently the materials should be so arranged that every element is connected either directly or indirectly with the proposition, and the connection so clearly established that it will be understood without effort. If a fact or an idea is set up as if for its own sake or is left ambiguous in its bearing on the facts in issue, it turns attention in the wrong direction, gives a mistaken impression of the whole position taken by the arguer, and destroys the coöperation between the parts, which is necessary to unity.

This harmony within the proof itself is largely a matter of proper subordination of the parts, and may better be treated under the heading of coherence.

II. Coherence

Closely akin to unity is the quality of coherence. The purpose of all argumentation is to convey ideas to others and make them believe as we do ; and, however well settled our own conceptions may be, if we beget confusion in presenting them to others, our efforts are in vain. However truly our facts and our inferences have a bearing on the proposition we uphold, if the bearing is not clear to those we seek to convince, our argumentation is a failure. The principle of coherence, then, demands that all the materials of the proof be so arranged as to make clear their relation to each other and to the proposition.

Of the elements of coherence in argumentation, perhaps the most important is what may be called "subordination." We have seen, in the treatment of the finding of the issues, that in any argumentative composition, the proof is made up of materials of widely different values. There are some facts that are so vital that, if we can make sure of them, they will establish our whole case ; and there are others that are truly valuable, but that have no meaning or importance in themselves. These secondary facts find no excuse for their introduction, except that they serve to prove the existence of some other fact. It follows that to put them into the proof without making clear just what is their bearing on these other larger facts, and just what is the part they are intended to perform, is to lose their only value. In the progress of the argument from point to point, they will be passed by without any understanding of their significance, and so are almost as well not given at all.

In contrast with these materials of a tributary nature are those facts and ideas in the proof that are themselves of prime importance. The nature of the human mind is such that, in reasoning, there are always a few points that stand out boldly, while all else sinks into a background of support. No reader or hearer can carry in mind and thoroughly assimilate more than a half dozen important ideas on any question in debate; so that the greatest care must be taken to enforce upon his attention and fix in his memory the facts in the case that are really decisive. He may be permitted to forget the details of evidence, but the existence of these decisive facts he must be brought to remember. If a reader or hearer is really to comprehend the meaning of any proofs, he must be made to understand what is large and what is small, what is important and what trivial. A traveller on the prairie gazes out over the unbroken level of the plain, but he sees nothing and remembers nothing save a feeling of weariness and monotony. The same is even more strikingly true of the mind of a man who is being reasoned with. He must see hills and valleys, light and darkness, great and small, or his mental vision is little more than a blank stare that leaves nothing behind to be remembered or believed.

Therefore, in arranging our materials: (1) We must first find out what are the critical points to be established. (2) Then these points must be made to stand out above all the rest of the proofs. (3) Finally, all the secondary materials must be carefully grouped about these centres of proof.

A second element of coherence in arrangement is a quality that may be called "sequence." Not only is it true that, in the proof, the lesser facts are dependent upon the greater for their value and their meaning, but it is also hardly less true that all the facts and ideas are, in like manner, dependent upon each other. Rarely is any one fact sufficient to establish another larger fact; more rarely is any one single fact or idea sufficient to establish the proposition. Usually the process is: many lesser bits of evidence are set forth to prove each larger fact; then a number of these larger facts combine and coöperate to prove the whole. Where the proofs are of such a nature, the effectiveness of the coequal facts depends, in large degree, upon the way in which they are made to work together.

This coöperation is largely a matter of sequence. Much evidence, not intelligible in itself, becomes full of meaning and force when viewed in the light of other correlative evidence. In any part of the proof, then, it is important that such facts be not set forth till after those from which they get their importance. For a fact misunderstood or neglected when it is first given, "falls back dead" and is rarely called to mind again; it must in most cases be appreciated when it is given, or it is lost. Especially is this true of the treatment of the larger ideas in a composition. Often an audience listens inattentively for many minutes to a speaker who is giving his best energy to the establishment of some idea of the first importance, because they are not possessed of those other facts that they must know to realize the meaning of his proof. Again, it often happens that, before an audience will follow the arguments of a disputant, he must first overthrow certain of the proofs of his opponent. As long as they remain unanswered, the audience remain suspicious and incapable of rightly understanding or crediting anything else; their viewpoint must be corrected before anything else can be done with good effect.

To secure coherence, it is also necessary to arrange the ideas so that they follow one another with easy and natural transitions. A reader or hearer should not feel that he is being arbitrarily picked up, carried around, and dropped, at the whim of the speaker or writer; he should rather have the sensation of being led easily, yet firmly, along in the most natural paths of reasoning. Readers or listeners are easily confused by sudden breaks in the chain of reasoning, and readily become lost if their mental scenes are shifted too suddenly. As the speaker proceeds, an audience should see the way opening gradually before them, feeling that each step is natural; so that when they have come to the end they will believe they have reached a proper destination.

In arranging for proper sequence, then, we need

to consider two requisites: (1) Proofs must be presented in such an order that every fact is clear in its full import at the time when it is presented. (2) Each idea must follow logically from the one preceding, in such a way that a single chain of reasoning runs all through the proof.

III. Emphasis

Well-directed emphasis is one of the prime qualities of all successful composition, and nowhere does it do a greater service than in argumentation. In the first place, as we have already seen, there are some things in our proof that are important and some that are trivial; emphasis distinguishes between them. Again, a disputant always has some points in his case that are strong and can be relied on, while he has others that are weak and vulnerable; emphasis gives prominence to his strong points and covers up his weak points.

Many qualities of arrangement that make for coherence are as truly matters of emphasis. The grouping of lesser facts around the greater, which is so essential to coherence, is equally important in emphasizing the important points in the proof. But, in addition to this discrimination between the lesser and the greater facts, it is also necessary to discriminate between the various more important points of the proof. Some are more warmly contested than others, and the proof on these critical points must be made to stand out over everything else. Again, on some issues, one contestant or another has the bad side for facts; the truth is against him, and he must conceal his defects. So it becomes necessary to know what are the places for the display of strength, and what the places for the hiding of weakness.

The emphatic parts of the proof are the beginning and the end. At the beginning the audience is expectant and critical, and first impressions are enduring; at the end comes "the last word," the part which gives the final impulse to conviction and persuasion. The parts between are most easily forgotten; so it is the middle of the proof that receives what is to be neglected or concealed.

The most important point should usually be placed at the end, for that is the position of maximum emphasis. The importance of the beginning depends somewhat on the circumstances; but it is rarely safe to make a feeble beginning. The first impression must not be weak, for it too often creates a prejudice that is an obstacle to later progress. Sometimes the beginning is made exceptionally important by the necessity for an immediate answer to some argument advanced by an opponent. His arguments may have been so strong and may have made such an effect that the answer to them becomes a turning-point of the proof; the refutation of them must be made emphatic. This refutation may, if the answer is very strong, and if it concerns the most vital point of the

whole question, be reserved till the end. But sometimes the arguments need to be answered at once, in
order to remove hostility on the part of the audience,
and in order to influence them favorably for the
reception of the other proofs that are to come. In
such cases both emphasis and tact require that the
refutation be placed at the beginning.

General refutation may be massed at particular
points, or it may be scattered along at different places
through the proof. Lesser arguments are usually
best answered wherever they happen to be suggested in the course of the proof; for distinct attention to them would give them an undue prominence.
The decision whether a point is of sufficient importance to require separate notice is a matter of individual judgment.

It may readily be seen from the preceding discussion of the general principles of arrangement that
unity, coherence, and emphasis in argumentation
imply more than in most kinds of composition. The
fusing of a multitude of thoughts into one thought,
the careful leading of a man's reason from one point
to another, the indispensable discrimination between
great and small, the painstaking establishment of
unmistakable relations between each small fact and
the whole question, the impressing of the few vital
points on the attention and the memory, — all these
tasks are exaggerated and made more critical than
in any other kind of writing or speaking.

It follows that much more care must be taken here

than in other kinds of composition, in the arrangement of our materials, before we finally put them in
rhetorical form for presentation. In description or
narration, all the work of preliminary arrangement
that is desirable may be embodied in a short outline
of a few headings. All that is needed is a few
rough jottings to state the main ideas and suggest
the general lines of their development; facts, rhetorical figures, mental pictures are properly left to
the suggestion of the minute. In argumentation the
requisites are far different. So much depends upon
the exact relations of fact to fact and point to point,
in order to make our appeals to the reasoning facul-
ties clear and effective, that we must give much more
time and consideration to the arrangement of our
materials. We must not only arrange our main
ideas and indicate the general trend of the development of these ideas, but also the details of fact and
of explanation must be accurately established in their
proper relations with each other.

The work of arrangement in argumentation is best
embodied in what is commonly called a " brief." A
complete " brief " is not, like outlines in many other
kinds of composition, a mere cursory sketch composed of paragraph or sentence headings. An argumentative outline, to do the work of arrangement
properly, should contain a statement and an arrangement of all the materials of the proof. In it should
be found all the essential points of explanation and
introduction, all the evidence, arguments, and ideas

that go to prove the proposition, and all the summarizing required to make the proof effective.   In short, a complete brief differs from the finished composition that may be created from it only in the fact that it lacks rhetorical form and the arts of persuasion.   It contains practically all that is necessary for a successful appeal to the intellect.   The brief is a composition in itself, and, when it is completed, it embodies the greater part of the work of preparation.

CHAPTER II

BRIEF–DRAWING

In the previous chapter we have seen what is the nature of the outline, or "brief," which is to be used in the work of arrangement. This brief is not a mere rough sketch, made as in many other kinds of composition, simply to suggest to our own minds a few main lines of thought. Rude outlines may well be serviceable in argumentation, in helping to clarify our ideas. But they are not the ultimate form in which we should arrange our materials : they are merely helpful steps by which we finally reach a completed brief. On the contrary, the completed brief should contain nearly all the proof of the whole case, even to the statement of the evidence, and should be an argument in itself. The brief is not a mere sketch that may be suggestive to our own minds, but it is a fully developed proof that may well serve to convince others. Further, we have seen that the qualities to be sought in arrangement are unity, coherence, and emphasis.

It is the purpose of this chapter to develop a system by which we can make briefs that will embody these three desirable qualities and fulfil all the requirements of effective arrangement. The plan of the chapter will be: to take some actual proposition for debate, to begin with a rough outline on the negative side of the question, then, step by step, to find the modifications that are necessary to make it an effective brief, finally stating these modifications in the form of rules for brief-drawing.

Let us take first a rough topical outline such as might commonly be made the rude beginning of any ordinary composition.

Question, *Resolved*, that in the United States the contract system of employing convict labor should be abolished.

BRIEF A[1]

NEGATIVE

The convict labor problem.

 Necessity of employment. Experiments with different systems.

Effect of contract system on reformation.

 Control by prison officers, habits of industry (regulations of the contract), and learning trades.

 Competition with free labor under the different systems.

 Competition under piece-price system.

 Competition under contract system.

 Public-account system.

 Methods of removing evils of competition under contract system.

 Contract system is the most profitable.

[1] The term "brief" is hardly the exact name for this rough outline, but it is used for convenience.

Examples.

On the whole the contract system is preferable to
any other.

This outline and the two or three immediately following are little more than a meaningless jumble of
headings to any one but the writer himself, and yet it
is the kind of outline that a student will sometimes
present as the basis of a composition.

What then shall be the first step in giving form to
this material? In the last chapter we saw that in
any piece of argumentation the important part is the
proof itself, and that in order to secure unity it is
necessary to subordinate the introduction and conclusion, making them simply a means in the more
effective presentation of the points in the proof.
In the outline just given it is evident that a part is
introductory in nature, a part is a discussion of the
proof, and part is merely a word of conclusion. This,
then, is the first step: to separate the parts and show
their relationship.

RULE I. *The brief should be divided into three
parts, marked respectively, introduction, discussion,
and conclusion.*

Taking Brief A and separating the parts according
to this rule we have:—

BRIEF B

INTRODUCTION

The convict labor problem.

Necessity of employment. Experiments with different systems.

Effect of contract system on reformation.

> Control by prison officers, habits of industry (regulations of the contract), and learning trades.
>
> Competition with free labor under the different systems.
>
> Competition under piece-price system.
>
> Competition under contract system.
>
> Public-account system.
>
> Methods of removing evils of competition under contract system.
>
> Contract system is the most profitable.
>
> > Examples.

On the whole the contract system is preferable to any other.

To secure unity and coherence in a brief we found not only that it was necessary to consider the introduction and conclusion ancillary to the discussion itself, but also that it was necessary to arrange the material so that it will make clear what is important and what is subordinate. The most natural method of securing this result is to arrange the material of the brief in headings and subheadings.

Take, for instance, this from Brief A : —

> Competition with free labor under the different systems.
>
> Competition under piece-price system.

L

Competition under contract system.
Public-account system.

Although these points are made here as of equal value, it is obvious after a moment's observation that they are of unequal value. Take the first two headings : the second is certainly subordinate to the first, and should be so arranged. Evidently there is some central idea in this group of headings, and we must find this idea and state it in such a way that the minor points can all be grouped under it. What, then, is the central idea ? It involves a comparison of the contract system and the other systems as regards its competition with free labor, and it may be stated as follows : —

BRIEF C

Competition with free labor is less harmful under the contract system than under the other systems.

Effects of competition under the piece-price system.

Effects of competition under the public-account system.

Ways of removing any evil effects under the contract system.

In general, then : —

RULE II. *The ideas in the brief should be arranged in the form of headings and subheadings.*

In taking up Brief B the most obvious fault is the lack of clearness. For the purpose of conveying the ideas to any other person than the maker of the brief, the outline is useless. Take, for illustration, the introduction to this brief : —

The convict labor problem.

    Necessity of employment. Experiments with different systems.

Here no one of the statements carries a clear idea of what was in the mind of the writer. " Necessity of employment." What about it ? Does the writer mean there is no necessity of employment, or that there is a general necessity ? Employment for what purpose ? Under what conditions ? These questions and others may justly be asked, and the brief cannot be said to be even tolerable, until the ideas are so stated that they cannot be misunderstood. Evidently, the principal difficulty lies in the fact that the writer has failed to make his statements *complete*. A word, or even a number of words, taken out of their connection may often have a number of different meanings, and the way to guard against vagueness and ambiguity is to make complete sentences. Let us then expand these phrases into complete statements.

BRIEF D

The problem of employment of the convict is one of the serious problems of criminology.

    It is admitted that the convict must be employed in some kind of work. Several different systems of employment have been tried in this country ; the most important of which are :

the piece-price system, the public-account system, and the contract system.

RULE III. *Each heading and subheading should be in the form of a complete statement.*

Another common fault of brief-drawing, and one closely akin to the one just considered, is that of crowding too much into one heading. It is as important to have each heading a *single* statement as it is to have each heading a *complete* statement. Take, for instance, the first point from the discussion, Brief B : —

Effect of the contract system on reformation.
> Control by prison officers, habits of industry (regulations of the contract), and the learning of trades.

Expanding this into complete statements in accordance with Rule III we have : —

The contract system is effective in the work of reforming the criminal. Under this system criminals are under the direct and responsible control of the prison officers, and are taught habits of industry, for the regulations of the contracts prescribe these things. The criminals have an opportunity to learn practical trades.

The subordinate heading here is an incoherent jumble, or, as it may be called, a crowded heading. The results of a crowded heading are : a lack of evident connection between the different subordinate headings, and a similar lack of connection, between the subordinate headings and the main heading. For instance, the statement "for the regulations of the contracts prescribe these things" evidently has no direct connection with the main heading, "The contract system is effective in the work of reforming the criminal," and to show justification for its presence in the brief some change must be made. This change must be made by a separation of the different ideas of this heading into headings each containing a single statement. It would then read as follows:—

BRIEF E

The contract system is effective in the work of reforming the criminal.

Convicts are under the direct and responsible control of the prison officers.

The contract provides that the contractor shall have no control over the discipline of the prison.

The convicts are taught habits of industry.

The contract provides that they shall be continually employed.

Convicts have an opportunity to learn a practical trade.

RULE IV. *Headings and subheadings should contain but a single statement.*

Thus far we have seen the importance of so stating our headings that the main and the subordinate

parts shall stand in their proper relations. It is difficult, however, to suggest the varying importance of
the different parts simply by the indentation of the
margins and by the form of statement. The only
way, then, seems to be to mark the various headings
by symbols. In doing this some definite system ought
to be followed. In this book the system of marking
will be as follows: —

I.

    A.

        1.

           a.

              x.

II.

    A. etc.

Brief E, then, with these marks, or symbols, added
will read: —

BRIEF F

I. The contract system is effective in the work of
reforming the criminal.

    A. Convicts are under the direct and respon-
sible control of the prison officers.

        1. The contract provides that the contractor
shall have no control over the discipline
of the prison.

    B. The convicts are taught habits of industry.

        1. The contract provides that they shall be
continually employed.

    C. Convicts have an opportunity to learn a
practical trade.

RULE V. *The relation between the headings and subheadings should be indicated by means of letters, numbers, or other symbols.*

In applying any system of lettering there is a common fault which leads to confusion, namely, using more than one symbol for marking a single heading. For instance, in Brief F, the marking is done correctly; but a beginner in argumentation might easily fall into the mistake of marking it something as follows:—

BRIEF G

A. 1. Convicts are under the direct and responsible control of the prison officers.
　2. The convicts are taught habits of industry.
　3. Convicts have an opportunity to learn a practical trade.

In the first heading of Brief G the reason in the mind of the writer for marking it *A.* 1 probably is the more or less vague idea that the three headings, numbered 1, 2, 3, are to be grouped together. He feels that these headings are more or less connected in meaning, so he puts in the letter *A* to indicate the connection. This can be his only excuse for putting in the extra letter, for otherwise it has no meaning whatever.

However, the use of the extra letter does not serve the purpose he has in mind. It does not make clear just *how* the subheads 1, 2, and 3 are connected, but confuses the reader by making him stop and guess what is the connection between them. If any such headings are really associated, the association can be made clear only by definitely stating the connecting idea, in a separate heading. By reference to Brief F we see how the relation of the ideas is rightly expressed. The subheadings are clearly established in their proper relations to one another by stating in main heading (I) the larger idea of which they are subordinate parts. So we have the inviolable rule that no symbol should be put into the brief unless it marks a separate and distinct heading of its own.

RULE VI. *No heading or subheading should be marked with more than one symbol.*

We have now a fairly distinct idea of the general rules for arranging our ideas in the form of a brief. But there are certain particular requisites that are peculiar to the three divisions of the brief, the introduction, the discussion, and the conclusion. These three parts differ from one another in many ways, and must have certain rules of their own, in accordance with which they can best perform their respective functions.

INTRODUCTION

The most important rule for the introduction is:—

RULE VII. *The introduction should contain all the information necessary for the understanding of the discussion.*

The force of this rule is obvious from the very nature of the introduction. The introduction exists solely for the purpose of preparing the way for the effective operation of the actual proof; and it has obviously failed in its purpose if, when the evidence and arguments are presented to the reader or hearer, by reason of his lack of information about the question, he is incapable of understanding the proof.

For an example take Brief B. We find, in the discussion proper, references to "the contract system," "the public-account system," "the piece-price system," terms which are meaningless to any man who has not given particular study to the question. Again, we find the most important points of the proof to be concerned with "reformation," "competition with free labor," and "profitableness"; these words have meaning in themselves, but we cannot see the force of the arguments brought forward concerning them, because we do not understand why these points are important or how they tend to prove anything about the proposition. The introduction in this case, in the first place, should have explained the import of these words whose meaning is not clear in the discussion, *i.e.* it should have explained the piece-price system, the public-account system, and the contract system. And, in the second place, it should have put the reader in possession of the facts of the case which are necessary in order to make clear to him what the real points of issue are, and how the proofs in the discussion establish these points.

This is the work that is usually, though not always, necessary to the introduction, viz.: (1) an explanation of the meaning of the words of the proposition, and of all the other important terms in the question that need explanation in order to be perfectly clear in the discussion; (2) an explanation of the nature of the problem in dispute, in such a way as to make clear the real nature of the question and lead up to (3) a statement of the issues; and (4) the partition, stating the points to be made by the disputant in trying to establish his side of these issues.

The explanation of the terms of the question might take form somewhat as follows: —

BRIEF H

INTRODUCTION

I. The problem of the employment of the convict is one of the serious questions of criminology.

    A. It is admitted that convicts must be employed in some kind of work.

    B. Several different systems have been tried in this country.

        1. The principal systems are the piece-price system, the public-account system, and the contract system.

II. The three systems may be described as follows: —

    A. The characteristics of the piece-price system are three: —

        1. Contracts are made with persons, firms,

or corporations, under which the prison is furnished with raw material.

2. These raw materials are manufactured by the convicts at agreed prices per piece.

3. The work is done wholly under the supervision of prison officials.

B. The public-account system is as follows:—

1. The prison buys its own raw materials.

2. The prison manufactures like a private firm, and sells in the best available market.

C. The contract system involves the following characteristics:—

1. Contracts are made with persons, firms, or corporations, under which convicts are employed at certain agreed prices for their labor for fixed periods of time.

2. The contractors are usually furnished by the prison with power and machinery.

3. The convicts work under the immediate direction of the contractor, but subject to the supervision of the prison officials.

The work of explaining the nature of the question, and stating the points to be proved, is essentially the work that has been treated of in Chapter III, on Finding the Issues. By analyzing the question, studying the history of its discussion, and picking out the points that are vital to the success of either side, we shall find that the settlement of the question depends on the decision of three vital points, viz. : What system gives the best financial returns ? What system is most effective in reforming the criminal ? What system has the most beneficial effect on the general welfare of the free labor of the State ?

If the contract system can be shown on the whole to have the preponderance of virtue in these respects, it is the most desirable and should not be abolished. If, judged by these standards, it is inferior on the whole to some one of the other systems, it should be abolished. The explanation of the nature of the question and the statement of the issues might, then, take form as follows : —

BRIEF I

III. The real question is whether one of the other systems would best be substituted for the contract system.

    A. The value of each system must be judged by three standards : —

        1. Are the financial returns satisfactory ?

        2. How does it affect the reformation of the criminal ?

        3. How does it affect the general welfare of the State ?

The amount of explanation required in a brief depends entirely upon the nature of the particular question. In the brief given above, Brief H, the explanation of the nature of the question is short and takes the form of exposition. In treating any new or uncommon question, full and detailed explanations would be required, in order to give the reader the information necessary to an understanding of the issues and of the question as a whole. In such a generally known question as that of the contract-labor system, little explanation was necessary, and that simply of an expository nature. But very often the explanation of the question takes the form of a narration of facts or a history of the question. In the court room it commonly consists of a narration of the leading facts of the case to be presented. In a discussion of the question, "*Resolved*, that United States senators should be elected by a direct vote of the people," the explanation would take a similar form. It would require a history of the origin of the Senate and of the existing form of election, and a narration of the events leading up to the agitation for popular election.

Finally, it is *generally* desirable to state the points which the disputant proposes to prove in order to establish his case. This is the part of the introduction ordinarily called the partition. Though the points in the partition may well correspond quite closely with the statement of the issues, they are not always identical. With the addition of this statement of the points of the proof, the completed introduction might read as follows : —

BRIEF J

INTRODUCTION

I. The problem of the employment of the convict is one of the serious questions of criminology.

    A. It is admitted that convicts must be employed in some kind of work.

    B. Several different systems have been tried in this country.

        1. The principal systems are the piece-price system, the public-account system, and the contract system.

II. The three systems may be described as follows : —

    A. The characteristics of the piece-price system are three : —

        1. Contracts are made with persons, firms, or corporations, under which the prison is furnished with raw material.

        2. These raw materials are manufactured by the convicts at agreed prices per piece.

        3. The work is done wholly under the supervision of prison officials.

    B. The public-account system is as follows : —

        1. The prison buys its own raw materials.

        2. The prison manufactures like a private firm and sells in the best available market.

    C. The contract system involves the following characteristics : —

    1. Contracts are made with persons, firms, or corporations, under which convicts are employed at certain agreed prices for their labor, for fixed periods of time.

    2. The contractors are usually furnished by the prison with power and machinery.

    3. The convicts work under the immediate direction of the contractor, but subject to the supervision of the prison officials.

III. The real question is, whether one of the other systems would best be substituted for the contract system.

    A. The value of each system must be judged by three standards : —

        1. Are the financial returns satisfactory ?

        2. How does it affect the reformation of the criminal ?

        3. How does it affect the general welfare of the State ?

IV. The negative intends to prove its case by establishing four facts : —

    A. The contract system brings the best financial returns.

    B. The contract system is effective in the work of reforming the criminal.

    C. Any defects of the system can be remedied without destroying the system.

    D. The contract system is the most desirable for its effect on the general welfare of the State.

This introduction, of course, is susceptible to many changes and improvements, but it fulfils with reasonable accuracy the functions of a good introduction for this particular question. In addition to Rule VII, which is explanatory of the general nature of this part of the brief, it should be borne in mind that there are generally three things necessary in the introduction, in order to make it conform to this general rule: (1) a definition and explanation of all the terms of the proposition and of any other important terms in the discussion that need explanation; (2) an explanation of the nature and real meaning of the question as found by analyzing its essential parts, in such a way as to *lead up to* (3) a statement of the issues and of the points to be proved by the disputant in establishing his case. These three elements of the introduction are, however, variable in importance, and their necessity is not in all cases so imperative as to make them all properly part of our Rules for Brief-drawing. But the statement of the issues and of the points to be proved in the discussion is so important as to justify the incorporation of it among the principles of good brief-drawing. We have seen how indispensable it is for the disputant himself to find and understand the issues; it is also generally desirable that the reader or hearer understand them. For him, as for the writer himself, it is knowledge of the issues that helps him to get a clear view of the real question in its entirety; it is the issues that enable him to follow readily the subsequent development of the proof; it is by an understanding of the issues that he may be made to feel the force of the evidence and the arguments, and their full effect upon the proposition.

The work of explaining the issues is like the work of the mill-race. The waters of the river go rushing by with impressive sound and force; but they do not make paper or spin cotton till the raceway gathers in their power and directs it straight at the turbine wheel. So evidence, arguments, and proof of all kinds may impress an audience with their volume and loud sound, but they do not actually convince anybody until they are controlled and effectively directed straight at the proposition. This is the true work of the issues. They are the agency by which the proofs given in the discussion are brought into connection with the proposition, in such a way that every blow in the proof strikes the question fairly and helps the disputant to win his cause. It is sometimes desirable, as a matter of tact, to conceal the points to be proved in the discussion; but such cases are exceptional, and are more properly provided for in the presentation than in the drawing of the brief.

RULE VIII. *The introduction should generally contain a statement of the issues and of the points to be proved in the discussion.*

There is one other desirable precept with respect to the making of an introduction : —

M

RULE IX.   *The introduction should contain only statements, the truth of which is admitted by both sides.*

To recur again to the general principles of arrangement, the introduction never exists for its own sake, and does not properly contain the proof of the proposition.   It is the servant of the discussion and merely preparatory in nature.   If we put into it prejudiced statements, that an opponent must deny and that we must consequently support by proof, it is no longer an introduction, but merely one part of the discussion.   We have destroyed our real introduction entirely.   This is a serious mistake, for with very few exceptions it is indispensable to success that the minds of readers or of an audience be prepared for the reception of the proofs before they are thrust upon them, and this work cannot be well done if the writer is actually arguing, and fighting an opponent all the way.   There is nothing in the work of the introduction to require any prejudice or controversial attitude to make it effective.   It is merely an explanation of the matters that the disputants are reasoning about, and of the facts that the audience must know in order to follow and understand the real discussion. The writings and speeches of the masters of the argumentative art all show their appreciation of the true functions of the introduction and of the necessity of keeping it free from signs of prejudice.   Although it may seem at the moment to be helpful to put a little unfairness and prejudice in at the beginning, it turns out in the end that the final effect is surer, if we withhold our proof till the proper time and place, and use the introduction for its rightful purposes.

THE DISCUSSION

The discussion contains the real proofs of the composition. These proofs are always of the nature of flights of stairs ascending from different directions toward the proposition. There are the smallest details of evidence, which serve to establish certain facts; these facts go to prove some larger facts; and so on, till all meet and are made one in the proposition itself.

Now there are two ways in which these proofs may be arranged to make clear this relation to one another. By one method we proceed from lesser to greater; the smallest details are stated first, then follow the facts these details are meant to prove, and finally the result of it all is stated in the proposition. *C* is true, hence *B* is true; *B* is true, hence *A* is true, and so on.

The other method is just the inverse of this. The fact that is directly connected with the proposition is put first; next come the facts that are the reasons for the truth of these facts that were first alleged; then, following in series, are the lesser and still lesser ideas, each statement reading as a reason for the truth of the statement next above it. *A* is true because *B* is true; *B* is true because *C* is true, etc.

The first method may be illustrated briefly as follows : —

a. The convicts are generally employed within the walls of the prison, and
b. The instructors employed by the contractors are under the control of the prison officers, and
c. The conditions of the employment of the convict are specified in the contract or by legislation; *hence:* —
    1. The system gives opportunity for proper control of the convicts, *hence:* —
        A. Deficiences in reformatory methods and prison discipline can be remedied by careful administration, therefore:—
III. Any defects in the contract system can be remedied without destroying the system.

The second method would make this part of the brief read as follows: —

III. Any defects in the contract system can be remedied without destroying the system because,
    A. Deficiencies in reformatory methods and prison discipline can be remedied by careful administration, for,
        1. The system gives opportunity for proper control of the convicts, for,
            a. The convicts are generally employed within the walls of the prison.

    b. The instructors employed by the con-
tractors are under the control of the
prison officers.

    c. The conditions of the employment of
the convict are specified in the contract or by legislation.

For the purposes of drawing a brief, the second
method is clearly far better than the first. In some
cases it is wise in presenting proof to conceal till the
end the point that is being proved, but these cases
are exceptional; and even where such concealment
is desirable, it is properly carried out in the final
presentation rather than in the making of the brief.
The defects of the first method, which may perhaps be called the "hence and therefore" method,
are obvious. When a brief or an argument founded
upon such a brief is presented, the reader or hearer
does not understand what the disputant is "driving
at," till after long wanderings he reaches the point
to be proved; then the reader is forced to go back
over all the ground again, in order to estimate the
real force of what he has been reading, and an audience, who cannot be given the privilege of hearing it
explained again, have irretrievably lost many of the
good points of the proof.

Again, the "hence and therefore" arrangement
has the disadvantage of presenting a deceptive appearance to the eye. It puts the least important
proof in the most prominent places and makes it

hard to appreciate, at a glance, the real coördination of the points. Finally, it makes the work of lettering and numbering difficult.

So we arrive at the two most important rules for the discussion, the rules that are the fundamentals of clearness in the arrangement of the proof in the form of a brief : —

RULE X. *In the discussion, each main heading should read as a reason for the truth or falsity of the proposition.*

RULE XI. *In the discussion, each subheading or series of subheadings should read as a reason for the truth of the heading above it.*

The last rule of the discussion may be stated as follows : —

RULE XII. *In phrasing refutation, the heading should clearly state the argument to be answered.*

This precept is of great importance, because it guards against a serious error. Refutation is the name that is given to any attack directed against the proof of an opponent. With the importance of refutation and the methods of handling it, we are not now concerned ; but there must always be more or less of it in any brief, and its effectiveness depends very largely upon the way it is introduced. The writer of a brief, knowing in his own mind what is the position of his opponent which he desires to assail, very naturally falls into the mistake of unconsciously attributing a like knowledge to others, and so goes on to array his answers, without making clear to his audience or readers just what it is he is answering. This carelessness often proves troublesome; for in order to make refutation achieve its purposes, it is necessary that the attention of an audience be first directed toward the exact point in controversy, in order that they may see the comparison of the two sides and so feel the destructive force of the answer.

For example, it is urged by opponents of the contract system, that the system enables the prison authorities and the contractors to become rich at the expense of the prisoners. In refuting this point, the student would be guilty of ambiguity if he should say, "The contract system does not allow the prison authorities and the contractors to become rich at the expense of the prisoners." It might very naturally be supposed from the statement that this is a point of positive proof rather than a point in refutation, that the writer is upholding this as one of the virtues of the system. This makes his proof weak, for he is "damning the system with faint praise." Again, this statement of the point might be interpreted to mean, that the writer was comparing the contract system with other systems, and declaring it to be preferable in this respect. As a matter of fact, what he means is, that the arguments made by his opponent to prove this objection to the contract system are false. To make his position clear and to bring his own arguments into proper contrast with those of his opponent, he should have stated his refutation something as follows : "The objection that this system allows the prison authorities and the contractors to become rich at the expense of the prisoners is groundless, for," etc.

This is, in general, the desirable way to phrase refutation ; state briefly and clearly the argument to be answered, and suggest the general nature of the answer. As for instance, "The contention that free silver causes prosperity is founded upon a false assumption, for," etc. "The evidence of Madden that Swift was married to Stella Johnson is unreliable, for," etc. "The argument that the incorporation of labor unions will prevent strikes is weak, for," etc. Whatever the form of the statement, it should so proclaim the argument to be answered that the attention of a reader or hearer cannot be misdirected.

The Conclusion

The function of the conclusion in the brief is obvious from the word itself. Its duty is merely to sum up the essential points that have been established by the proof, and to make clear their bearing as a whole on the proposition. This work is best done by a summary in brief form, lettered and numbered.

The summary should generally contain a statement of all the main headings of the discussion, and of as many of the subheadings as are necessary finally to present the proof as a whole. An illustration of the form of such summary is given in the conclusion of the brief printed at the end of this chapter.

· RULE XIII. *The conclusion should contain a summary of the essential points of the proof.*

The following brief is, with slight emendations, a student's brief presented in class work. It is not presented as perfect or as approaching perfection, but it illustrates the principles that work toward the making of a brief, effectively embodying the general laws of the arrangement of materials.

INTRODUCTION

I. The problem of the employment of the convict is one of the serious questions of criminology.

   A. It is admitted that convicts must be employed in some kind of work.

   B. Several different systems have been tried in this country.

      1. The principal systems are the piece-price system, the public-account system, and the contract system.

II. These three systems may be described as follows : —

   A. The characteristics of the piece-price system are three : —

      1. Contracts are made with persons, firms, or corporations under which the prison is furnished with raw materials.

      2. These raw materials are manufactured by the convicts at agreed prices per piece.

    3. The work is done wholly under the supervision of prison officials.

B. The public-account system is as follows : —

    1. The prison buys its own raw materials.

    2. The prison manufactures like a private firm, and sells in the best available market.

C. The contract system involves the following characteristics : —

    1. Contracts are made with persons, firms, or corporations, under which convicts are employed at certain agreed prices for their labor, for fixed periods of time.

    2. The contractors are usually furnished by the prison with power and machinery.

    3. The convicts work under the immediate direction of the contractor, but subject to the supervision of the prison officials.

III. The real question is whether some one of the other systems would best be substituted for the contract system.

    A. The value of each system must be judged by three standards : —

        1. Are the financial returns satisfactory ?

        2. How does it affect the reformation of the criminal ?

        3. How does it affect the general welfare of the State ?

IV. The negative intends to prove its case by establishing four facts : —

A. The contract system brings the best financial returns.

B. The contract system is effective in the work of reforming the criminal.

C. Any defects of the system can be remedied without destroying it.

D. The contract system is the most desirable for its effect on the general welfare of the State.

DISCUSSION

I. The contract system brings the best financial returns, because,

 A. The system avoids expenses necessary in the other systems, for,

  1. It avoids the expense of machinery.

  2. It avoids the necessity of supplying working capital.

  3. It avoids the employment of high-priced officials and salesmen.

  4. It avoids the risks and losses of trade.

  5. It diminishes opportunities for peculation, because,

   a. Extravagance and peculation are common under the other systems, for,

    x. The Commissioner of Labor of New York declares, "The large outlay of funds under the public-account system gave opportunity for wholesale extravagance and peculation."

B. The public-account system is seriously defective from a financial standpoint, for,

    1. In Illinois in four years and five months the loss to the state was $314,212.

    2. In New York it was found that the expenses of the sales department were such as to make the system financially impracticable.

C. According to the report of the United States Commission of Labor, the income of this system is sixty-five per cent of the running expenses of the prison.

D. The Commission, comparing this system with others, declares these returns to be more satisfactory than those from any other system, for,

    1. This Commission says, "In a financial sense the contract system is the most profitable of any to the State, except the so-called lease system."

II. The contract system is effective in the work of reforming the criminal, because,

A. The convicts are under the direct and responsible control of the State, for,

    1. In every contract there is a clause providing that the contractor shall have no control over, and shall in no way interfere with, prison discipline.

    2. Punishment cannot be inflicted on the complaint of instructors without full investigation by the wardens.

3. The penalty for any violation of the rules by a contractor or instructor is immediate dismissal.

B. The system teaches the prisoner a practical trade by which he can earn an honest living after release, because,

1. The Labor Commissioners of New York say that the convicts learn exactly the same trades and specialize in the same way as in factories and other places of work outside.

2. It proved effective in Pennsylvania in teaching trades for practice after leaving the prison.

C. It teaches habits of industry, because,

1. Under it the convict must be constantly employed, for,

a. The contractor engages to keep a certain number of men continually employed.

D. The contract system promotes the health of the convicts, because,

1. Mr. Pillsbury of New York says that the system is very beneficial to the health of the convicts, and that they leave the prison in better physical condition than when they came.

III. Any defects in the contract system can be remedied without destroying the system, because,

A. Deficiencies in reformatory methods and prison discipline can be remedied by careful administration, for,

    1. The system gives opportunity for proper control of the convicts, for,

        a. The convicts are generally employed within the walls of the prison.

        b. The instructors employed by the contractors are under the control of the prison officers.

        c. The conditions of the employment of the convict are specified in the contract or by legislation.

    2. The work of reform depends largely upon the character of the officers in charge.

    3. The character of the officials can be improved by legislation, for,

        a. Making the offices non-partisan would remove inefficiency due to politics.

        b. Efficiency of the officers would be improved by making the term of office permanent during good behavior.

B. Any possible evils of competition can be remedied by legislation, because,

    1. Competition can be prevented by limiting the production of any article by convicts to one-tenth of the total product in that State.

    2. Competition could be lessened by pro-

viding for a greater diversity of products by the convicts, for,

 a. The Labor Commissioner of Massachusetts recommends this as a remedy.

 3. Competition could be lessened by a law requiring the public advertisement for proposals for contracts, because,

  a. This would tend to prevent injuriously low prices in competition, for,

   x. The advertisement of the proposals would raise the cost of production to the contractor by stimulating competition in bids for the labor.

IV. The contract system is the most desirable for its effect on the general welfare of the State, because,

 A. The argument that the competition of convict labor with free labor under the contract system is detrimental to the welfare of the State is weak, for,

  1. The competition must exist under any system of employment, because,

   a. The products of the convict must be sold in the market.

  2. The competition is more serious under the public-account system, for,

   a. Goods can be sold below the market price in competition, because, *x.* The state cannot be forced into bankruptcy.

      y. The whole cost of production is the cost of the material.

   b. The tendency is to centralize manufactures on a few lines of production, for,

      x. It is impossible to manage many different lines of manufacturing.

   c. The United States Industrial Commission says, " It has been shown by numerous investigations that under the public-account system there is greater competition with the products of free labor than under any other."

3. The competition is at least no less harmful under the piece-price system, because,

   a. The Industrial Commission in their report of 1900 say that the piece-price system does not affect the competition with free labor.

   b. The first biennial report of the Bureau of Labor of California declares that under the piece-price system the effects of competition were no different from the effects under the contract system.

   c. The Prison Labor Reform Commission of New York stated that, in practical operation, the piece-price

system was shown to be more oppressive to competitive free labor
than the contract system.

  d. In New Jersey this system was found
  to be worse in its competitive effects
  than the contract system.

B. It is conducive to the effective administration of the prison, for,

  1. The officers of the prison are chosen
  solely for their efficiency as prison
  keepers, for,

    a. They are not required to act as busi-
    ness managers, because

      x. The manufacturing is done under
      the direction of outside contrac-
      tors.

  2. The contract system restricts prisons to
  the use for which they are intended, for,

    a. It relieves the management of the
    prison from the necessity of managing
    large manufacturing establishments,
    as under the other systems.

CONCLUSION

The negative has proved the following : —

I. The contract system brings the best financial
returns, because,

  A. It avoids expenses necessary in the other
  systems.

N

    B. The public-account system is seriously defective financially.

    C. The income from the contract system is sixty-five per cent of the running expenses.

    D. Students of the subject declare that the returns are largest from the contract system.

II. The contract system is effective in the work of reforming the criminal, for,

    A. The convicts are under the direct control of the State.

    B. The system furnishes a trade to the convict, and thus furnishes a means of honest livelihood on his release.

    C. The convict is taught habits of industry.

    D. The contract system promotes the health of the convicts.

III. Any defects in the contract system can be remedied without destroying the system, for,

    A. Disciplinary and reformatory deficiencies can be remedied by careful administration.

    B. Any possible evils of competition can be remedied by legislation.

IV. The contract system is the most desirable for its effect on the general welfare of the State, for,

    A. The argument that it introduces undesirable competition with free labor is weak.

    B. It gives effective prison administration.

We therefore maintain that the contract system of employing convict labor should not be abolished.

RULES FOR BRIEF–DRAWING
General Rules

I. The brief should be divided into three parts, marked respectively, introduction, discussion, and conclusion.

II. The ideas in the brief should be arranged in the form of headings and subheadings.

III. Each heading and subheading should be in the form of a *complete* statement.

IV. Each heading and subheading should contain but a *single* statement.

V. The relation between the headings and the subheadings should be indicated by means of letters, numbers, or other symbols.

VI. No heading or subheading should be marked with more than one symbol.

Rules for Introduction

VII. The introduction should contain all the information necessary for an understanding of the discussion.

VIII. The introduction should generally contain a statement of the issues and of the points to be proved in the discussion.

IX. The introduction should contain only statements the truth of which is admitted by both sides.

Rules for Discussion

X. In the discussion, each main heading should read as a reason for the truth or falsity of the proposition.

XI. Each subheading or series of subheadings should read as a reason for the truth of the heading above it.

XII. In phrasing refutation the heading should state clearly the argument to be answered.

RULE FOR CONCLUSION

XIII. The conclusion should contain a summary of the essential points of the proof.

In concluding this chapter there is one other matter of detail, to which reference should be made, though it is a matter of individual discretion rather than of rule or precept, that is the method of inserting references to authorities. The method may be adopted which is used in the text of the present volume, of putting numbers in the body of the text (or brief) with the title and exact citation of the authority appended at the foot of the page. Or, it is simpler, and just as clear, merely to add the reference at the end of the quotation or statement which it supports. Probably the best method, on the whole, and the one to be recommended, is to insert the reference in the margin of the brief, opposite the heading in connection with which it is quoted.

Whatever the method, the exact citation for every authority used should *always* be given.

BOOK IV.   PRESENTATION

CHAPTER I

GENERAL PRINCIPLES OF PRESENTATION

UNDER invention, selection, and arrangement, we have considered the methods of finding materials, of estimating their value, and of arranging them so as best to utilize their strength.   The product of our work has been embodied in a brief.   It sometimes happens that our preparation ends here; the brief itself may be the presentation of our argument.   But as a rule other preparation is required.   The brief is usually but the foundation-stones and the beams which sustain and shape the building, but which in the end are hidden from view by outward forms that are more sightly and more useful.   To achieve our purposes, we generally need to put the materials in more pleasing and effective rhetorical form.

Now, in this ultimate presentation of the proof, we need to bear in mind that the labors of argumentation are twofold.   In our earlier consideration of the general nature of the art, we have seen that there are two elements in all argumentation: (1) conviction, or the appeal to the reason, which is the act of inducing another to accept the truth of an idea or proposition; and (2) persuasion, or the appeal to the emotions, which is the act of moving the will of another by affecting his feelings. We have further seen that both are essential to effectiveness.

How much conviction and how much persuasion to use must be determined by circumstances. In an intercollegiate debate, the element of persuasion is slight. It is usually no more than tact and vigor in the work of conviction. The lawyer before the jury needs a judicious mixture of both. Danton before the French Convention made his appeal wholly to the most turbulent passions of a passionate mob. But though the relative amounts of the two elements may vary, both are almost always necessary for success.

Conviction

The most important work of conviction is done when the brief is completed. When the materials have been gathered and arranged, it only remains to put the proof in words that will impress it clearly and forcibly on the understanding of those we would convince. To be able to do this, obviously the first requisite is a knowledge of rhetoric. The effect of well-arranged and well-chosen proofs is often neutralized by confused and halting English. The man who cannot express himself is always a weakling in argumentation.

Then, in addition to the general principles of rhetoric, there are certain adaptations of these rhetorical principles to the peculiar work of argumentation.

A general treatment of rhetorical forms lies beyond the necessary limits of this book. The principles that are peculiar to argumentative composition will be treated in the following chapters on the introduction, the discussion, and the conclusion.

Persuasion

Persuasion has been defined as the act of moving the will by affecting the emotions. The ultimate aim of argumentation is to make others believe as we desire. This can be done only through the medium of the will. If the volition of the audience or reader is left untouched, our strivings are in vain. Consequently, it is the work of persuasion to establish a connection between the will and the ideas communicated to the intellect by conviction. But the moving power of the human will is emotion. So that persuasion is an appeal to the emotions.

Persuasion may come before conviction, or after it, or the two may accompany one another at each step. We may touch the emotions first, to prepare them for the reception of the proof to come. We may first convince, and afterward carry over the effects on the intellect till they reach and compel the will. We may — and with best results — play on reason and emotion simultaneously, and so keep understanding and volition always in sympathy. However it is done, the essential thing is, that, **in** some way, reason and emotion shall be brought together and made coöperant to the common end.

Professor Robinson, in his excellent book on "Forensic Oratory," has given a classification of the emotions that it is sometimes helpful to have in mind.

"That fundamental principle out of which all noble impulses arise is the tendency of human nature toward perfection. . . . Perfection is predicable of human nature as to its action, as to its character, and as to its attainment. A man is perfect as to action when he fulfils his duty; as to character, when his predominant ideas and impulses are pure and virtuous; as to attainment, when he possesses the highest happiness which human nature is able to enjoy. And thus in actual life the fundamental tendency toward perfection manifests itself in three subordinate tendencies: the tendency toward duty, the tendency toward virtue, and the tendency toward happiness. . . .

"These natural dispositions render the heart susceptible to certain impulses, each of which corresponds to some one of the many forms in which the ideas of duty, virtue, and happiness are presented to the mind. The idea of duty yet to be fulfilled awakens zeal; of duty heretofore performed, complacency; of duty which another had omitted, anger; of duty as discharged by another, approbation. The idea of virtue as an attribute of character engenders admiration; as exemplified in individuals, good will, esteem, friendship, or even love for them and emulation of their excellence; as contrasted with vice, abhorrence of the vice itself and aversion or contempt toward those in whose character depravity is manifested. The idea of happiness as possible begets courage, desire, and hope; as unattainable, despair; as already possessed, joy;

as derived from others, gratitude; as endangered, fear; as denied to others, pity; as prevented or destroyed by others, indignation. These are the universal impulses to which all men are subject. These are the weapons of the orator to which no human heart can ever be invulnerable."[1]

The course of successful argumentation is, then: (1) to set forth our proofs in such a way that they will be understood and accepted as true; (2) to establish these proofs in connection with some one or more of the emotions, and (3) to rouse the emotions to such a degree that they will move the will. Take for an illustration the advocate. He presents his witnesses, his arguments, his evidence, and so seeks to convince the reason of the jury that his client has the truth on his side. But that is not all. Before making this appeal, he prepares the jury for a favorable reception of his proofs by a tactful appeal to their emotions. He tells them of his own sincerity and longing for justice, and so rouses the instincts of virtue and duty to give him attention and sympathy. As he proceeds he discourses on the demeanor of witnesses, on the "exemplary conduct of his client" and the malice of the parties of the other side, again touching the chords of virtue in his hearers. He appeals to their instincts of happiness, by portraying the misfortunes of his client, as the evidence is made to tell the story. In his peroration he summons them to the performance of their duty.

In handling persuasion we have always to con-

[1] Robinson, "Forensic Oratory," pp. 14–15.

sider : (1) what emotions to appeal to, and (2) how to make the appeal.

(1) In deciding what emotions are best appealed to, there are to be considered : first, the audience, using the word to embrace both hearers and readers, and, second, the circumstances.   In order to persuade, a speaker or writer must identify himself with his audience.   If they are mentally his inferiors, he must descend to their level.   If their most common instincts are different from those natural to him, he must yield to their spirit and make their feelings his. The debater cannot command from a height ; he must descend and lead.

Contrast, for example, the methods of persuasion in the two following selections : the first is an introduction taken from a speech by Edmund Burke, showing one of the serious defects of the great English statesman as an orator; he was wholly lacking in tact and in the powers of handling men.   On one occasion, in addressing the House of Commons, he said : —

"Mr. Speaker, I rise under some embarrassment occasioned by a feeling of delicacy toward one-half of the house, and of sovereign contempt for the other half."

The second selection is taken from the speech by Governor Livingstone of New Jersey before the legislature of New Jersey in 1777 : —

"Having, already, laid before the assembly, by messages, the several matters that have occurred to me, as more particularly demanding their attention, during the present session, it may seem less necessary to address you in the more ceremonious form of a speech. But, conceiving it my duty to the state to deliver my sentiments on the present situation of affairs, and the eventful contest between Great Britain and America, which could not, with any propriety, be conveyed in occasional messages, you will excuse my giving you the trouble of attending for that purpose."[1]

But men are not always moved by the same appeals under different circumstances. The following is the eloquent conclusion of one of Henry Ward Beecher's sermons in the pulpit of the Plymouth Church, Brooklyn : —

"We are children of God in proportion as we are in sympathy with those who are around about us, and in proportion as we bear with each other. How sacred is man, for whom Christ died! And how ruthlessly do we treat him! Oh, my brother, oh, my sister, oh, father and mother, you are of me, and I am of you! We have the same temptations. We are walking to the same sounds. We are upon the same journey, out of darkness toward light; out of bondage toward liberty; out of sin toward holiness; out of earth toward heaven; out of self toward God. Let us clasp hands. Let us cover each other's faults. Let us pray more and criticise less. Let us love more and hate less. Let us bear more and smite less. And by and by, when we stand in the unthralled land, in pure light, made as the angels of God, we will pity ourselves for every stone that we threw, but we shall not be sorry for any tear that we shed, or any hour of

[1] "Eloquence of the United States," Vol. V, p. 64. Compiled by E. B. Williston, 1827.

patient endurance that we experienced for another. Not the songs that you sang, not the verses that you wrote, not the monuments that you built, not the money that you amassed, but what you did for one of Christ's little ones, in that hour will be your joy and your glory above everything else.

"Brethren, this is a sermon that ought to have an application to-day, on your way home, in your houses, and in your business to-morrow. From this time forth, see that you are better men yourselves, and see that your betterment is turned to the account of somebody else. And consider yourselves as growing in grace in proportion as you grow in patience and helpfulness. Consider yourselves as growing in piety and as growing toward God in proportion as you grow in sympathy for men." [1]

With this, contrast the following appeal by the same speaker to a hostile public meeting in Liverpool, England. Mr. Beecher had already made several speeches in the cities in England in behalf of the Northern interests in the Civil War, and this was his greatest effort. Liverpool was the recognized headquarters of the Southern sympathizers in England; so that the audience that confronted him was largely hostile, and he was compelled to fight for a hearing in the face of hisses, catcalls, and every form of indecent interruption. Mr. Beecher began : —

"For more than twenty-five years I have been made perfectly familiar with popular assemblies in all parts of my country except the extreme South. There has not for the whole of that time been a single day of my life when it

[1] "Plymouth Pulpit," Eighth Series, March-September, 1872, p. 245.

would have been safe for me to go south of Mason and Dixon's line in my own country, and all for one reason : my solemn, earnest, persistent testimony against that which I consider to be the most atrocious thing under the sun — the system of American slavery in a great free republic. [Cheers.] I have passed through that early period when right of free speech was denied to me. Again and again I have attempted to address audiences that, for no other crime than that of free speech, visited me with all manner of contumelious epithets ; and now since I have been in England, although I have met with greater kindness and courtesy on the part of most than I deserved, yet, on the other hand, I perceive that the Southern influence prevails to some extent in England. [Applause and uproar.] It is my old acquaintance ; I understand it perfectly — [laughter]—and I have always held it to be an unfailing truth that where a man had a cause that would bear examination he was perfectly willing to have it spoken about. [Applause.] And when in Manchester I saw those huge placards, 'Who is Henry Ward Beecher?' [laughter, cries of "Quite right," and applause], and when in Liverpool I was told that there were those blood-red placards, purporting to say what Henry Ward Beecher has said, and calling upon Englishmen to suppress free speech, I tell you what I thought. I thought simply this, 'I am glad of it.' [Laughter.] Why? Because if they had felt perfectly secure, that *you* are the minions of the South and the slaves of slavery, they would have been perfectly still. [Applause and uproar.] And, therefore, when I saw so much nervous apprehension that, if I were permitted to speak — [hisses and applause] — when I found they were afraid to have me speak — [hisses, laughter, and " No, no ! "] — when I found that they considered my speaking damaging to their cause — [applause] — when I found

that they appealed from facts and reasonings to mob law —
[applause and uproar] — I said, no man need tell me what
the heart and secret counsel of these men are.   They
tremble and are afraid.   [Applause, laughter, hisses, " No,
no ! " and a voice, " New York mob."]   Now, personally,
it is a matter of very little consequence to me whether I
speak here to-night or not.   [Laughter and cheers.]   But
one thing is very certain, if you do permit me to speak here
to-night, you will hear very plain talking.   [Applause and
hisses.]   You will not find a man — [interruption] — you
will not find me to be a man that dared to speak about
Great Britain three thousand miles off, and then is afraid
to speak to Great Britain when he stands on her shores.
[Immense applause and hisses.]   And if I do not mistake
the tone and temper of Englishmen, they had rather have
a man who opposes them in a manly way — [applause
from all parts of the hall] — than a sneak that agrees with
them in an unmanly way.   [Applause and " Bravo ! "]
Now, if I can carry you with me by sound convictions, I
shall be immensely glad [applause] ; but if I cannot carry
you with me by facts and sound arguments, I do not wish
you to go with me at all ; and all that I ask is simply FAIR
PLAY.   [Applause, and a voice, " You shall have it, too."]

" Those of you who are kind enough to wish to favor my
speaking, — and you will observe that my voice is slightly
husky from having spoken almost every night in succession for some time past, — those who wish to hear me
will do me the kindness simply to sit still ; and I and
my friends the Secessionists will make all the noise.
[Laughter.] " [1]

It hardly seems possible that these two speeches
were from the same lips.   They are both strong emo-

[1] " Patriotic Addresses," Beecher, p. 516.

tional appeals, and the power of each depends, in no small degree, upon the fitness for the time and place. In the case of the sermon, Mr. Beecher spoke to an audience gathered on a quiet Sabbath day, in a consecrated edifice, in whose "dim religious light" were felt all the sacred influences of architecture and of music. The minds of his hearers were open to high thoughts and ready to meet in close communion of sympathy and feeling with the orator. So he might well touch the chords of mutual love and of aspiration. In Liverpool, before a strange audience in a strange hall, his coming heralded by scurrilous placards and threats against his life, the orator was compelled to fight for even the privilege of speech itself. To have addressed such a crowd in terms of "holiness" and "temptation" would have been to raise a riot. On the other hand, if the pastor of the Plymouth pulpit had appealed to his congregation for "fair play," he would have been charged with insanity.

Beecher's speech in Liverpool also affords a good illustration of the need of knowing the character and previous opinions of an audience. His audience was largely made up of laboring men. They were struggling from day to day to make an honest living, and their standard of value was wages; they commonly estimated ideas in terms of pounds, shillings, and pence. The master of persuasion knew their thoughts and directed his appeal accordingly. He founded his reasoning on the basis of the benefits to English industry and wages, from the freeing of the Southern slaves.

English industry, he said, needs not cotton, but consumers; slaves are not consumers, but make them free, and they become the patrons of British cotton and linen, machines and books. Furthermore, he spoke in terms that would reach and stir a workingman.

" It is a necessity of every manufacturing and commercial people that their customers should be very wealthy and intelligent. Let us put the subject before you in the familiar light of your own local experience. To whom do the tradesmen of Liverpool sell the most goods at the highest profit? To the ignorant and poor, or to the educated and prosperous? [A voice, " To the Southerners." Laughter.] The poor man buys simply for his body; he buys food, he buys clothing, he buys fuel, he buys lodging. His rule is to buy the least and the cheapest that he can; he brings away as little as he can; and he buys for the least he can. . . .

" A savage is a man of one story, and that one story a cellar. When a man begins to be civilized, he raises another story. When you christianize and civilize the man, you put story upon story, for you develop faculty after faculty, and you have to supply every story with your productions. The savage is a man one story deep, the civilized man is thirty stories deep. [Applause.] Now, if you go to a lodging-house where there are three or four men, your sales to them may, no doubt, be worth something; but if you go to a lodging-house like some of those which I saw in Edinburgh, which seem to contain about twenty stories [" Oh, oh! " and interruption], every story of which is full, and all who occupy buy of you — which is the better customer, the man who is drawn out or the man who is pinched up? " [1]

[1] " Patriotic Addresses," Beecher, p. 519.

(2) The question how to appeal to the emotions is more serious. The first requisite is a knowledge of human nature. We have seen that one of the prime qualities of effectiveness is adaptation to the audience. To get such adaptation a speaker or writer must know the peculiarities of the men he addresses. However, such knowledge alone will not enable him to persuade. If he does not understand human nature in general, he is powerless to reach the emotions which he knows are before him. He must know how men in general think and act; when a man is best persuaded by silence and when he needs to be reassured; when to wait and when to strike. Such knowledge is not gained from books and cannot be explained. It comes only from contact with men and close study of their habits of mind. The master of persuasion is never a recluse.

Closely akin to the persuasive powers arising from the knowledge of human nature, are the influences that come from the personality of the speaker or writer. The influence of personality is felt most strongly in oratory; but personal character shows itself in print as well, and wherever it goes it persuades, favorably or unfavorably. Every quality of mind or heart that may make enemies or make friends is a proper part of persuasive power.

There are two qualities that may be mentioned as particularly desirable in argumentative persuasion. The first is sincerity or earnestness. No man will be persuaded by any one who he thinks is trying to

o

deceive him or play with his convictions for personal ends. A suspicious audience is the hardest kind to handle, and undoubtedly an audience does not require much to make it suspicious. Sometimes the hearers have occasion to suspect that a speaker is positively dishonest and designing; but more often they believe simply that the speaker is arguing for argument's sake or "to be worthy of his hire," and that he really has no interest or confidence in his cause. Such suspicion is seriously damaging to persuasive power. Enthusiasm in an audience can be roused only by enthusiasm in the speaker, and earnest conviction is only begotten by a belief in the earnestness of him who persuades. Consequently, whatever his real motives, no great orator, no effective writer, neglects to be sure at every step that his audience have confidence in the honesty and earnestness of his endeavors. Hence it is, that the following exordium is an example of one of the most common methods of introduction. It is taken from the speech of Sir James McIntosh in behalf of Jean Peltier before the Court of the King's Bench, February, 1803, and shows how necessary a man, of even so great eloquence, thought it to be that his audience believe in his sincerity.

"I must begin with observing that, though I know myself too well to ascribe to anything but to the kindness and good nature of my learned friend, the attorney-general, the unmerited praises which he has been pleased to bestow on me, yet, I will venture to say, he has done me no more than justice in supposing that in this place and on this occasion, where I exercise the functions of an inferior minister of justice, an inferior minister, indeed, but a minister of justice still, I am incapable of lending myself to the passions of any client, and that I will not make the proceedings of this court subservient to any political purpose." [1]

Another element of persuasion is a quality in the speaker or writer that may be termed *modesty*. Modesty, in this connection, does not mean an attitude of subservience or self-suspicion. Proper modesty does not require that a speaker apologize for his poor abilities, his "inadequacy to the task before him," etc. There is such a thing — even in public discussion — as false modesty, and it is a detriment to him who plays with it. Self-confidence and manly courage are perfectly consistent with every attribute of real modesty. True modesty requires simply, that the man should be made secondary to the subject. If it be an arguer's purpose to display his own abilities and dazzle his audience, conceit is no hindrance; but if it be his aim to win his case, it is different. If he makes it evident that he thinks he is himself more important than what he has to say, the men whom he is addressing will readily share his disrespect for the cause he represents, and, however much they may envy his brilliancy, they will be likely to give their allegiance elsewhere. Furthermore, an audi-

[1] Howell's State Trials, Vol. 28, p. 566.

ence has a natural tendency to doubt the modesty
of a speaker. For the moment he is on a plane a
little above his auditors; he stands as their leader in
thought and action. Now an audience are willing to
be led, but they object to being driven. They will
accept leadership, but they will rebel against dictation, and they are quick to notice any assumption of
superiority or command. The line between leadership and dictation, between equality and assumed
superiority, is the dead-line of friendship with the
audience, and a speaker who crosses the line has
lost much of the power of persuasion. This is the
essence of the art of persuasion; *the relation of the
speaker to his audience and of the writer to his reader
must always be an attitude of leadership.*

Assuming that the arguer knows the character of
his audience, has learned by study of human nature
how to reach the emotions he sees before him, and is
keeping in sympathy with the men he is seeking to
persuade, it still remains for him to apply his own
particular subject to the particular audience. In
order to do this, he needs to consider carefully *what
ideas in his proof will most forcibly affect the emotions
of his hearers or readers.* There are in every question certain phases of it that have a particular interest for any particular audience. The workingmen
of Liverpool in 1863 were most interested in the
industrial side of the slavery question, and Beecher
showed his consummate tact in choosing this as the
one phase to be treated above all others at the mass-

meeting in Philharmonic Hall (see p. 192). It would have been folly to have discussed the question from the standpoint of American patriotism. On the other hand, before a council of clergymen in the United States, it would have been the immorality of "man owning man" that would have been the theme of persuasion.

It often happens that speakers and writers treat their subjects from too many points of view. They turn the question over and examine it on every side, when the men whom they address are moved in mind or heart by only one aspect of it all. Intellect may be the same in every audience, varying only in the degree of its keenness; but the emotional interests of audiences differ widely in their very nature. In any subject there are only certain phases that can touch these varying emotions, and it is a fundamental duty of one who would persuade, to consider well what these interesting phases are. Then his appeals will be well directed toward the vulnerable points, and his blows will be of some effect on the will of his audience.

The work of persuasion as here outlined takes varied forms in the different parts of the presentation. These particular forms are best discussed in the following chapters, on the introduction, the discussion, and the conclusion.

CHAPTER II

THE INTRODUCTION

THE duty of the introduction is to prepare the way for the work of the discussion proper. This duty of the introduction is twofold. Both the intellect and the emotions must be reached in the discussion, and so both must be made ready by the work of the introduction. The intellect must be prepared, so that all the proofs may have their fullest effect; the emotions, in order that the speaker or writer may, from the first, be brought into harmony with the forces that will ultimately sway his audience. So the introduction must contain both conviction and persuasion.

Conviction

We have seen that, with respect to conviction, it is the duty of the introduction to give all the information necessary for an understanding of the discussion; also that the parts usually necessary for the accomplishment of this purpose are, briefly: (1) a definition of terms; (2) an explanation of the question in such a way as to lead up to (3) the issues, and (4) the partition or statement of the points to be proved in the discussion.

I. Definition.

Definition in argumentation serves two purposes. It serves, first, to enable the writer himself, in the beginning of his work in preparation, to find out the real meaning of the question. Secondly, it serves to make the meaning of the question clear to the reader or hearer. In the execution of the former of these two purposes the definitions do not need to be expressed at all; it is sufficient that the investigator find and understand them himself. But in presenting his proofs to others, the arguer must consider the methods he will need to use, in order to make his definitions effective with the persons he is seeking to convince.

To present a definition forcibly is not always easy. A mere dictionary definition, which we have seen to be of little or no value in finding out the meaning of the question, is of even less value in the work of presentation. If a person does not understand the meaning of a word or phrase, his confusion will not usually be cleared away by the quotation of a mere sentence from a dictionary. In the first place, such a definition is nearly always too short and too compact to be grasped in its full meaning, in the short time given for the statement of it. Moreover, it will probably not be convincing. If the person who is being argued with is to be made to accept fully the definition, he must be persuaded of its reasonableness; he must be made to see *why* the term means what the disputant says, and so be brought to accept it without mental reserve or qualification. It is for these reasons that we find all the best argumentative writers and speakers taxing the resources of their ingenuity for interesting, clear, and forcible methods of presenting their definitions.

The following are some of the most common and effective ways : —

(1) *Definition by authority.*

The argument from authority, which we have already considered elsewhere, may be used with good effect in the explanation of definitions. We have seen that a dictionary statement is of little value ; but there are few ways of defining more persuasive with an audience, than to quote to them an explanation of the term, as given by some recognized specialist in that branch of human affairs with which the word or phrase is concerned. The quotation, however, should not be too short or too dogmatic in form. It should be an explanation rather than a mere sentence statement. Also, care should be taken, as in any argument from authority, that the reliability of the person quoted is fully recognized, so that the definition may have the full force of expert evidence. In using this method, also, it is usually desirable to explain the quotation, either before or after reading it, in order to be sure that it is understood and accepted by the persons addressed. It will be noticed that in the selection that follows, the speaker, after citing his definition, goes on at considerable length to comment on the reasonableness of the statements of his authority, and to show the bearing of the definition on the question before the court. The illustration is from the speech by Mr. William A. Beach before a military commission in Washington, D.C., 1865. He is here defining the term " military law " : —

" ' Military law may be defined to be a body of rules and ordinances prescribed by competent authority for the government of the military state considered as a distinct community. . . . The general law claims supreme and undisputed jurisdiction over all. The military law puts forth no such pretensions. It aims solely to enforce on the soldier the additional duties he has assumed. It constitutes tribunals for the trial of breaches of military duty only. It attempts not to regulate or adjust the civil rights of those who fall under its cognizance, nor does it affect to redress civil injuries or private wrongs, unless they be, in some degree, connected with the safety and good order of the military state as having a tendency to disturb its peace and quiet. Civil injuries or private wrongs, not immediately related to the rights of a soldier as such, are left, like his civil rights, to the redress of the general or common law.' . . .

" Your Honors perceive how completely the extract justifies my reasoning. It will impress Your Honors with its obvious propriety. It assigns to Courts like yourselves their true position. It enables them to accomplish their full office, without interference, with the ordinary tribunals of the country. It disturbs none of the relations of civil life. It assigns to you exclusively the field of military discipline and efficiency. It maintains a wise harmony between the necessity which called you into existence and the functions you should exercise." [1]

[1] " Great Speeches by Great Lawyers," p. 459.

(2) *Etymological derivation of the term.*

The meaning of a term may often be made clear, by tracing the etymological derivation of the word or the history of the development of its meaning. This method is, perhaps, not so common as many others, for ambiguity in a word does not, in argumentation, usually arise from any confusion of its common meanings such as might be removed by a study of its life history. But wherever this method may be used it is always persuasive, because such an explanation is logical and clear.

John Quincy Adams, in his Sixteenth Lecture on Rhetoric and Oratory at Harvard University in 1807, thus defined the word " passion " : —

" There is, however, a more restricted sense in which the term ' passion ' is used, and of which the precisest idea will be formed by tracing its etymology. In this sense it is equivalent to sufferance, distress, anguish. In this sense it has emphatically been applied to the last sufferings of the Saviour ; and to this sense it must be confined when we are inquiring into those pathetic powers of oratory which awaken the sympathies of the audience. These very words themselves, ' pathetic ' and ' sympathy,' are both derived from the Greek πάθος, of which the Latin *passio* is merely a translation. And the meaning, universally annexed to them, has kept closer to their original derivation than the Latin term." [1]

Blackstone, in Chapter XXVII of his " Commentaries," defines " heirlooms " by this method : —

[1] J. Q. Adams's Lectures, Vol. I, pp. 380–381.

" Heirlooms are such goods and personal chattels as, contrary to the nature of chattels, shall go by special custom to the heir along with the inheritance, and not the executor of the last proprietor. The termination, *loom*, is of Saxon original, in which language it signifies a limb or member; so that an heirloom is nothing else but a limb or member of the inheritance." [1]

(3) *Definition from context.*

The meaning of a term often depends upon the way in which it is used in connection with certain other words, in the same sentence or paragraph. Under such conditions, the best way to define the terms is to explain fully how they are connected with one another. Such an explanation is sure to be forcible, if the reasoning is sound, for it shows the person addressed just why the term means what is alleged. An excellent illustration of this method was given by Daniel Webster in his speech before the Supreme Court in the case of Ogden *vs.* Saunders, 1807. Mr. Webster is here defining the word " contracts " : —

" The most conclusive argument, perhaps, arises from the connection in which the clause stands. The words of the prohibition, so far as it applies to civil rights, or rights of property, are, that ' no State shall coin money, emit bills of credit, make anything but gold and silver coin a tender in the payment of debts, or pass any law impairing the obligation of contracts.' . . . The parts of the prohibition are connected by the subject-matter, and ought, therefore, to be construed together. Taking the words

[1] Chase's Blackstone, p. 536.

thus together, according to their natural connection, how is it possible to give a more limited construction to the term ' contracts,' in the last branch of the sentence, than to the word ' debts,' in that immediately preceding ? Can a State make anything but gold and silver a tender in payment of future debts ? This nobody pretends. But what ground is there for a distinction ? No State shall make anything but gold and silver a tender in the payment of debts, either existing or future, but that contracts spoken of are subsisting contracts only. Such a distinction seems to us wholly arbitrary." [1]

(4) *Definition by analogy.*

It is sometimes effective to show an analogy between the terms to be defined and some other term whose meaning is better known. By comparing the ambiguous phrase with some standards, with which the audience are well acquainted from their everyday experience, the ambiguity is removed. Mr. Seward, in his defence of William Freeman before the Cayuga Oyer and Terminer, Auburn, N.Y., 1846, defined " insanity " by the method of analogy as follows : —

" Although my definition would not perhaps be strictly accurate, I should pronounce insanity to be a derangement of the mind, character, and conduct resulting from bodily disease. I take this word ' derangement,' because it is one in common everyday use. We all understand what is meant when it is said that anything is ranged or arranged. The houses on a street are ranged, if built upon a straight line. The fences on your farms are ranged. A tower, if justly built, is ranged ; that is, it is ranged by the plummet.

[1] The Works of Daniel Webster, Vol. VI, p. 38. Little, Brown and Co., Boston, 1851.

It rises in a perpendicular range from the earth. A file of men marching in a straight line are in range. 'Range yourselves, men,' though not exactly artistical, is not an uncommon word of command. Now what do we mean when we use the word '*de*ranged'? Manifestly that a thing is not ranged, is not arranged, is out of range. If the houses on the street be built irregularly, they are deranged. If the fences be inclined to the right or left, they are deranged. If there be an unequal pressure on either side, the tower will lean, that is, it will be deranged. So if a man be insane. There was a regular line which he was pursuing, not the same line which you or I follow, for all men pursue different lines, and every sane man has his own peculiar path. All these paths are straight, and all are ranged, though all divergent. . . . If the fond mother becomes the murderer of her offspring, it is easy to see that she is deranged. If the pious man, whose steps were firm and whose pathway led straight to Heaven, sinks without temptation into criminal debasement, it is easy to see that he is deranged. But in cases where no natural instinct or elevated principle throws its light upon our research, it is often the most difficult and delicate of all human investigations to determine when a person is deranged.

" We have two tests. *First*, to compare the individual after the supposed derangement with himself as he was before. *Second*, to compare his course with those ordinary lines of human life which we expect sane persons of equal intelligence and similarly situated to pursue."[1]

(5) *Definition by illustration.*

One of the most common ways of explaining a term is to give illustrations of the interpretation put

---

[1] Works of William H. Seward, Vol. I, p. 425.

upon it. The greatest virtue of such a method lies
in its vividness. A person will commonly remember
a concrete example long after he has forgotten the
statement of a principle.

William Pinckney, in his defence of John Hodges
before the Circuit Court of Maryland, at the opening
of his speech gave an extended definition of "treason." The following is an excerpt from the first
part of his explanation : —

"It may be affirmed as an universal proposition that
criminal intention is the essence of every species of
crime. . . .

"Take the case of a man who, in time of war, is charged
with the defence of an important fortress or castle, which
he surrenders to an incompetent force. What more effectual means could he have adopted to aid the enemy than
the delivery of this fortress? The books will tell you
that if he was bribed to this desertion of his duty, if he
did it with a view to benefit the enemy, he is guilty of
treason. But if pusillanimity was the cause, or if it arose
from a false calculation of his own means, or the force of
the enemy, he is not a traitor. You may banish him with
ignominy from the ranks which he has disgraced, or try
him by martial law as a coward or a fool; but he has committed no treason.

"Suppose a powerful force to invade the country, to
which resistance is hopeless. They levy contributions,
they do not proclaim that they will hang me if I neglect
to comply with this order, but they threaten plunder and
desolation. I know they have the power to execute that
threat, and I comply accordingly. Now the paying of
money or the furnishing of provisions is an assistance; it
is 'giving aid and comfort' much more effectually than

the delivery of a few prisoners or a deserter. Yet no man will call this treason, because there is no evidence of hostility to the interests of the country. The authorities say it is not treason." [1]

(6) *Definition by exclusion.*

The meaning of a term is often ambiguous because it is commonly understood to include more than it really ought to include. Various attributes, closely connected with the attributes properly implied in the term, may easily become confused with the term itself. The confusion may arise from the misrepresentation of an opponent, or — the common difficulty — from a careless confusion of ideas. In either case, the term is most satisfactorily defined by drawing the line of distinction between the essential and the unessential attributes, and by excluding the ideas that are extraneous, thus leaving the term to include only its natural and proper intent.

An excellent example is found in the speech by James T. Brady in defence of the Savannah privateers, before the Circuit Court of the United States. Mr. Brady is here defining the term "piracy" : —

" What are the circumstances, what are the acts, that, in view of the law, amount to piracy ? You will understand me that, for the present, I entirely exclude from your consideration any of the particular circumstances which are supposed to give to the actual crime perpetrated a public character, lifting it out of the penal law that you administer, and out of the regions of private crime, into a field of quite different considerations. They are, undoubt-

[1] " Great Speeches by Great Lawyers," p. 38.

edly, that the act done shall be with intent of depriving the person who is in possession of property, as its owner, or as the representative of that owner, of that property. . . . There must be actual violence, or the presence or exhibition of power and intent to use violence, which produces the surrender and delivery of the property. Such are the ingredients of robbery and piracy. And, gentlemen, these two ingredients are all ; and you must rob one or the other of them of this, their poison, or the crime is completely proved, when the fact of the spoliation, with these ingredients, shall have been proved. The use that the robber or the pirate intends to make of retaliation, by way of injury, by way of provocation, by way of any other occasion or motive that seems justifiable to his own conscience to any form whatever of the higher law, has nothing to do with the completeness of the crime." [1]

(7) *Definition by analysis.*

Any definition, by whatever method, before it can be presented, requires that the term be analyzed and the attributes essential to its meaning determined upon. The name "analysis," as denoting one of the modes of presenting a definition, does not mean that any more careful preliminary analysis of the terms by the writer or speaker is required than is necessary in any other case. It means only that a definition is often best presented by directly explaining to the audience what these essential attributes are, as they have been found by analysis. The method here called by the name "analysis" consists, then, in explaining the attributes that are properly implied

---

[1] " Great Speeches by Great Lawyers," p. 381.

in the term. For example, Mr. Beach, in defence of Samuel North, defined "crime" as follows:—

" It will be conceded that all crime, punishable by human authority, consists in the violation of some rule of conduct declared and published by some competent source. The principle is fundamental. It underlies the administration of criminal justice by all tribunals, whether military or civil. To constitute offence there must be law existing and law violated; and the law which declares it must be proclaimed and public. If it exist in the form of positive enactment, it must be published. If it be customary law, it must be general, uniform, acknowledged. The citizen cannot be entrapped into crime. He must be notified of the demands of society in all the departments of its action, whether of peace or war, before obedience can be exacted, and disobedience punished. In a government of laws those acts only are criminal which the law condemns; and publicity is one of its material requisites. The idea of secret statutes, withheld from the subject whose conduct they are to regulate, is hostile to every principle of just government, and excites the sternest indignation."[1]

There are, of course, many other ways in which a definition may be presented; the foregoing are simply examples of some of the most desirable methods. The choice of method depends entirely upon the circumstances,—on the intelligence of the audience, the nature of the question, and the nature of the term itself.

II. **Explanation of the question, the issues, and the partition**.

In considering the presentation of the remaining

[1] *Idem*, p. 453.

P

parts of the introduction, viz., the explanation of the question, the issues, and the partition, the three parts are best treated together. In any introduction the three must be very closely related : the explanation of the question must make the problem clear in such a way as to lead up to the issues, and make them seem the only natural outgrowth from the very nature of the case; the partition, in like manner, must be made to seem the natural outgrowth from the issues. The purpose of the partition is, to make the persons to be convinced understand just how the proofs of the disputant meet the issues of the case, and establish his side of them. Consequently, the value of the partition depends largely upon its close and evident relation to the statement of the issues; sometimes the points of the issues are identical with the points of the partition. An excellent illustration of the clear and forcible presentation of these three parts of the introduction is found in the speech of David Dudley Field in the case of the United States *vs.* Cruikshank, 2 Otto. In this case Mr. Field's clients were indicted for acts declared to be criminal by the so-called Enforcement Act, passed by Congress in 1870. He is here trying to prove that this Enforcement Act is unconstitutional. He said : —

"Let us reduce and formulate the question, if we can, so as to separate the incidental from the essential, in order that our attention may be withdrawn from all other considerations than that of the one fundamental and permanent theory, upon which this legislation must stand, if it stand at all."

He then quoted and briefly explained the thirteenth, fourteenth, and fifteenth amendments to the Constitution. Continuing, he said : —

" Professing to act under the authority of these amendments, Congress has passed five acts, four only of which were in existence at the time of the indictment now under consideration : one called the Civil Rights Act, passed April 9, 1866 ; the second called the Enforcement Act, passed May 31, 1870; the third, amending this, passed February 28, 1871 ; and a fourth act, passed April 20, 1871."

He then quoted the terms of these acts and explained their provisions. Continuing : —

" By authority of this legislation ninety-seven persons were indicted together in the Circuit Court of the United States for the District of Louisiana, and three of them, the present defendants, were found guilty upon the first sixteen counts. The indictment was found under the 6th and 7th sections of the Enforcement Act, sixteen counts being for simple conspiracy under the 6th section, and the other sixteen being for conspiracy, with overt acts resulting in murder."

He then explained the sixteen counts on which his clients had been indicted. Continuing : —

" This indictment, or that portion of it upon which these defendants have been convicted, is supposed to be justified by the 6th section of the Enforcement Act, and that section is said to rest upon the late amendments. In considering the question, whether it is or is not supported by them, I assume, what cannot be disputed, that before the late amendments this section, and the same may be said of the other sections, would have been beyond the competency of Congress.   The point of contention, therefore, is whether the amendments have conferred the power."

This last contains the statement of the issue of the case.   It is to be observed how carefully, step by step, Mr. Field leads up to this statement, so that its accuracy is clearly and fully understood by the court. It only remains for him to complete his introduction by the statement of the partition.   After a word of explanation, connecting the issue with the points of the partition, he finished as follows : —

" My argument, therefore, will consist of an endeavor to establish the following two propositions : —

" I. The natural interpretation of the language of the new amendments does not justify the present legislation.

" II. If the natural interpretation did justify it, yet, as the language is susceptible of a different one, the latter must be preferred as that alone in which it was understood by the people."

In the introduction given above, the circumstances of the case made it necessary to have the explanation of the question long and detailed, and — as is common in cases at law — the explanation took the form of a narration of events.   Also the nature of the case made it possible to reduce the question to a *single* issue.   This is not always possible or desirable. More often — as in the brief on the contract labor question — the issues are two or three in number.

An illustration of an argument where there were two issues is found in Webster's speech in the case of Gibbons *vs.* Ogden. The state of New York had passed a law giving to Robert Fulton and others exclusive rights of navigation "by fire or steam" within the waters of the state. Mr. Webster was here endeavoring to prove that the law was unconstitutional. He began by citing the terms of the acts in question and explaining the origin and history of the controversy before the court. He then stated the issues as follows : —

"On these pleadings the substantial question is raised, Are these laws such as the legislature of New York has a right to pass? If so, do they secondly, in their operation, interfere with any right enjoyed under the Constitution and laws of the United States, and are they therefore void, as far as such interference extends?"

He then proceeds directly to the partition : —

"In regard to these acts, I shall contend, in the first place, that they exceed the power of the legislature ; and, secondly, that, if they could be considered valid for any purpose, they are void still, as against any right enjoyed under the laws of the United States with which they come in collision ; and that in this case they are found interfering with such rights."[1]

It is to be noticed, in this case, that the points of the partition correspond exactly with the points of the issues. This is frequently desirable. It is a

[1] The Works of Daniel Webster, Vol. VI, p. 8. Little, Brown and Co., Boston, 1851.

particularly clear method because it makes the relation between the issues and the partition so evident. But it is to be observed that the two parts are not identical. The issues are merely a statement of the points on which the controversy must turn, and so are unprejudiced in nature; the partition, on the other hand, is the statement of the points the disputant means to establish in proving his side of the case. They are closely related, but not the same.

In the example given above, the issues are presented in the form of a bare statement. But often this is not sufficient. Usually, the critical point or points need to be emphasized, and so presented rhetorically, that they will be impressed on the attention and the memory of the audience. For example, Mr. Jeremiah Black, in his argument in the case of *ex parte* Milligan, 4 Wall. 2, presented the issues of the case briefly and forcibly as follows : —

" The case before you presents but a single point, and that an exceedingly plain one. . . . Keeping the character of the charges in mind, let us come at once to the simple question upon which the court below divided in opinion : Had the commissioners jurisdiction — were they invested with legal authority to try the relaters and put them to death for the offence of which they were accused ? We answer, no ; and, therefore, the whole proceeding from beginning to end was utterly null and void. On the other hand, it is absolutely necessary for those who oppose us to assert, as they do assert, that the commissioners had complete legal jurisdiction both of the subject-matter and of the parties, so that their judgment upon the law and the facts is absolutely conclusive and binding, not subject to correction nor open to inquiry in any court whatever. Of these two opposite views, you must adopt one or the other; for there is no middle ground on which you can possibly stand."

One very common method of presenting the issues consists in excluding irrelevant or mutually admitted matter. It is the error of confusing other kindred questions with the question really in hand that most often makes necessary a careful definition of the issues; and this confusion may very effectively be cleared away by explaining in the introduction what these kindred questions are, and just why they ought to be excluded from consideration. Burke, in his speech in the House of Commons on the Marriage Act, 1781, made clear the issue of the debate by excluding irrelevant matter. The bill in question provided that the power of marrying, without consent of parents, should not exist till twenty-one years of age. Mr. Burke, in his introduction, said: —

" The question is not now, whether the law ought to acknowledge and protect such a state of life as minority, nor whether the continuance, which is fixed for that state, be not improperly prolonged in the law of England. Neither of these in general is questioned. The only question is, whether matrimony is to be taken out of the general rule, and whether the minors of both sexes, without the consent of their parents, ought to have a capacity of contracting the matrimonial, whilst they have not the capacity of contracting any other engagement." [2]

[2] Burke's Speeches, p. 402. James Duffy, London, 1871.

Persuasion

The function of conviction in the introduction is to prepare the minds of the audience for a reception and appreciation of the proof to be offered later in the argument. The function of persuasion is analogous. The emotions of an audience need to be prepared no less than their intellect. A man's emotions cannot be wildly and roughly attacked any more than his reason; if the audience is antagonistic to the speaker or out of harmony with him, his emotional appeals will be unavailing. Consequently, before a speaker can control these moving impulses of his audience, he must establish with them close relations of fellow-feeling. He must bring them into close sympathy with himself so that whatever moves him may be transmitted freely to them. Here, in the introduction, the speaker often first touches on that emotion which he wishes most to affect in his later efforts, and so prepares it for stronger appeals that are to come. Persuasion in the introduction is also a very valuable help in preparing for the work of conviction in the discussion. If an audience is inattentive or hostile to a speaker, much of his proof may pass by without effect; so, in order to make his audience listen and do justice to his demonstrations in the discussion, he must interest them in his cause, and create in them a willingness to be convinced. In general, then, persuasion in the introduction must bring the thought and feeling of the audience into working harmony with the speaker or writer.

In trying to win favor with the audience, a speaker may make an appeal in his own behalf, or in behalf of his subject. A plea for personal sympathy is dangerous and must be used with the most delicate tact. It must always be the dignified appeal of a strong man to his equal; to overdo the sentiment will surely beget contempt. A plea for the subject, however, may be made somewhat more openly. The lawyer may with boldness seek pity for his client; the legislator, enthusiasm for his cause. But even such an introduction requires a knowledge of human nature and a careful observation of the changing moods of an audience, in order to avoid an excess of emotion. An excellent example, of the tactful use in combination of both kinds of appeal, is found in the following introduction by Mr. W. H. Seward in his defence of William Freeman. His client in this case was a negro, the son of a slave. He had committed a triple murder, and public sentiment was wrought to a high pitch of indignation against him. After the murderer's death, an examination of his brain proved him to have been insane; but, at the time of the trial, he was generally believed to be a criminal of the most debased order, and Mr. Seward was censured for undertaking his defence. He said, in part: —

"I plead not for a murderer. I have no inducement, no motive to do so. I have addressed my fellow-citizens in many various relations, when rewards of wealth and fame awaited me. I have been cheered on other occasions by manifestations of popular approbation and sympathy; and where there was no such encouragement, I had at least the gratitude of him whose cause I defended. But I speak now in the hearing of a people who have prejudged the prisoner, and condemned me for pleading in his behalf. He is a convict, a pauper, a negro, without intellect, sense, or emotion. My child, with an affectionate smile, disarms my careworn face of its frown whenever I cross my threshold. The beggar in the street obliges me to give, because he says 'God bless you' as I pass. My dog caresses me with fondness if I will but smile on him. My horse recognizes me when I fill his manger. But what reward, what gratitude, what sympathy and affection can I expect here? There the prisoner sits. Look at him. Look at the assemblage around you. Listen to their ill-suppressed censures and their excited fears, and tell me where, among my neighbors or my fellow-men, where, even in his heart, I can expect to find the sentiment, the thought, not to say of reward or of acknowledgment, but even of recognition. I sat here two weeks during the preliminary trial. I stood here, between the prisoner and the jury, nine hours, and pleaded for the wretch that he was insane and did not even know he was on trial; and, when all was done, the jury thought, at least eleven of them thought, that I had been deceiving them, or was self-deceived. They read signs of intelligence in his idiotic smile, and of cunning and malice in his stolid insensibility. They rendered a verdict that he was sane enough to be tried — a contemptible compromise verdict in a capital case; and then they looked on, with what emotions God and they only know, upon his arraignment. The district-attorney, speaking in his adder ear, bade him rise, and, reading to him one indictment, asked him whether he wanted a trial, and the poor fool answered no. Have you counsel? No. And they went through the same mockery, the prisoner giving the same answers, until a third indictment was thundered in his ears, and he stood before the court silent, motionless, and bewildered. Gentlemen, you may think of this evidence what you please, bring in what verdict you can, but I asseverate, before Heaven and you, that, to the best of my knowledge and belief, the prisoner at the bar does not, at this moment, know why it is that my shadow falls on you instead of his own." [1]

Often there is no more effective appeal than that of honesty and earnestness. Confidence, on the part of the audience, in a speaker's motives is indispensable for success in either convincing or persuading, and the existence of such motives may well be emphasized in the introduction. Then, too, sympathy always goes out quickly and strongly to a man who is honest in his motives, and always creates a solid basis of confidence and understanding.

Patrick Henry's introduction in his famous speech, before the Convention of Delegates, is a model of magnanimity and earnestness : —

" No man thinks more highly than I do of the patriotism, as well as abilities, of the very worthy gentlemen who have just addressed the House. But different men often see the same subject in different lights ; and, therefore, I hope that it will not be thought disrespectful to those gentlemen, if, entertaining as I do opinions of a charac-

1 Works of William H. Seward, Vol. I, p. 413.

ter very opposite to theirs, I shall speak forth my sentiments freely and without reserve. This is no time for
ceremony. The question before the House is one of awful
moment to this country. For my own part, I consider it
as nothing less than a question of freedom or slavery; and
in proportion to the magnitude of the subject ought to be
the freedom of the debate. It is only in this way that we
can hope to arrive at truth, and fulfil the great responsibility which we hold to God and our country. Should I
keep back my opinions at such a time through fear of giving offence, I should consider myself as guilty of treason
toward my country and of an act of disloyalty toward
the majesty of Heaven, which I revere above all earthly
kings."

It sometimes happens that the speaker or writer is
a stranger to those whom he addresses. Under such
circumstances his first duty is to create some bond of
fellow-feeling with his audience. Here modesty is
clearly one indispensable quality. To this should be
added, when possible, the bonds of some common
interest or common emotion; again, an appeal may
well be made for a charitable hearing and for fair
play. Sergeant Prentiss, in his defence of Edward
C. Wilkinson, felt the need of creating such a union
of feeling with the members of the jury he rose to
address, and based his appeal upon the sympathy of
common emotional instincts.

" I came before you an utter stranger, and yet I feel
not as a stranger towards you; I have watched during the
course of the examination the various emotions which the
evidence was so well calculated to arouse in your bosoms,

both as men and as Kentuckians ; and when I beheld the flush of honorable shame upon your cheeks, the sparkle of indignation in your eyes, or the curl of scorn upon your lips, as the foul conspiracy was developed, I felt that years could not make us better acquainted. I saw upon your faces the mystic sign which constitutes the bond of union among honest and honorable men, and I knew that I was about to address those whose feelings would respond to my own. I rejoiced that my clients were, in the fullest sense of the term, to be tried by *a jury of their peers*." [1]

Sometimes the audience is worse than a stranger ; it may be an enemy. To handle an audience that is hostile at the outset, is the most difficult task with which an arguer is ever confronted. It calls for a rare combination of courage and patience, of modesty and self-confidence, of tact and determination. The emotions best appealed to under such conditions are commonly those of honesty, courtesy, or a desire for fair play. The skill needed on such an occasion is well illustrated in Beecher's Liverpool speech already given on page 188. His plea for a hearing then consisted largely in a demand for fair play — a plea that Englishmen take pride in respecting. Moreover, there was no little persuasive power in the display of a manly courage such as an enemy must respect. A similar plea, full of dignity, courage, and firm modesty, is found in the opening words of William Pinckney's speech in the Maryland Assembly, in 1788, in behalf of a petition for the relief of oppressed slaves : —

[1] " Great Speeches by Great Lawyers," p. 88.

"Before I proceed to deliver my sentiments on the sub-ject-matter of the report under consideration, I must en-treat the members of this House to hear me with patience, and not to condemn what I may happen to advance in support of the opinion I have formed, until they shall have heard me out.   I am conscious, sir, that upon this occa-sion, I have long-established principles to combat and deep-rooted prejudices to defeat; that I have fears and apprehensions to silence, which the acts of former legisla-tures have sanctioned, and that (what is equivalent to a host of difficulties) the popular impressions are against me.   But if I am honored with the same indulgent atten-tion which the House has been pleased to afford me, on past subjects of deliberation, I do not despair of surmount-ing all these obstacles, in the common cause of justice, humanity, and policy." [1]

If prejudice has been created by the appeals of a preceding speaker, these prejudices must, as far as possible, be mitigated in the introduction, for such an unfavorable attitude may nullify the effect of all proof or persuasion, as long as the vision of the audi-ence is thus distorted.   At such a time, the "retort courteous," ridicule, sarcasm, or even invective are good weapons of defence.   Whatever weapon of reply is chosen, there is one precaution that must always be remembered : the disputant must never permit himself to lose his temper in the smallest degree.   This temptation is sure to arise in the heat of any earnest discussion where persuasion plays any great part, and it is a temptation that must be always

[1] "Eloquence of the United States," Vol. V, p. 92.   E. and H. Clark, Middletown, Conn., 1827.

repressed, for ill temper in discussion hurts only him who uses it.

There are few better models of personal retort in the history of oratory than can be found in Webster's famous Reply to Hayne, in the debate on the Foote Resolution. Another illustration of the great senator's power in personal debate is found in his reply to Calhoun on the 22d of March, 1838. Humor, sarcasm, and defiance are wielded with power, yet all is courteous and firmly dignified.

"MR. PRESIDENT: I came rather late to the Senate this morning, and, happening to meet a friend on the Avenue, I was admonished to hasten my steps, as 'the war was to be carried into Africa,' and I was expected to be annihilated. I lost no time in following the advice, Sir, since it would be awkward for one to be annihilated without knowing anything about it.

"Well, Sir, the war has been carried into Africa. The honorable member has made an expedition into regions as remote from the subject of this debate as the orb of Jupiter from that of our earth. He has spoken of the tariff, of slavery, and of the late war. Of all this I do not complain. On the contrary, if it be his pleasure to allude to all or any of these topics, for any purpose whatever, I am ready at all times to hear him.

"Sir, this carrying the war into Africa, which has become so common a phrase among us, is, indeed, imitating a great example; but it is an example which is not always followed with success. In the first place, every man, though he be a man of talent and genius, is not a Scipio; and in the next place, as I recollect this part of Roman and Carthaginian history, — the gentleman may be more accurate, but as I recollect it, when Scipio resolved upon carrying the war into Africa, Hannibal was not at home. Now, Sir, I am very little like Hannibal, but I am at home; and when Scipio Africanus South Caroliniensis brings the war into my territories, I shall not leave their defence to Asdrubal, nor Syphax, nor anybody else. I meet him on the shore, at his landing, and propose but one contest.

" Concurritur; horæ
Momento cita mors venit, aut victoria læta." [1]

A hostile audience is less common than an inattentive one. It is well-nigh impossible to convince an audience whose minds are wandering away from the subject or who are carelessly half-listening. At the very beginning, if any such danger is present, — and it is unfortunately a common danger, — the attention of the audience must be roused and centred on the topic of the hour. For this reason, probably the most common of all forms of persuasive introduction is that which emphasizes the importance of the question in discussion. There are many ways of arousing interest in an audience. It may be shown that the question is of great inherent importance; that it is of a peculiar significance because of its relation to current events and conditions; that it is one of the growing problems of the future; or, perhaps, that it has some especially close bearing on the interests of the particular audience. A good example is found in the introduction of Charles James Fox to one of his speeches on the East India Bill: —

[1] The Works of Daniel Webster, Vol. IV, p. 500. Little, Brown and Co., Boston, 1856.

" I did not intend, Sir, to have said anything in addition to that which has been already urged so ably in favor of the resolution now agitated. In my own opinion, its propriety and necessity are completely and substantially established. A few particulars, suggested in the course of the debate by gentlemen on the other side of the House, may be thought, however, to merit some animadversion. And, once for all, let no man complain of strong language. Things are now arrived at such a crisis as renders it impossible to speak without warmth. Delicacy and reserve are criminal where the interests of Englishmen are at hazard. . . .

" This, at least, has made such an impression on my mind that I never felt so much anxiety ; I never addressed this House under such a pressure of impending mischief ; I never trembled so much for public liberty as I now do. The question before the House involves the rights of Parliament in all their consequences and extent. These rights are the basis of our Constitution, and form the spirit of whatever discriminates the government of a free country. And have not these been threatened and assaulted ? " [1]

[1] "The World's Orators" (England), pp. 317–318. G. P. Putnam's Sons, New York, 1900.

CHAPTER III

THE DISCUSSION

THE work of presenting the proof of the discussion, is largely a matter of applying the principles of composition. If the proofs have been well invented and arranged, to make them accomplish their purpose only requires the use of words that will convey them to the minds of others. So that the first requisite for forceful presentation is a working knowledge of rhetoric in general.

But immediately the question arises as to the proper relation of the finished composition to the brief. How closely shall the brief be followed in the final presentation? Shall the exact words of the brief be repeated? In answering these questions there are two extremes that are generally to be avoided. On the one hand, rhetorical embellishment or rhetorical carelessness may destroy all the advantage gained by a good arrangement. On the other hand, the bare bones of the outline may be exposed so rudely as to be offensive. Of these two faults the beginner undoubtedly tends toward the latter; he does not take pains enough to make his dish enticing or even palatable. The speech or the finished composition is too often a mere repetition of heads and subheads, with the addition of a few conjunctions and a trite phrase here and there. This defect is far more pardonable than that of the beginner, who talks at random and buries what little he has to say in the confusion of vague and formless rhetoric; but it is, nevertheless, a defect.

One of the rhetorical elements most commonly lacking, in the presentation of proof by a beginner, is *variety*. It is sometimes assumed that less variety in presentation is desirable in argumentation than in most of the other forms of composition or oratory. It is said that in a story or in a demonstrative oration, since the purpose of the writer or speaker is to please or make display, variety is indispensable; but that in argumentation, since the appeal is only to the reason, variety is superfluous. In truth, the fact that argumentation (*i.e.* conviction in argumentation) addresses only the reason, instead of making variety superfluous, makes it the more necessary. In a narrative or a lecture there is variety in the very subject-matter to give it interest; but in argument, the natural coldness of logic needs to be dressed more attractively to hold attention. It is easy, in presenting proof after proof, to fall into some formula of statement or some "stereotyped" method of arrangement. This habit should be carefully avoided, and variety in word, phrase, and manner should be sought from the beginning.

But, in seeking for the qualities that attract, the qualities that convince must not be forgotten. In

order to convince, it is not sufficient that the materials
of the proof are well arranged in the mind of the
speaker; the arrangement must be made clear to
the audience.   Variety and smoothness do not require
that the relative importance of the points of the brief,
or their connection with one another, be obscured.   In
fact, in spoken discourse, even more care needs to be
taken in the final presentation than in the brief itself,
to make clear the importance and the mutual relation
of the points.   In the brief, the indenting of the headings and subheadings and the use of the symbols,
show to the eye how the evidence and arguments are
related to one another and to the whole question, and
distinguish between the important and the incidental
parts.   But in spoken and in written presentation,
where there are not headings or subheadings, these
things must be made evident by explanation; the
large and vital facts must be enforced by repetition,
by illustration, by direct explanation of their significance, or by some other of the many possible methods
of emphasis; the relation of one piece of evidence to
another must often be fully explained, or the purpose
and effect of various arguments must be made evident to the reader.

The following quotation illustrates the effectiveness
of one method of gaining emphasis, viz., by digressing
in the middle of an argument to explain the significance of a piece of evidence.   The selection is taken
from the speech by William C. Plunkett in the case of
Rex *vs*. Forbes and others.   The defendants were on

trial for participation in a riot. They were charged
with hurling bottles and other missiles at the Lord-
lieutenant of Ireland in a public theatre.

" When I state that a bottle was thrown at the king's
representative, and that implements of violence were flung
at his person, such is the state of the public mind that it
is listened to as if it were a mere bagatelle, a *jeu d'esprit*,
a trifle of which the Lord Lieutenant need not take any
notice, and which is below the attention of the government
and the law officers. Why, gentlemen of the jury, are we
awake? Can we be insensible to the effect of such occur-
rences upon the honor and safety of the country? Can
we reflect, without indignation, that such an outrage should
be committed in a civilized country against the person of
his majesty's representative, because he had the presumption, in opposition to a desperate gang, to execute the
parting injunctions of the king in a manner not calculated
to give offence or excite animosity? " [1]

Iteration, the persistent repetition of a word or
phrase, may also be forcibly used to impress an idea
on a reader's memory. This device is well illustrated
in the following passage from Matthew Arnold : —

" The practical genius of our people could not but urge
irresistibly to the production of a real prose style, because
for the purposes of modern life the old English prose, the
prose of Milton and Taylor, is cumbersome, unavailable,
impossible. A style of regularity, uniformity, precision,
balance, was wanted. These are the qualities of a serviceable prose style. Poetry was a different *logic*, as
Coleridge said, from prose. But there is no doubt that a

---

[1] " Great Speeches by Great Lawyers," p. 638.

style of regularity, uniformity, precision, balance, will acquire a yet stronger hold upon the mind of a nation if it
is adopted in poetry as well as in prose, and so comes to
govern both. This is what happened in France. To the
practical, modern, and social genius of the French a true
prose was indispensable. They produced one of conspic-
uous excellence, supremely powerful and influential in the
last century, the first to come and standing at first alone,
a modern prose. French prose is marked in the highest
degree by the qualities of regularity, uniformity, precision,
balance. With little opposition from any deep-seated and
imperious poetic instincts, the French made their poetry
also conform to the law which was moulding their prose.
French poetry became marked with the qualities of regularity, uniformity, precision, balance. . . . Our literature
required a prose which conformed to the true law of prose;
and that it might acquire this the more surely, it compelled
poetry, as in France, to conform itself to the law of prose
likewise. . . . Poetry, or rather the use of verse, entered
in a remarkable degree, during the [eighteenth] century,
into the whole of the daily life of the civilized classes;
and the poetry of the century was a perpetual school of
the qualities requisite for a good prose, qualities of regularity, uniformity, precision, balance." [1]

There are few methods of making a vivid impression on the attention and memory of an audience,
more forcible than the use of the so-called rhetorical
question. The rhetorical question is one in which
the answer is implied in the form of the question;
as, for example, " Is the United States a republic or
a despotism ? " The value of this device lies largely,
in the effect of variety and incisiveness which it im-

[1] Genung, "The Working Principles of Rhetoric," p. 304.

parts.   The following illustration is from Webster's
speech in the case of Ogden *vs.* Saunders: —

" We come before the court alleging the law to be void
and unconstitutional; they stop the inquiry by opposing
to us the law itself.   Is this logical? . . .   Is it not obvious, that, supposing the act of New York to be a part of
the contract, the question still remains as undecided as
ever.   What is that act?   Is it a law, or is it a nullity? a
thing of force, or a thing of no force?   Suppose the parties
to have contemplated this act, what did they contemplate?
its words only, or its legal effect? its words, or the force
which the Constitution of the United States allows to it?
If the parties contemplated any law, they contemplated all
the law that bore on their contract, the aggregate of all
the statute and constitutional provisions." [1]

In contrast with the defects of lack of variety and
emphasis, stands the great weakness of lack of unity.
Emphasis puts stress upon the significant points
of the proof.   However, as we have already seen, to
be convincing, a speaker or writer must make his
audience or reader accept, not this point or that, but
his *whole case*.   In order thus to establish the proposition as a whole, in presenting the proof the different elements must be firmly bound together in
one.   The introduction and the conclusion are of
great service in gaining this effect; but it is dangerous to leave this work entirely to these external aids.
There must be coherence within the proof, as well as
ropes and bands without.   To depend for unity en-

[1] The Works of Daniel Webster, Vol. VI, p. 30.   Little, Brown
and Co., Boston, 1851.

tirely upon the partition at the beginning and the summary at the end, is likely to make it seem artificial and forced; to gain an effect that is natural and convincing, the unity must be made evident in the proof itself.

There are three valuable aids in getting unity in the proof itself, viz.: (1) transitions, (2) summaries, (3) partitions. It is not true that these devices are desirable in every piece of argumentation. Often the proofs are of such a nature, their connection with one another is so obvious, that summaries and partitions within the proof are unnecessary; sometimes these devices are positively undesirable, because they give an air of exactness and formality that is inappropriate. The practice of such methods may easily be carried to an extreme; but the common danger is that of deficiency rather than that of excess.

Transitions, summaries, and partitions are also of high value as aids to *coherence*. A speaker, leading an audience along new paths, needs to keep in close touch with them, lest they lose the way and become confused. By the use of transitional sentences and paragraphs he holds them always under a firm control, and is enabled to guide them carefully, so that the way is constantly opening ahead at each step.

John Ward, in his "System of Oratory," explains a transition as follows: —

"*A transition*, therefore, is *a form of speech by which the speaker in a few words tells his hearers both what he has said already and what he next designs to say*. Where a discourse consists of several parts this is often very proper in passing from one to another, especially when the parts are of a considerable length ; for it assists the hearers to carry on the series of the discourse in their mind, which is a great advantage to the memory. It is likewise a great relief to the attention to be told when an argument is finished and what is to be expected next."[1]

Mr. Ward also gives an excellent illustration of the use of the simple transition : —

" Cicero, as I have had occasion to observe formerly, divides his *oration for the Manilian law* into three parts, and proposes to speak, *first of the nature of the war against king Mithridates, then of its greatness, and lastly of the choice of a general*. And when he has gone thro' the first head, which is pretty long, he connects it with the second, by this short transition : *Having shown the nature of the war, I shall now speak a few things of its greatness*. And again, at the conclusion of his second head, he reminds his hearers of his method in the following manner : *I think I have sufficiently shewn the necessity of this war from the nature of it, and the danger of it from its greatness. What remains is to speak concerning the choice of a general, proper to be intrusted with it*."[2]

The following is a good example of a clear and easy simple transition, from George William Curtis's report to the President of the United States, in behalf of the Civil Service Commission, 1876 : —

" But while these are the necessary results of the present system of admission, both upon the service itself and upon the character of those who are employed in it, there are evils to be considered still more serious."

[1] John Ward, " A System of Oratory," Vol. I, p. 290.
[2] *Ibid.*, Vol. I, p. 291.

The use of the summary within the discussion contributes to unity, by gathering together proofs that
are closely associated, and relating them clearly to
the whole proposition. They bring the materials
thus summarized into one single strong point, instead
of a number of scattered and incomplete points.
Also the summary contributes to clearness, by closing
up the division of the proof that is completed, and
making it evident that a new line of argument is to
be undertaken. Finally, these occasional summaries
help greatly in making intelligible the final summary
in the conclusion.

In the report of the Civil Service Commission of
1871, is an excellent example of the short, simple,
and direct style of summary that is most effective for
use within the proof itself : —

"These are some of the serious and threatening evils
of the present practice of treating the inferior posts of administration as party prizes. It exasperates party spirit
and perverts the election. It tends to fill the public service with incapacity and corruption, destroying its reputation and repelling good men. It entices Congress to desert
the duties to which it is especially designated by the Constitution, and tempts the Executive to perilous intrigue."

The writer then takes up a new line of argument
with the following introductory sentence : —

"The arguments by which the present pernicious practice is justified seem to us wholly unsound." [1]

[1] George William Curtis, Orations and Addresses, Vol. II, p. 43.

Internal partitions perform much the same office as the external partition of the introduction. They turn the attention in the desired direction and explain what will be done next, so that the audience can follow the line of thought that is to come. Webster showed his mastery of the arts of clearness by his frequent use of this kind of partition. No better model can be found than the following, taken from his speech before the Supreme Court in the case of Luther *vs.* Borden *et al:* —

" Having thus, may it please your honors, attempted to state the questions as they arise, and having referred to what has taken place in Rhode Island, I shall present what further I have to say in three propositions : —

" 1. I say, first, that the matters offered to be proved by the plaintiff in the court below are not of judicial cognizance ; and proof of them, therefore, was properly rejected by the court.

" 2. If all these matters could be, and had been, legally proved, they would have constituted no defence, because they show nothing but an *illegal* attempt to overthrow the government of Rhode Island.

" 3. No proof was offered by the plaintiff to show that, in fact, another government had gone into operation, by which the Charter government had become displaced." [1]

The summary and partition are very effective in combination ; the summary showing what has been done, and the partition what remains to be done, thus establish beyond a doubt the unity of the demon-

[1] The Works of Daniel Webster, Vol. VI, p. 236. Little, Brown and Co., Boston, 1851.

stration, and give to the readers a clear understanding of what is being accomplished. This combination should, however, be used with judgment, for it is the most formal of all the methods of transition. It is most properly used where the proof is very long, and where the quality most to be sought for is that of logical perfection. For example, it is most appropriate in such an effort as that of Mr. Webster before the Supreme Court in the case of Gibbons *vs.* Ogden : —

" I contend, therefore, in conclusion on this point, that the power of Congress over these high branches of commercial regulation is shown to be exclusive, by considering what was wished and intended to be done, when the convention for forming the Constitution was called; by what was understood, in the State conventions, to have been accomplished by the instrument; by the prohibitions on the States, and the express exception relative to inspection laws; by the nature of the power itself; by the terms used, as connected with the nature of the power; by the subsequent understanding and practice, both of Congress and the States; by the grant of exclusive admiralty jurisdiction to the federal government; by the manifest danger of the opposite doctrine, and the ruinous consequences to which it directly leads. . . .   But I contend, in the second place, that whether the grant were to be regarded as wholly void or not, it must, at least, be inoperative, when the rights claimed under it come in collision with other rights, enjoyed and secured under the laws of the United States; and such collision, I maintain, clearly exists in this case." [1]

[1] The Works of Daniel Webster, Vol. VI, pp. 18–19.   Little, Brown and Co., Boston, 1851.

Persuasion

Of persuasion in the discussion little need be said. The reason for not giving it more extended treatment is not that it is unimportant. On the contrary, persuasion is necessary in order to make the proofs effective. Certain general suggestions as to the methods of persuasion have been given in the chapter on Presentation ; but beyond this, particular directions as to how to persuade are impracticable. In general, the things to be sought are a knowledge of the audience, a close sympathy with their emotions, alertness to seize on any opportunity for an appeal, and tact in the handling of human nature. Much may be gained from a study of the use of persuasion by the great orators.

CHAPTER IV

THE CONCLUSION

TWENTY-TWO centuries ago Aristotle said that the object of the epilogue or conclusion was fourfold: first, to conciliate the audience in favor of the speaker and to excite them against his adversary; secondly, to amplify and diminish; thirdly, to rouse the emotions; and fourthly, to recapitulate. Time has not changed the truth of his statement; these are to-day the offices of the conclusion. Clearly, two of these are concerned with conviction and two with persuasion. To recapitulate and to "amplify and diminish" are desirable, in order to make complete the appeal to reason; to gain sympathy and to rouse the passions are desirable, in order to appeal successfully to the emotions.

Conviction

In argumentation the first object of the conclusion is, to recapitulate or summarize. The concluding summary is generally necessary, in order to make the proof clear and forcible. In the first place, the points made in the discussion must finally be gathered together into a single point, in order to convince the audience of the strength of the demonstration *as a whole;* again, the various points must be repeated and emphasized, in order to impress them on the memory of the audience.

The summary may take a variety of forms, with varying degrees of length and formality. In nearly all student argumentation the summary needs to be careful and detailed; the main heads of the proof must be repeated, and usually many of the subordinate points of the evidence. Rhetorically, the summary may take the form of a plain recapitulation, or it may be amplified by explanation and enforcement.

One of the best examples of a simple recapitulation is found in the conclusion of Webster's speech in the case of Ogden *vs.* Saunders : —

"To recapitulate what has been said, we maintain, first, that the Constitution, by its grants to Congress and its prohibitions on the states, has sought to establish one uniform standard of value, or medium of payment. Second, that, by like means, it has endeavored to provide for one uniform mode of discharging debts, when they are to be discharged without payment. Third, that these objects are connected, and that the first loses much of its importance, if the last, also, be not accomplished. Fourth, that, reading the grant to Congress and the prohibition on the States together, the inference is strong that the Constitution intended to confer an exclusive power to pass bankrupt laws on Congress. Fifth, that the prohibition in the tenth section reaches to all contracts, existing or future, in the same way that the other prohibition, in the same section, extends to all debts, existing or future. Sixthly, that, upon any other construction, one great political object of the Constitution will fail of its accomplishment." [1]

[1] The Works of Daniel Webster, Vol. VI, p. 40.

Usually, however, the summary is less formal than the above in its phrasing, and less abrupt in its ending. The more common style is such as that in Burke's speech, on a bill for shortening the duration of Parliaments : —

" Thus, in my opinion, the shortness of a triennial sitting would have the following ill effects : it would make the member more shamelessly and shockingly corrupt, it would increase his dependence on those who could best support him at his election, it would wrack and tear to pieces the fortunes of those who stood upon their own fortunes and their private interest ; it would make the electors infinitely more venal, and it would make the whole body of the people who are, whether they have votes or not, concerned in elections, more lawless, more idle, more debauched ; it would utterly destroy the sobriety, the industry, the integrity, the simplicity of all the people, and undermine, I am much afraid, the deepest and best laid foundations of the commonwealth." [1]

" Amplify and diminish " is the name given to the practice of magnifying the importance of certain points in the discussion, and belittling the importance of others. In doing this, a disputant may diminish certain of his own proofs and amplify certain others, his purpose being to bring out the force of the greater points, by contrast with the lesser. But usually, the practice consists in diminishing, not one's own proof, but the proof of an opponent. In such a case, its effectiveness consists in the direct contrasting of the

[1] The Speeches of Edmund Burke, p. 400. James Duffy, Dublin, 1871.

arguments on the opposite sides. The decision of any question is determined by a comparison, in the minds of those addressed, of the relative weight of the proofs of the two arguers, so that a disputant may help his cause just as truly, by diminishing the weight of the proof against him, as by adding to that of his own. In any question, there are always some phases of it that are favorable to one side, and others that are favorable to the other side; on certain points, the facts support the affirmative, on others, they support the negative. So, the beliefs of the audience or readers about the proposition, as a whole, will be determined largely by their opinions as to which phase, or what points, are really important. For illustration, in a discussion of the question as to whether a protective tariff would be beneficial to the United States, the affirmative might successfully maintain that such a tariff would help to build up the industries of the country, whereas, the negative might be able to prove that the tariff would tend to diminish our foreign commerce. Then, in this case, if the audience thought that foreign commerce was more desirable than new industries, they would support the negative of the question, and *vice versa*. Clearly, then, it would be the policy of the affirmative to persuade the audience that the building up of industry at home was of more importance to the country as a whole than the building up of commerce abroad. In this way the affirmative could weaken its opponents, by belittling the significance of the points they had

R

proved and magnifying the significance of its own
points, just as surely as it could by a direct attack
upon their arguments or evidence. This is one of
the most common kinds of amplifying and diminishing. It may, however, take various forms; it may
consist in a contrasting of the results of two opposite
policies, a contrasting of the evidence of the two
sides, or a contrasting of the motives of the two parties; but in all these the purpose is the same, viz. :
to compare the two proofs as a whole, and show the
preponderance of the one over the other. In student
debates, where both the materials of the discussion
and the time are narrowly limited, so that the conflict
of the opposing proofs is peculiarly direct, to amplify
and diminish is especially effective.

Mr. Evarts, in his argument in the case of the
Savannah Privateers, uses this artifice, diminishing
the case of the defence and amplifying his own case
in prosecution : —

" And now, here is your duty, here your post of fidelity,
not against law, not against the least right under the law,
but to sustain, by whatever sacrifice there may be of sentiment or of feeling, the law and the Constitution. I need
not say to you, gentlemen, that if, on a state of facts which
admits no diversity of opinion, with these opposite forces
arrayed, as they now are, before you — the Constitution of
the United States, the laws of the United States, the commission of this learned court, derived from the government of the United States, the venire and impanelling of
this jury, made under the laws and by the authority of the
United States, on our side ; met, on their side, by nothing,

on behalf of the prisoners, but the commission, the power, the right, the authority of the rebel government, proceeding from Jefferson Davis — you are asked by the law, or under the law, or against the law, in some form, to recognize this power, and thus to say that the vigor, the judgment, the sense, and the duty of a jury, to confine themselves to their responsibility on the facts of the case, are worthless and yielding before impressions of a discursive and loose and general nature. Be sure of it, gentlemen, that, on what I suppose to be the facts concerning this particular transaction, a verdict of acquittal is nothing but a determination that our government and its authority, in the premises of this trial, for the purposes of your verdict, are met and overthrown by the protection thrown around the prisoners by the government of the Confederate States of America, actual or incipient." [1]

Persuasion

The necessity of an appeal for sympathy, in the conclusion, is too obvious to need explanation. When the speech is over, or the essay is finished, the time has come for the hearer or reader to act or deliberate on action; he must, then, be favorably disposed in his feelings toward the speaker or writer, in order to give his side a fair and favorable consideration. All the labors of persuasion, in the introduction and in the discussion, may be lost, if the emotions aroused there are allowed to lapse at the end. The sympathy for the speaker and his subject, which has already been stirred, must be left active in the minds of the

[1] "Great Speeches by Great Lawyers," p. 420.

audience, when he at length submits his case to their hands for judgment.

The conclusion reaps the harvest of sympathy, sowed in the earlier parts of the argument. Aristotle suggests that this last effort of persuasion may be an appeal by the speaker for favor for himself and his cause, or it may be an attack on the character or cause of an opponent. A good use of these methods, in combination, is found in the argument of Sergeant Prentiss in defence of Edward C. Wilkinson, who was on trial for murder. In the beginning of the selection he directly attacks the instigator of the trial, and later, the chief witnesses for the prosecution, clos- . ing with a brief appeal for sympathy for himself : —

"But there is a murderer ; and, strange to say, his name appears upon the indictment, not as a criminal, but as a prosecutor. His garments are wet with the blood of those upon whose deaths you hold this solemn inquest. Yonder he sits, allaying for a moment the hunger of that fierce vulture, conscience, by casting before it the food of pretended regret, and false but apparent eagerness for justice. He hopes to appease the manes of his slaughtered victims — victims to his falsehood and treachery — by sacrificing upon their graves a hecatomb of innocent men. By base misrepresentations of the conduct of the defendants, he induced his imprudent friends to attempt a vindication of his pretended wrongs by violence and bloodshed. . . .

"Upon his head rests not only all the blood shed in this unfortunate strife, but also the soul-killing crime of perjury ; for, surely as he lives, did the words of craft and falsehood fall from his lips, ere they were hardly loosened from the Holy Volume. But I dismiss him, and do consign him to the furies — trusting, in all charity, that the terrible punishment he must suffer from the scorpion lash of a guilty conscience will be considered in his last account.

"Johnson and Oldham, too, are murderers at heart. But I shall make to them no appeal. There is no chord in their bosoms which can render back music to the touch of feeling. They have both perjured themselves. The former cut up the truth as coolly as if he had been carving meat in his own stall. The latter, on the contrary, was no longer the bold and hot-blooded knight, but the shrinking, pale-faced witness. Cowering beneath your stern and indignant gaze, marked you not how 'his coward lip did from its color fly'; and how his quailing eye sought from floor to rafter protection from each honest glance. . . .

"Gentlemen of the Jury : — I shall detain you no longer. . . . I had hoped, when the evidence was closed, that the commonwealth's attorney might have found it in accordance with his duty and his feelings to have entered at once a *nolle prosequi*. Could the genius of 'Old Kentucky' have spoken, such would have been her mandate. Blushing with shame at the inhospitable conduct of a portion of her sons, she would have hastened to make reparation.

"Gentlemen : Let her sentiments be spoken by you. Let your verdict take character from the noble State which you in part represent. Without leaving your box, announce to the world that here the defence of one's own person is no crime, and that the protection of a brother's life is the subject of approbation rather than of punishment.

"Gentlemen of the Jury : I return you my most profound and sincere thanks for the kindness with which you have listened to me, a stranger, pleading the cause of strangers. Your generous and indulgent treatment I shall ever remember with the most grateful emotions. In full confidence that you, by your sense of humanity and justice, will supply the many defects in my feeble advocacy, I now resign into your hands the fate of my clients. As you shall do unto them, so, under like circumstances, may it be done unto you." [1]

But gaining sympathy for one's self is not the whole of persuasion. The emotions, which, as we have seen, are the mainsprings of action, must be given a final stimulus. It is never safe to leave all appeal to the emotions to be made in the conclusion; the feelings must be stirred in the introduction, and kept constantly active through all the discussion. But there the work of persuasion is only begun; in order to bring the emotions finally into play, they must be wrought to the highest pitch of all at the close, and directed to the desired end. Consequently, in any great oration, it is in the peroration that we find the most impassioned eloquence; it is here that the orator spends his powers freely in the final appeal. The conclusion must complete, and give carrying force to the work of persuasion, as it does to the work of conviction.

The emotions are so many, and the possible ways of stirring them so varied, that examples are not of any real value. To gain such power requires a study of the whole field of the persuasive art — a study of human nature, a study of audiences, a study of the world's oratory. Finally, to develop the fruits

1 "Great Speeches by Great Lawyers," pp. 121–123.

of study into real power, demands, in the words of Demosthenes, "*Practice ! practice ! practice !*"

To choose an example of persuasion in the conclusion, involves discrimination among many of the most brilliant passages in the world's oratory. The following, from the speech by Grattan on the " Declaration of Irish Right," is not given as, in any sense, the best; it is simply an illustration : —

"I might, as a constituent, come to your bar and demand my liberty. I do call upon you by the laws of the land, and their violation ; by the instruction of eighteen centuries ; by the arms, inspiration, and providence of the present movement — tell us the rule by which we shall go ; assert the law of Ireland ; declare the liberty of the land ! I will not be answered by a public lie, in the shape of an amendment ; nor, speaking for the subject's freedom, am I to hear of faction. I wish for nothing but to breathe in this our island, in common with my fellow-subjects, the air of liberty. I have no ambition, unless it be to break your chains and contemplate your glory. I never shall be satisfied so long as the meanest cottager in Ireland has a link of the British chain clanking to his rags. He may be naked, he shall not be in irons. And I do see the time at hand ; the spirit has gone forth ; the declaration of right is planted, and though great men should fall off, the cause will live ; and though he who utters this should die, yet the immortal fire shall outlast the organ that conveys it, and the breath of liberty, like the word of the holy man, will not die with the prophet, but survive him." [1]

[1] Hardwicke, " History of Oratory and Orators," p. 138.

CHAPTER V

REFUTATION

" REFUTATION consists in the destruction of opposing proofs." As suggested in this definition, refutation is, in form, destructive rather than constructive; but in its purposes and results it is no less serviceable than positive proof. With respect to any given proposition, there are always two contrary beliefs that a person may hold: he may believe that the proposition is true or that it is not true. Consequently, if we can induce him to reject the opposite of what we uphold, we are thereby preparing him to accept our own views. Negative argument pure and simple is rarely, if ever, sufficient; for belief is always essentially positive in nature, so that to destroy without building up will not serve our purpose. Refutation, therefore, is properly auxiliary and supplementary to positive proof. In our attempt to convince or persuade any man, we must realize that he will, almost surely, have in his own mind many preconceived ideas and preëstablished opinions about the matter in discussion, and that many of those ideas and opinions are liable to be antagonistic to what we are trying to make him believe. In such circumstances, our success must often depend upon our ability to destroy these hostile conceptions, thus preparing the way for the acceptance of our own contentions. The necessity for such destructive effort is, of course, peculiarly pressing in any form of disputation where the arguer is confronted by some definite opponents, as in debate, or perhaps in a newspaper controversy; for here, the audience or readers are consciously balancing the two sides of the question, and they must be made to see with perfect clearness, that one side overthrows and destroys the other. But in any form of argumentative discussion there are always opponents of some kind, either real or imaginary, and they must be mastered before we can hope to make others fully accept our own beliefs.

The partial or complete destruction of such opposing opinions and arguments often calls for a keener insight and a more adroit attack, than does any of the positive work of construction. It therefore becomes of the first importance to decide how much one ought to refute, and what are the various methods that may be used.

How much to refute

Concerning the question of *how much* to refute, John Quincy Adams, in his Lectures on Rhetoric and Oratory (Lecture XXII), says : —

" There are three very common errors in the management of controversy against which I think it proper here to guard you, and from which I hope you will hereafter very sedulously guard yourselves. The first may be termed

answering too much ; the second answering too little ; and
the third answering yourself, and not your opponent."

Speaking of the first of these mistakes, he says : —

" You answer too much when you make it an invariable
principle to reply to everything which has been or could
be said by your antagonist on the other side. . . .   If you
contend against a diffuse speaker, who has wasted hour
after hour in a lingering lapse of words, which had little
or no bearing upon the proper question between you, it is
incumbent upon you to discriminate between that part of
his discourse which was pertinent, and that which was
superfluous.   Nor is it less necessary to detect the artifice
of an adversary, who purposely mingles a flood of extraneous matter with the controversy, for the sake of disguis-
ing the weakness of his cause.   In the former of these
two cases, if you undertake to answer everything that has
been said, you charge yourself with all the tediousness
of your adversary, and double the measure by an equal
burden of your own.   In the latter you promote the cause
of your antagonist by making yourself the dupe of his
stratagem.   If, then, you have an opponent whose redun-
dancies arise only from his weakness, whose standard of
oratory is time, and whose measure of eloquence is in
arithmetical proportion to the multitude of his words,
your general rule should be to pass over all his general,
unappropriate declamation in silence ; to take no more
notice of it than if it had never been spoken.   But if you
see that the external matter is obtruded upon the subject
with design to mislead your attention, and fix it upon
objects different from that which is really at issue, you
should so far take notice of it as to point out the artifice,
and derive from it an argument of the most powerful
efficacy to your own side."

The objections to answering too many of the lesser arguments of an opponent are two. In the first place, it involves a loss of time and energy. This is particularly true in the case of the arguments of an opponent who wastes himself in "a lingering lapse of words," which have little or no bearing upon the proper question. But it is also true, even when the efforts of an opponent are well directed at the points in issue. The greater part of the materials in any proof are, as we have seen, only secondary in nature; they are of force merely because they tend to establish some larger, more vital fact. The important thing is, to reach and overthrow these more significant and critical parts of the proof: if they can be destroyed, the secondary facts fall with them. To sink a battle-ship does not demand that every foot of its armor be twisted and torn, that every turret and smoke-stack be demolished; a half dozen well-aimed shots is enough. It is only necessary that the vulnerable spot be well chosen, and that the aim be sure. Consequently it should be the purpose of the debater, in his refutation, to let the lesser points of his opponent pass unheeded, and to give his attention only to vital elements. In the second place, answering too much results in confusion. To attempt to refute too many petty arguments, weakens the discrimination between the important and the unimportant, which is always necessary in argumentation, if we are to make a distinct and lasting impression. Emphasis, as a means to clearness and force, is just as desirable in refutation as elsewhere, and emphasis cannot be attained, if attention is given alike to the great and the small points. Furthermore, answering too much gives undue dignity and importance to many points of the other side. One way to dispose of a foolish or trivial point is illustrated by Cicero in his defence of Q. Ligarius : —

"When Tubero, in his accusation of Ligarius before Cæsar, had made it part of his charge, that Ligarius was in Africa during some part of the civil war between Cæsar and Pompey ; Cicero in his answer, not thinking it deserved a serious reply, contents himself with barely mentioning it ironically. For thus he begins his defence of Ligarius, *Cæsar, my kinsman Tubero has laid before you a new crime, and till this day unheard of, that Q. Ligarius was in Africa.*" [1]

Insignificant proofs are better left insignificant. To bring them anew to the attention of the audience, and give them the compliment of a special reply, helps, rather than hinders, an opponent.

Of the second fault, which consists in answering too little, Mr. Adams says : —

"The second error in controversy, against which I am anxious of warning you, is that of answering too little. It is not unfrequently found united with that against which I have last admonished you. When too much of our strength is lavished upon the outworks, the citadel is left proportionately defenceless. If we say too much upon points extrinsic to the cause, we shall seldom say enough upon those on which it hinges. To avoid this fault, therefore, it is as essential to ascertain which are the strong parts of

[1] John Ward, " A System of Oratory," Vol. II, p. 366.

your adversary's argument as it is to escape the opposite error of excess." [1]

The safeguards against the errors of both these extremes are the same : analyze your adversary's case, pick out his "strong parts," and answer them. It is also well to remember that, "It is much easier to despise than to answer an opponent's argument, that whenever we can indulge our contempt we are apt to forget that it is not refutation." Sarcasm and scorn may be *aids* to refutation, but they are not *substitutes* for it. In refutation, then, the first essential is to understand what are the few vital points of the other side.

Concerning the last and very common error, which consists in "answering yourself," the comment made by Mr. Adams cannot be improved upon : —

" But the most inexcusable of all the errors in confutation is that of answering yourself, instead of your adversary, which is done whenever you suppress, or mutilate, or obscure, or misstate, his reasoning, and then reply not to his positions, but to those which you have substituted in their stead. This practice is often the result of misapprehension, when a disputant mistakes the point of the argument urged by his adversary ; but it often arises also from design, in which case it should be clearly detected and indignantly exposed. The duty of a disputant is fairly to take and fully to repel the idea of his opponent, and not his own. To misrepresent the meaning of your antagonist evinces a want of candor which the auditory seldom fail to perceive, and which engages their feelings in his favor.

[1] Adams, Lectures on Rhetoric and Oratory, Vol. II, p. 88.

When involved in controversy, then, never start against
yourself frivolous objections for the sake of showing how
easily you can answer them.   Quinctilian relates an anecdote of the poet Accius, which every controversial writer
or speaker will do well to remember.   Accius was a writer
of tragedies, and being once asked why he, whose dialogue
was celebrated for its energy, did not engage in the practice of the bar, answered, because in his tragedies he could
make his characters say what he pleased ; but that at the
bar he should have to contend with persons who would say
anything but what he pleased.   There can be no possible
advantage in supposing our antagonist a fool.   The most
probable effect of such an imagination is to prove ourselves so." [1]

The words of Accius should be observed by every
student of argumentation.   It is easy to set up men
of straw and knock them down, but it is dangerous.
To suggest possible arguments, unless you are sure,
either that they have already been advanced, or that
they must be advanced by the other side, is foolish.
If the arguments are worth while, do not help your
adversary by suggesting them ; if they are not worth
while, it is a waste of time to notice them.   Furthermore, it gives an opponent the opportunity to ridicule
the effort, by admitting or ignoring the points thus
suggested.

Methods of Refutation

It must not be presumed that refutation is a separate and distinct kind of argumentation.   To refute

[1] Lectures on Rhetoric and Oratory, Vol. II, pp. 90–91.

demands just as thorough a mastery of the general principles of handling evidence and arguments, as is needed for positive demonstration. But, in addition to all these things, there are certain peculiar methods of arranging and presenting the materials of destructive proof.

(1) *State clearly the argument to be answered.*

Before taking up any of the particular methods there is one principle of refutation that is noteworthy. Always make perfectly clear to the audience or reader, just what is the point that is to be attacked. The statement to which objection is made should almost always be distinctly stated at the start, and the statement should be supplemented, while the reply is being presented, by whatever explanations are necessary, in order to make evident the purposes and results of the answer. It must be made clear that there are two opposing arguments which directly meet, and that one overthrows the other. The force of refutation is destructive, and it cannot achieve its full effect unless the audience understands just what is to be destroyed, and just how the refutation accomplishes the destruction.

A study of forensic and deliberative oratory shows the painstaking care used by the ablest speakers and writers. The following is an example of Webster's method in forensic refutation, a model of clearness in introducing refutation. The quotation is from his speech in the case of Ogden *vs*. Saunders: —

"Here we meet the opposite arguments, stated on different occasions in different terms, but usually summed up in this, that the law itself is a part of the contract, and therefore cannot impair it. What does it mean? Let us seek for clear ideas. It does not mean that the law gives any particular construction to the terms of the contract, or that it makes the promise, or the consideration, or the time of performance, other than is expressed in the instrument itself. It can only mean that it is to be taken as a part of the contract or understanding of the parties, that the contract itself shall be enforced by such laws and regulations respecting remedy and for the enforcement of contracts as are in being in the State where it is made at the time of entering into it. This is meant, or nothing very clearly intelligible is meant, by saying the law is part of the contract. . . .

"Against this we contend : —

"1st. That, if the proposition were true, the consequence would not follow.

"2d. That the proposition itself cannot be maintained." [1]

To take an illustration from a deliberative oration : Webster, in replying to Mr. Calhoun in the Senate, on the question of the protective tariff, divided his speech into five parts, corresponding to the five main points of his opponent. The following are the sentences introductory to these parts respectively : —

"I. In treating of protection, or protective duties, the first proposition of the honorable member is, that all duties laid on imports really fall on exports; that they are a toll paid for going to market.

[1] The Works of Daniel Webster, Vol. VI, p. 29. Little, Brown and Co., Boston, 1851.

" II. Another opinion of the honorable member is, that increased production brings about expansion of the currency, and that such increase makes a further increase necessary. His idea is, that, if some goods are manufactured at home, less will be imported ; if less goods are imported, the amount of exports still keeping up, the whole export being thus paid for by the import, specie must be brought to settle the balance ; that this increase of specie gives new powers to the banks to discount ; that the banks thereupon make large issues, till the mass of currency becomes redundant and swollen; that this swollen currency augments the price of articles of our own manufacture, and makes it necessary to raise prices still higher, and this creates a demand for the imposition of new duties. This, as I understand it, is the honorable member's train of thought.

" III. There is a third general idea of the honorable gentlemen, upon which I would make a few observations. It is, that the South and West are the great consumers of the products of the manufactures of the North and East; that the capacity of the South to consume depends on her great staples ; and that the sale of these depends mainly on a foreign market.

" IV. A fourth sentiment of the honorable member is, that the removal of all duties increases the exportation of articles manufactured at home.

" V. Finally, the honorable member is of opinion that the whole system of protection was prostrated, and is prostrated, cut up, root and branch, and exterminated forever, by the State interposition of South Carolina." [1]

(2) *Exposing any fallacy.*

The first method that suggests itself for the over-

[1] The Works of Daniel Webster, Vol. IV, pp. 528–538. Little, Brown and Co., Boston, 1856.

throw of opposing proof is to point out, by an explanation, any fallacy in the arguments, or any weakness
in the evidence of the other side. The ways of
detecting flaws in evidence and errors in arguments,
have already been shown. We have also noted several of the more common general fallacies, such as
begging the question and arguing beside the point.
The two last-mentioned fallacies are frequently encountered, and some forceful method of exposing the
error is a good weapon to have ready at hand. To
lay bare any such defects in the processes of an
opponent's proof is, of course, to refute him.

(3) *Reductio ad absurdum.*

One of the most commonly used methods of proof
peculiar to refutation is that of reducing an argument
to an absurdity, or, as it is named, the *reductio ad
absurdum*. The refuter adopts for the moment the
line of argument of his opponent; then, by carrying
it out to its logical conclusion, shows that it results in
an absurdity. For example, A contends that women
ought to be allowed to vote, because, with respect to
political rights, "all men are free and equal." B
answers him by showing that the same argument
carried out to its logical conclusion would prove that
all criminals, idiots, and minors should have the right
of suffrage, thus reducing the argument to a manifestly absurd proposition.

This method is effective because of its simplicity
and directness; it also has in it an element of ridicule

that is persuasive against an opponent. William
Ellery Channing, in a reply to Henry Clay on the
slavery question, used this method as follows: —

" But this property, we are told, is not to be questioned
on account of its long duration. ' Two hundred years of
legislation have sanctioned and *sanctified* negro slaves as
property.' Nothing but respect for the speaker could
repress criticism on this unhappy phraseology. We will
trust it escaped him without thought. But to confine ourselves to the argument from duration ; how obvious the
reply ! Is injustice changed into justice by the practice
of ages ? Is my victim made a righteous prey because I
have bowed him to the earth till he cannot rise ? For
more than two hundred years heretics were burned, and
not by mobs, not by Lynch law, but by the decrees of
councils, at the instigation of theologians, and with the
sanction of the laws and religions of nations ; and was this
a reason for keeping up the fires, that they had burned
two hundred years ? In the Eastern world, successive
despots, not for two hundred years, but for twice two
thousand, have claimed the right of life and death over
millions, and, with no law but their own will, have be-
headed, bowstrung, starved, tortured unhappy men without number who have incurred their wrath ; and does the
lapse of so many centuries sanctify murder and ferocious
power ? "

Again : —

" But the great argument remains. It is said that this
property must not be questioned, because it is established
by law. ' That *is* property which the law declares *to be*
property.'[1] Thus human law is made supreme, decisive,

[1] The italics are by Mr. Clay.

in a question of morals.   Thus the idea of an eternal,
immutable justice is set at naught.   Thus the great rule
of human life is made to be the ordinance of interested
men.   But there *is* a higher tribunal, a throne of equal
justice, immovable by the conspiracy of all human legisla-
tures.   'That is property which the law declares to be
property.'   Then the laws have only to declare you, or
me, or Mr. Clay, to be property, and we become chattels
and are bound to bear the yoke!   Does not even man's
moral nature repel this doctrine too intuitively to leave
time or need for argument?"[1]

(4) *Dilemma.*

The dilemma is one of the oldest of all known
rhetorical forms.   As a method of refutation, it consists in reducing an issue to an alternative, and then
showing that both members of the alternative are
untenable.   These two members are called the "horns
of the dilemma."   The refuter says in substance:
"Now, with respect to this point at issue, there are
two and only two possibilities, viz., A and B.   But
A is not true, and B is not true; consequently your
contention falls."   In order to make the dilemma
conclusive, obviously two things are necessary.
(*a*) The two horns of the dilemma must include all
the possibilities in the case, *i.e.* the alternative must
be exact.   (*b*) Both members of the alternative must
be destroyed.

James Wilson, speaking in the convention for the

[1] The Works of William E. Channing, D.D., Vol. V, pp. 48–49.
G. G. Channing, Boston, 1846.

province of Pennsylvania, in vindication of the colonies, January, 1775, used the dilemma as follows:—

"In the first place, then, I say that the persons who allege that those employed to alter the charter and constitution of Massachusetts Bay act by virtue of a commission from his majesty for that purpose, speak improperly, and contrary to the truth of the case. I say they do not act by virtue of such commission; I say it is impossible they can act by virtue of such a commission. What is called a commission either contains particular directions for the purpose mentioned, or it contains no such particular directions. In either case can those, who act for that purpose, act by virtue of a commission? In one case, what is called a commission is void; it has no legal existence; it can communicate no authority. In the other case, it extends not to the purpose mentioned. The latter point is too plain to be insisted on: I [will] prove the former." [1]

Jeremiah S. Black, in defence of the right of trial by jury, thus attacked the contention of his opponents, which was that the law of nations was binding in the trial of the cause in question:—

"Our friends on the other side are quite conscious that when they deny the binding obligation of the Constitution they must put some other system of law in its place. Their brief gives us notice that, while the Constitution, and the acts of Congress, and *Magna Charta*, and the common law, and all the rules of natural justice shall remain under foot, they will try American citizens according to *the law of nations!* But the law of nations takes no

[1] "Eloquence of the United States," Vol. V, p. 56. E. and H. Clark, Middletown, Conn., 1827.

notice of the subject.   If that system did contain a special provision that a government might hang one of its own citizens without a judge or jury, it would still be competent for the American people to say, as they have said, that no such thing should ever be done here.   That is my answer to the law of nations." [1]

Sometimes the possibilities with respect to the point in issue cannot be reduced to two.   There may be a choice offered of any one of three or more possible conditions, or courses of action.   In such a case, to state the issue in the form of a dilemma, presenting a single alternative, would not be an exact division, and so would be fallacious; to be truthful it is always necessary to state *all* the possibilities of choice, whatever their number.   When more than two possibilities are to be considered, the method is, properly speaking, not a dilemma; but the *modus operandi* is similar.   Webster, in his argument in the case of the Providence Railroad Co. *vs.* City of Boston, made a division into three possibilities.   Mr. Webster is here contending against the proposition that a certain street or piece of land is a public highway : —

" If this street, or land, or whatever it may be, has become and now is a public highway, it must have become so in one of three ways, and to these points I particularly call your honors' attention.

" 1st.   It must either have become a highway by having been regularly laid out according to usage and law ; or

" 2d.   By *dedication* as such by those having the power

---

to dedicate it, and acceptance and adoption so far as they are required ; or

" 3d. As a highway by long user, without the existence of proof of any original laying out, or dedication.

" It is not pretended by any one that the land in question is a highway, upon the last of these grounds. I shall therefore confine myself to the consideration of the other two questions ; namely, ' Was there ever a formal and regular laying out of a street here ? or was there ever a regular and sufficient dedication and acceptance ? ' " [1]

(5) *Residues.*

The method of residues, like that of the dilemma, is founded upon a division of the point in question into parts. The difference is, that in the dilemma all the parts are destroyed, whereas, in the method of residues, one of the parts is left standing. By the method of residues, the matter in dispute is divided into two or more sections, which include all the possibilities in the case ; then all but one of these are demolished, the one left standing being the aspect of the issue which the refuter wishes to establish. " There are," says the refuter, " three possibilities, A, B, and C. But A and B are false, consequently the presumption is that C is true." This method is not, strictly speaking, a method of refuting. It is rather a method of using refutation : the ultimate purpose of the speaker or writer is not destructive, but constructive ; he destroys some of the parts into

---

[1] The Works of Daniel Webster, Vol. VI, p. 186. Little, Brown and Co., Boston, 1851.

which he divides the question, in order that he may establish the remaining part. He uses refutation to accomplish his end ; but the end itself is constructive proof.

The first requisite in using the method of residues is, that the division of the whole into parts shall be exhaustive. The strength of the method depends entirely upon the assumption, that all the possibilities in the case are destroyed save one. If, then, the disputant omits, in his division, to mention one of the possibilities, he has proved nothing, for it still remains uncertain which possibility is true, — the one he seeks to establish or the one he failed to mention. Again, in order to make the work complete, it is necessary that the residuary part be enforced by positive demonstration. The refuting of all but one of the possibilities, leaves a presumption that the remaining possibility is true ; but there may well be a suspicion that even this last part too is false, or that there is some fallacy in the division. Consequently, to be at all convincing the residuary part must be enforced by positive proof.

There is no better example of the use of the method of residues, than that found in Thomas H. Huxley's Lectures on Evolution, delivered in New York in 1876. Professor Huxley was here endeavoring to establish the theory of evolution, as the true theory respecting the genesis and history of the universe. In his first lecture he divided the question into three possible hypotheses as follows : —

" So far as I know, there are only three hypotheses which ever have been entertained, or which well can be entertained, respecting the past history of Nature. I will, in the first place, state the hypotheses, and then I will consider what evidence bearing upon them is in our possession, and by what light of criticism that evidence is to be interpreted.

" Upon the first hypothesis, the assumption is, that phenomena of Nature similar to those exhibited by the present world have always existed ; in other words, that the universe has existed from all eternity in what may be broadly termed its present condition.

" The second hypothesis is, that the present state of things has had only a limited duration ; and that, at some period in the past, a condition of the world, essentially similar to that which we now know, came into existence, without any precedent condition from which it could have naturally proceeded. The assumption that successive states of Nature have arisen, each without any relation of natural causation to an antecedent state, is a mere modification of this second hypothesis.

" The third hypothesis also assumes that the present state of things has had but a limited duration ; but it supposes that this state has been evolved by a natural process from an antecedent state, and that from another, and so on ; and, on this hypothesis, the attempt to assign any limit to the series of past changes is, usually, given up." [1]

He then proceeded, in his series of lectures, to overthrow the first two hypotheses, leaving the third — the theory of evolution — standing as the residuary part, and finally he supported this theory by positive proof of its probability.

[1] *Popular Science Monthly*, Vol. X, p. 44.

Burke, in his speech on "Conciliation with America," used the method of residues. He began : —

"Sir, if I were capable of engaging you to an equal attention, I would state, that as far as I am capable of discerning, there are but three ways of proceeding relative to this stubborn Spirit which prevails in your Colonies, and disturbs your Government. These are, to change that Spirit, as inconvenient, by removing the Causes. To prosecute it as criminal. Or, to comply with it as necessary. I would not be guilty of an imperfect enumeration ; I can think of but these three. Another has indeed been started, that of giving up the Colonies ; but it met so slight a reception that I do not think myself obliged to dwell a great while upon it. It is nothing but a little sally of anger, like the frowardness of peevish children, who, when they cannot get all they would have, are resolved to take nothing."

He then considered the first two ways at length and proved them impracticable, and concluded : —

"If then the removal of the causes of this Spirit of American Liberty be, for the greater part, or rather entirely, impracticable ; if the ideas of Criminal Process be inapplicable, or if applicable are in the highest degree inexpedient, what way yet remains ? No way is open, but the third and last, to comply with the American Spirit as necessary ; or, if you please, to submit to it as a necessary Evil."

(6) *Showing an opponent's proof to be a proof of your own side of the case.*

To turn the argument of an opponent against him is not often possible. But circumstances sometimes give the opportunity. A piece of testimony may be used by a writer, when he has not fully considered all the interpretations that may be put upon it. It not infrequently happens that evidence, or an argument, is introduced to give support to some particular point, and, in its bearing on that phase of the question, the evidence may be favorable to the speaker or writer that introduces it ; but as the discussion proceeds, it may turn out that, with respect to some other phase of the question, the evidence or the argument may be interpreted in another way, adversely to its inventor. The effect of such an unexpected turn of affairs is obvious; the opponent is "hoist with his own petard." The very manner of introducing the proof adds to its effectiveness. Webster, in the Girard Will Case, used this method in attacking one of the proofs of the defendants : —

"The arguments of my learned friend, may it please your honors, in relation to the Jewish laws as tolerated by the statutes, go to maintain my very proposition ; that is, that no school for the instruction of youth in any system which is in any way derogatory to the Christain religion, or for the teaching of doctrines that are in any way contrary to the Christian religion, is, or ever was, regarded as a charity by the courts. It is true that the statutes of Toleration regarded a devise for the maintenance of poor Jewish children, to give them food and raiment and lodging, as a charity. But a devise for the teaching of the Jewish religion to poor children, that should come into the Court of Chancery, would not be regarded as a charity, or entitled to any peculiar privileges from the court."[1]

[1] The Works of Daniel Webster, Vol. VI, p. 166. Little, Brown and Co., Boston, 1851.

(7) *Refutation should be followed by positive proof*.
With respect to the method of handling refutation,
the final word of advice is, to follow up refutation
with positive proof.   This suggestion is of a general
nature and is open to exceptions.   But it must not be
forgotten that refutation is destructive; it demolishes,
but does not build up.   To make men act or thoroughly believe, it is not enough to make them see
there is no reason why they should not be convinced;
they must be made to see that there is a positive
reason why they should be convinced.   Consequently,
pure refutation is weak and lacks the strongest elements of conviction; it is a necessary help, but is
not sufficient in itself.   It is, therefore, generally an
anticlimax to place refutation at the end of the discussion, or at the end of any important division of
the argument.   Positive proof rather than refutation
should be given the emphatic places.

This leads to the matter of the *arrangement* of
refutation.   With respect to the strength and the
weakness of the points of refutation, the same rules
apply as in positive proof : the emphatic places are
the beginning and the end.   If, then, the answer to
be made is strong, it may well be put first or toward
the last.   Weaker answers are best hidden in the
middle.   However, it often happens that an opponent makes a point or presents some idea, which must
be overthrown before the speaker or writer can proceed with his own proof.   In such circumstances,
clearly the answer to the point must be made at the

very beginning. Doubt often arises as to whether it is best to make the answer a distinct point in the discussion, or to introduce it as merely an incident to some other point. This depends upon the importance of the argument to be answered, and so is a question of personal judgment in each particular case. In general, however, any answer to what would correspond to a "subhead" in an opponent's brief, should rarely be made a main head in refutation. Such lesser arguments of an opponent are best answered, in connection with those parts of one's own proof with which they are naturally associated; they should be considered wherever they happen to arise in the course of one's own argument. It is true in general that, with the exception of the most vital of the proofs of the opposition, refutation is best made as the occasion for the answers arises in the course of one's own demonstration. But if the answer to an opponent's argument is, from the circumstances, of such importance as to make any large part of the question depend upon it, there should be no hesitation in making it one of the main issues of the proof, and emphasizing it as such.

Finally, it should never be forgotten that arrangement of the materials is just as necessary in refutation as in positive proof. A rambling, incoherent, formless presentation is just as fatal to efficiency in destructive as in constructive argument. Just as in the arrangement of all other materials, the "main head" must be made to stand out clear and emphatic, and around it the lesser materials must be grouped in subordination. It is a common failing of inexperienced debaters, however accurate and firm they may be elsewhere, to become careless in refutation, forgetting many of the principles of arrangement and presentation. These principles apply equally to all kinds of proof, whether positive or negative.

PART II
DEBATE

CHAPTER I

DEBATE

In the preceding chapters the principles that have been set forth apply equally to written and to spoken argumentation. But in that form of discussion commonly known as debate, which consists in a direct oral contest between two opposing sides, on a definite question at a definite time, some of these principles must undergo slight adaptations, and to them must be added other new principles.

A good argumentative essayist is not necessarily a good debater, any more than a good writer is necessarily a good speaker. To begin with, a debater must know something of the arts of public speech; he may not be positively eloquent, but he must know how to express himself before an audience with a reasonable degree of ease and force. But elocution is not all. The debater, in addition to being an orator, must be something of a general. In polemic warfare there are ambuscades, unexpected reënforcements for the enemy, and critical situations of various kinds which cannot be foreseen. To meet these contingencies and master them demands a clear head, quick judgment, firm decision, and a certain amount of bold self-confidence. There is, moreover, a strategy of debate which must be learned by study and experience. How to open the battle, when to use light cavalry and when to use artillery, when to attack, when to give way, how to plan an ambuscade, how to retreat — a knowledge of these things belongs no less to the debater than to the military commander.

Finally, the work of preparation for debate is different in many ways from that for written disputation. In preliminary reading, attention must be given to matters that might under other conditions safely be neglected. In selecting evidence, the choice must often be determined by the special conditions; evidence that is good in an essay, is often ineffective in spoken argument. In drawing a brief, the choice of the main headings and the arrangement of the points must be planned, with regard to the exigencies and the strategy of the contest. Then, also, preparation for the refutation of an opponent's arguments must be much more thorough.

To attempt to make fixed and inexorable rules for many of these processes mentioned above would be a mistake; uniformity of method in debating is undesirable, as well as impossible. Consequently, the principles that follow are general rather than specific. Further, it should be understood that debate is not a form of argumentation entirely separate and distinct from other forms. Every principle enunciated in the preceding chapters, on argumentation in general, has full force in debate. The suggestions given here are merely additional.

I. Preliminary Reading

With respect to preliminary reading, there are but two things to be emphasized in addition to what has already been said in Chapter IV.

A. Particular study needs to be given to the opposite side of the question.

B. Especial attention needs to be given to the study of the broad, general principles of the problem to be discussed.

A. In debate, refutation is no less important than positive proof; in intercollegiate debates it is most often the rebuttal that is decisive; in any discussion it is the "last speech" that is coveted; Webster's famous Reply to Hayne was almost pure refutation. And it is very seldom that successful refutation is impromptu. An anecdote in point is told concerning one of the most brilliant advocates of the English bar. This lawyer was one day arguing an important case before one of the highest tribunals of the country. In the course of the trial he was made the object of an attack, personal and political in nature, from his opponent, the attorney for the prosecution. The attack was bitter, but forcible and persuasive. It seemed to be unexpected by any one; the court was surprised, but manifestly affected. The advocate arose to make reply, and in his introduction, with perfect calmness and great eloquence, he answered every charge, retrieved the lost favor of the court, and overpowered his assailant with an irresistible invective. After this trial was finished, one of the judges — a personal friend — expressed his surprise and admiration at the extraordinary eloquence of the reply, declaring the retort to be one of the most brilliant passages ever heard in an English court of law, and added, that he had never believed such impromptu oratory to be within the limits of human powers. In answer to these congratulations, the advocate invited the justice to accompany him to his law chambers. Entering his library, he walked to a desk, opened a drawer, and took from it a manuscript; it was his speech of the morning written out in full, nearly word for word as he had delivered it. He had foreseen a contingency that nobody else had expected or deemed possible, and had made ready to meet the situation. He won because he was prepared.

Daniel Webster declared that all the material of his Reply to Hayne had been gathering, and waiting in his desk for months before the debate. Speaking of Senator Hayne, he said to a friend: "If he had tried to make a speech to fit my notes, he could not have hit it better. No man is ever inspired with the occasion; I never was." Mere words and gestures do not make refutation any more than they make positive proof. There must be just as much evidence in the one as in the other. Refutation demands as careful a choice of weapons and as accurate a method of handling them as any other kind of proof. Invention, selection, and arrangement demand as much preliminary planning here, as elsewhere.

Clearly, the primary necessity in preparing refutation is to know just what points we shall be called upon to answer; we must have a clear and accurate understanding of the points our opponents need to establish, and of the methods they may adopt in the attempt. Furthermore, it is desirable to know the other side of the case in order wisely to prepare our own positive proof. Would any capable general ever lay the plans for an attack without first considering the position of his enemy, his location, his points of strength and weakness? As we shall see more clearly later, the selecting of the main heads of a brief in debate, depends very largely upon what the opposition may be able to "do about it." Those points must be chosen for emphasis, that will hit hardest and straightest at the necessary proof of the other side; and at the same time we must remember that these main heads will surely be attacked, and we must take up a position that is defensible against assault. All this means a study and comparison of the two sides of the question, so as to find out what arguments need to be attacked, and, on the other hand, what statement of one's own arguments will best stand defensible against the other side.

B. But it is rarely possible to foresee every argument that an opponent may advance. No two persons reason just alike : an opponent may well look at the question from some peculiar standpoint, or, as more often happens, he may plan a surprise. Then, too, there are many minor questions that are raised in such a discussion, which it is hardly worth while trying to anticipate, or which escape notice in preparation. Commonly, these minor points are best left unanswered; but sometimes circumstances make them worth notice. Whatever the reason, it is certain that all the incidents of a debate cannot be foreseen; we must always expect the unexpected. A successful debater must always be ready to meet strange situations, and to manufacture more or less of refutation and of proof on the scene of action.

Now a disputant who has read only on those phases of the question that are of interest to him, or who undertakes only those parts of the discussion that he treats in his own proof, is helpless in such circumstances. He has no resources to draw upon. If the discussion were in writing, he might think it over, consult new authorities, and plan his answer; but in debate there is no such opportunity. He must act at once. He is in the predicament of a military expedition that sets out on a long campaign, with a day's rations and no base of supplies. When a debater is thus surprised, his only hope must lie in having a thorough knowledge of the question as a whole, and in all its details, a knowledge so thorough as to be ready at the call of any exigency. Furthermore, a broad understanding of the foundations and general conditions of the question is necessary, in order to be able to estimate rightly, the force and bearing of arguments that are made by opponents. A superficial preparation always distorts the mental

vision of a speaker, and confuses in his mind the real
issues in the discussion. But debate demands an
especially clear perception and quick judgment of
what is vital : the debater must think as quickly and
act as decisively, as the broker on the exchange ; superficial information or a confused understanding
mean as sure disaster in the one case as in the other.
A debater in action must be able, when any argument or any evidence is brought against him, to
estimate in a few seconds just what the matter
amounts to, how it is related to his own case, how
much to say about it, and where — in what part of
his speech — to answer it. Here a stock of ready-
made arguments becomes useless. Only a deep
understanding of the subject to the very bottom can
give this clear, ready insight, and this steady judgment that alone avails.

These two foregoing suggestions are especially applicable in preparation for school or college debates.
There the limitations of time are very stringent : not
the smallest fraction of a minute can be lost in confusion or unnecessary deliberation ; the answer must
be in the debater's head as soon as the argument has
left his opponent's lips. The necessity for such preparation, important everywhere, is here intensified by
the circumstances.

II. The Introduction

A. In debate, to have the first speech is a privilege. This privilege, which arises from the influence

of the speech upon the remainder of the debate, is
twofold.   First, the speaker has an opportunity to
make the first impression on the audience; and, secondly, he has an opportunity to direct the course of
the debate.   This, then, is the duty of a speaker opening a debate, whom, for convenience, we will call
the "first speaker on the affirmative," viz., to win
sympathy for himself or his view of the subject, and
so to present the question as to persuade his audience that his method of treating this question is just
and sensible.   It always happens in such a controversy that there is one method of dividing up and
discussing the question that is advantageous to the
affirmative, and another method that is advantageous
to the negative.   Consequently, to force an opponent
to discuss the question according to your plan, to compel him to fight you on your own grounds, is a point
won.   To return to a military comparison, in war it
is a great advantage to be able to have the choice of
position; and this advantage generally goes to the
army that is first on the field.   An adroit and
aggressive first speaker can so explain the origin and
history of the question, and so present the issues, as
to compel his opponent to accept his partition of the
case, on penalty of losing favor with the audience,
by seeming to evade the issue.

Rhetorically, an opening speaker should use a
graceful and finished diction.   His general tone
should be conciliatory.   Above all, his exposition
should be lucid and interesting, avoiding fine

distinctions and technicalities in explaining the question.

The duty of the first speaker in opposition, who may be called the " first speaker on the negative," is clear. He may adopt the same tone and rhetorical style as the opening speaker, — clear, smooth, and conciliatory ; or he may take a different attitude, an attitude of open belligerency from the start. But he must, whatever the method, overthrow the influence of his opponent who has introduced the debate. This is a difficult task, calling for tact and aggressive force. Sometimes his opponent will have excited the audience against him, or will have won their sympathy for himself ; then the speaker must counteract these effects by the use of sarcasm, wit, invective, or whatever resources he may command. If the opening speaker has seemed to establish an interpretation of the question unfavorable to the negative, he must offer battle at the very start, and overthrow this interpretation by showing that " the preceding speaker has falsified history and distorted the facts," that he has "misrepresented the real issues in hand," or "unfortunately failed to grasp the real question," etc. Whatever the situation he finds left by his opponent, he must adapt himself to it and change it to his own advantage. He must take matters as he finds them. At such a time, a lecture or an essay is worse than nothing. The whole value of the introduction of a first speaker on the negative, depends on its adaptation to the circumstances.

An illustration directly in point may be taken from the famous Lincoln-Douglas debates of 1858. The circumstances of this controversy are well known. It occurred during the most intense period of the slavery struggle, just before the opening of the War of the Rebellion. The country was stirred to a passionate interest, by the fight in Congress over the admission of Kansas into the Union, by the conflict between slavery and anti-slavery factions in that state, and by the Dred Scott decision, just declared by the Supreme Court. Lincoln and Douglas were rival candidates for the Illinois senatorship. They were recognized representatives of the two great political factions of the North, and the whole country soon became the spectators of the contest.

In brief, the events immediately preceding, to which frequent reference was made by both speakers, were as follows. In 1820, a bill was passed in Congress containing what has since been known as the Missouri Compromise. This Compromise declared that thereafter slavery should be prohibited north of 36° 30′ in all the territory acquired from France by the Louisiana Purchase. This Compromise was looked upon as a sacred and permanently binding agreement, between the Northern and the Southern interests in the country. In 1854 Senator Douglas, from the Committee on Territories, reported the Nebraska Bill, in one section of which this Compromise was declared repealed, because "inconsistent with the principle of non-intervention by Congress with slavery in the states and territories as recognized by the Compromise of 1850." The shock to the country was great. The acting generation had come to look upon the Missouri Compromise as sacred, and almost a part of the Constitution itself. A long and hard-fought contest followed, the Nebraska Bill being finally forced through at the end of four months. The country soon saw, beneath all disguises, that the measure was purely a Southern proslavery move, and that the beginning of a struggle between the slave states and the free states was at hand. Then there followed immediately the struggle between the slavery and the free-soil factions, for the control of Kansas. If the question had been left to the actual settlers, slavery would have been excluded. But the neighboring inhabitants of Missouri invaded the territory, seized the polls, and fraudulently elected a proslavery legislature and delegate to Congress.

The Whig party was destroyed. The Republican party came into being and nominated their first presidential candidate, John C. Frémont. After Mr. Buchanan's inauguration, the effort to force slavery on Kansas was resumed with even greater zeal. The Supreme Court came to the aid of the Democrats by making the Dred Scott decision, the important part of which was the assertion that Congress had no power to exclude slavery from the territories.

The first quotation is the introduction to Senator Douglas's opening speech, given at Chicago, July 9, 1858: —

" MR. CHAIRMAN AND FELLOW-CITIZENS: I can find no language which can adequately express my profound gratitude for the magnificent welcome which you have extended to me on this occasion. This vast sea of human faces indicates how deep an interest is felt by our people in the great questions which agitate the public mind, and which underlie the foundations of our free institutions. A reception like this, so great in numbers that no human voice can be heard to its countless thousands, — so enthusiastic that no one individual can be the object of such enthusiasm, — clearly shows that there is some great principle which sinks deep in the heart of the masses, and involves the rights and liberties of a whole people, that has brought you together with a unanimity and a cordiality never before excelled, if, indeed, equalled on any occasion. I have not the vanity to believe that it is any personal compliment to me.

" It is an expression of your devotion to that great principle of self-government to which my life for many years past has been, and in the future will be, devoted. If there is any one principle dearer and more sacred than all others in free governments, it is that which asserts the exclusive right of a free people to form and adopt their own fundamental law, and to manage and regulate their own internal affairs and domestic institutions.

" When I found an effort being made during the recent session of Congress to force a Constitution upon the people of Kansas against their will, and to force that State into the Union with a Constitution which her people had rejected by more than ten thousand, I felt bound as a man of honor and a representative of Illinois, bound by every consideration of duty, of fidelity, and of patriotism, to resist to the utmost of my power the consummation of that fraud. With others I did resist it, and resisted it successfully until the attempt was abandoned. We forced them to refer that Constitution back to the people of Kansas, to be accepted or rejected as they shall decide at an election, which is fixed for the first Monday in August next. . . .

" Hence, my friends, I regard the Lecompton battle as having been fought and the victory won, because the arrogant demand for the admission of Kansas under the Lecompton Constitution unconditionally, whether her people wanted it or not, has been abandoned, and the principle which recognized the right of the people to decide for themselves has been submitted in its place.

" Fellow-citizens : While I devoted my best energies — all my energies, mental and physical — to the vindication of the great principle, and whilst the result has been such as will enable the people of Kansas to come into the Union, with such a Constitution as they desire, yet the credit of this great moral victory is to be divided among a large number of men of various and different political creeds. I was rejoiced when I found in this great contest the Republican party coming up manfully and sustaining the principle that the people of each Territory, when coming into the Union, have the right to decide for themselves whether slavery shall or shall not exist within their limits. I have seen the time when that principle was controverted. I have seen the time when all parties did not recognize the right of a people to have slavery or freedom, to tolerate or prohibit slavery, as they deemed best ; but claimed that power for the Congress of the United States, regardless of the wishes of the people to be affected by it, and when I found upon the Crittenden-Montgomery bill the Republicans and Americans of the North, and I may say, too, some glorious Americans and old line Whigs from the South, like Crittenden and his patriotic associates, joined with a portion of the Democracy to carry out and vindicate the right of the people to decide whether slavery should or should not exist within the limits of Kansas, I was rejoiced within my secret soul, for I saw that the American people, when they come to understand the principle, would give it their cordial support." [1]

Mr. Lincoln opened his speech in reply as follows : —

" My fellow-citizens : On yesterday evening, upon the occasion of the reception given to Senator Douglas, I was furnished with a seat very convenient for hearing him, and was otherwise very courteously treated by him and his friends, and for which I thank him and them. During the course of his remarks my name was mentioned in such a way as, I suppose, renders it at least not improper that I should make some sort of reply to him. I shall not attempt to follow him in the precise order in which he addressed the assembled multitude upon that occasion, though I shall perhaps do so in the main.

" There was one question to which he asked the attention of the crowd, which I deem of somewhat less importance — at least of propriety for me to dwell upon — than the others, which he brought in near the close of his speech, and which I think it would not be entirely proper for me to omit attending to, and yet if I were not to give some attention to it now, I should probably forget it altogether. While I am upon this subject, allow me to say that I do not intend to indulge in that inconvenient mode sometimes adopted in public speaking, of reading from documents ; but I shall depart from that rule so far as to read a little scrap from his speech, which notices this first

---

[1] Lincoln-Douglas Debates, pp. 5-6. Follett, Foster and Co., 1860.

topic of which I shall speak — that is, provided I can find it in the paper.

" ' I have made up my mind to appeal to the people against the combination that has been made against me! the Republican leaders have formed an alliance, an unholy and unnatural alliance, with a portion of unscrupulous federal office-holders. I intend to fight that allied army wherever I meet them. I know they deny the alliance, but yet these men who are trying to divide the Democratic party for the purpose of electing a Republican Senator in my place, are just as much the agents and tools of the supporters of Mr. Lincoln. Hence I shall deal with this allied army just as the Russians dealt with the allied forces at Sebastopol — that is, the Russians did not stop to inquire, when they fired a broadside, whether it hit an Englishman, a Frenchman, or a Turk. Nor will I stop to inquire, nor shall I hesitate, whether my blows shall hit these Republican leaders or their allies, who are holding the federal offices and yet acting in concert with them.'

" Well, now, gentlemen, is not that very alarming? Just to think of it! right at the outset of his canvass, I, a poor, kind, amiable gentleman, I am to be slain in this way. Why, my friend, the Judge, is not only, as it turns out, not a dead lion, nor even a living one — he is the rugged Russian Bear!

" But if they will have it — for he says that we deny it — that there is any such alliance, as he says there is — and I don't propose hanging very much upon this question of veracity — but if he will have it that there is such an alliance — that the Administration men and we are allied, and we stand in the attitude of English, French, and Turk, he occupying the position of the Russian, in that case, I beg that he will indulge us while we barely suggest to him that these allies took Sebastopol. . . .

" Popular sovereignty ! everlasting popular sovereignty !
Let us for a moment inquire into this vast matter of
popular sovereignty," etc.[1]

We have said, that the value of the introduction of
a first speaker on the negative depends upon its
adaptation to the circumstances. This is also true
of the introduction to any speech, after the opening
speech. The very essence of debate, as contrasted
with simple written argumentation, consists in seeing
situations and meeting them. A debater who demon-
strates and argues regardless of what the opposition
are doing, is like a fencer who lunges right and left
without looking at his opponent. Very seldom is it
safe to enter the discussion without taking notice of
what has been said and done by preceding speakers,
or without laying some foundation of sympathy and
understanding with the audience.

For example, contrast the two following introduc-
tions. They are both from the same man, Senator
Robert Y. Hayne of South Carolina. They were
both delivered in the same debate, the debate in the
Senate in 1830, on the famous Foote Resolution.
But there is this difference: the first is the introduction to Mr. Hayne's opening speech; the second
is part of the introduction to a second speech, delivered at a later stage of the discussion, after he had
been attacked and his position assailed by such
senators as Benton and Webster. The contrast

[1] Lincoln-Douglas Debates, pp. 14-15.   Follett, Foster and Co., 1860.

shows the difference in tone and method adapted to the different situations.

Mr. Hayne's opening speech began as follows: —

" It has been said, and correctly said, by more than one gentleman, that resolutions of inquiry were usually suffered to pass without opposition. The parliamentary practice in this respect was certainly founded in good sense and sound policy, which regarded such resolutions as intended merely to elicit information, and therefore entitled to favor. But I cannot give my assent to the proposition so broadly laid down by some gentlemen, that because nobody stands committed by a vote for inquiry, that, therefore, every resolution proposing an inquiry, no matter on what subject, must pass almost as a matter of course, and that, to discuss or oppose such resolutions, is unparliamentary. The true distinction seems to be this : where information is desired as the basis of legislation, or where the policy of any measure, or the principles it involves, are really questionable, it was always proper to send the subject to a committee for investigation ; but where all the material facts are already known, and there is a fixed and settled opinion in respect to the policy to be pursued, inquiry was unnecessary, and ought to be refused. No one, he thought, could doubt the correctness of the position assumed by the gentleman from Missouri, that no inquiry ought ever to be instituted as to the expediency of doing ' a great and acknowledged wrong.' I do not mean, however, to intimate an opinion that such is the character of this resolution. The application of these rules to the case before us will decide my vote, and every Senator can apply them for himself to the decision of the question, whether the inquiry now called for should be granted or refused. With that decision, whatever it may be, I shall be content.

U

"I have not risen, however, Mr. President, for the purpose of discussing the propriety of instituting the inquiry
recommended by the resolution, but to offer a few remarks
on another and much more important question, to which
gentlemen have alluded in the course of this debate — I
mean the policy which ought to be pursued in relation to
the public lands.   Every gentleman who has had a seat in
Congress for the last two or three years, or even for the
last two or three weeks, must be convinced of the great
and growing importance of this question.   More than half
of our time has been taken up with the discussion of
propositions connected with the public lands ; more than
half of our acts embrace provisions growing out of this
fruitful source.   Day after day the changes are rung on
this topic, from the grave inquiry into the right of the
new States to the absolute sovereignty and property in
the soil, down to the grant of a preëmption of a few
quarter sections to actual settlers.   In the language of a
great orator in relation to another 'vexed question,' we
may truly say, 'that year after year we have been lashed
round the miserable circle of occasional arguments and
temporary expedients.'   No gentleman can fail to perceive that this is a question no longer to be evaded ; it
must be met — fairly and fearlessly met.   A question that
is pressed upon us in so many ways ; that intrudes in such
a variety of shapes ; involving so deeply the feelings and
interests of a large portion of the Union ; insinuating
itself into almost every question of public policy, and
tinging the whole course of our legislation, cannot be put
aside or laid asleep.   We cannot long avoid it ; we must
meet and overcome it, or it will overcome us.   Let us,
then, be prepared to encounter it in a spirit of wisdom
and of justice, and endeavor to prepare our own minds
and the minds of the people for a just and enlightened

decision. The object of the remarks I am about to offer is merely to call public attention to the question, to throw out a few crude and undigested thoughts, as food for reflection, in order to prepare the public mind for the adoption, at no distant day, of some fixed and settled policy in relation to the public lands. I believe that, out of the western country, there is no subject in the whole range of our legislation less understood, and in relation to which there exists so many errors, and such unhappy prejudices and misconception.

"There may be said to be two great parties in this country, who entertain very opposite opinions in relation to the character of the policy which the Government has heretofore pursued, in relation to public lands, as well as to that which ought, hereafter, to be pursued."[1]

The introduction to his second speech, in part, was : —

"When I took occasion, two days ago, to throw out some ideas with respect to the policy of the Government in relation to the public lands, nothing certainly could have been farther from my thoughts than that I should be compelled again to throw myself upon the indulgence of the Senate. Little did I expect to be called upon to meet such an argument as was yesterday urged by the gentle-man from Massachusetts [Mr. Webster]. Sir, I questioned no man's opinions; I impeached no man's motives; I charged no party, or State, or section of country, with hostility to any other; but ventured, I thought in a becoming spirit, to put forth my own sentiments in relation to a great national question of public policy. Such was my course. The gentleman from Missouri [Mr. Benton], it is

[1] Debates in Congress, Vol. VI, Part I, pp. 21–32. Gales and Seaton, Washington, 1830.

true, had charged upon the Eastern States an early and continued hostility towards the West, and referred to a number of historical facts and documents in support of that charge. Now, sir, how have these different arguments been met ? The honorable gentleman from Massachusetts, after deliberating a whole night upon his course, comes into this chamber to vindicate New England, and, instead of making up his issue with the gentleman from Missouri, on the charges which he had preferred, chooses to consider me as the author of those charges, and, losing sight entirely of that gentleman, selects me as his adversary, and pours out all the vials of his mighty wrath upon my devoted head. Nor is he willing to stop there. He goes on to assail the institutions and policy of the South, and calls in question the principles and conduct of the State which I have the honor to represent. When I find a gentleman of mature age and experience, of acknowledged talents and profound sagacity, pursuing a course like this, declining the contest offered from the West, and making war upon the unoffending South, I must believe, I am bound to believe, he has some object in view that he has not ventured to disclose. Why is this ? Has the gentleman discovered in former controversies with the gentleman from Missouri that he is overmatched by that Senator ? And does he hope for a more easy victory over a more feeble adversary ? Has the gentleman's distempered fancy been disturbed by gloomy forebodings of 'new alliances to be formed,' at which he hinted ? Has the ghost of the murdered Coalition come back, like the ghost of Banquo, to 'sear the eye-balls ' of the gentleman, and will it not 'down at his bidding '? Are dark visions of broken hopes, and honors lost forever, still floating before his heated imagination ? Sir, if it be his object to thrust me between the gentleman from Missouri and himself, in order to rescue the East from the contest it has provoked with the West, he shall not be gratified. Sir, I will not be dragged into the defence of my friend from Missouri. The South shall not be forced into a conflict not its own. The gentleman from Missouri is able to fight his own battles. The gallant West needs no aid from the South to repel any attack which may be made on them from any quarter. Let the gentleman from Massachusetts controvert the facts and arguments of the gentleman from Missouri — if he can ; and if he win the victory, let him wear its honors : I shall not deprive him of his laurels." [1]

B. Definition of terms in the introduction is especially important in debate. We have seen that the purpose of all preliminary definition is, to enable the reader or hearer readily to comprehend the terms used in the discussion. In written argumentation, if the reader runs across a word or a phrase that he does not understand, he can pause and think it over till he does understand, or he can even lay aside the essay for a time until he can find out the meaning elsewhere. But in spoken discourse it is different. The audience must catch the meaning of every phrase and every idea as it falls from the lips of the speaker, or they will not get it at all, and the effect of the whole argument will be lost. Consequently, the greatest care must be taken that no term is left ambiguous. The methods of defining have already been explained ; it only needs to be emphasized that

[1] Debates in Congress, Vol. VI, Part I, p. 43. Gales and Seaton, Washington, 1830.

definition is more important in debate than in any other form of discussion.

For a similar reason the issues and the explanation of the question are important. And there is this additional reason for giving attention to the issues : in debate a great multiplicity of facts and arguments is thrown together in a short time ; and an audience may easily become perplexed in the midst of such confusion, unless they are given some standard of judgment. An audience cannot see the force or bearing of arguments, unless they understand what are the vital points in the question. If they know the issues, they can appreciate the meaning of any important fact that is presented, and they will be likely to remember it ; but an audience, left free to judge things according to their own previous knowledge and preconceived opinions, cannot be relied on to judge rightly as to what is worth remembering. For these reasons the issues should almost always be presented in the introduction in some form, and further, it is wise to repeat them in various forms in the discussion, keeping them always clear before the audience.

The desirability of the partition is always a matter of judgment, depending entirely on the circumstances. It always contributes to clearness ; but it is sometimes unwise to reveal to the enemy the line of attack you intend to pursue. Sometimes a distinct partition is impossible ; for example, in the Lincoln-Douglas debates a definite partition would have been awkward and inappropriate, for no particular question was under discussion, the debates being informal and extemporaneous, and really but a running fight.

In general a partition of some kind is desirable, unless there is some objection to it, such as those suggested above. A partition need not be formal in character; it does not necessarily imply a division of the proof into three, four, or five parts, stating exactly what is to be proved. The partition may be very cursory and informal, merely suggesting for the sake of clearness the general course to be followed in the discussion; for example, in the following, taken from the introduction to Charles Sumner's speech in the Senate, May 19 and 20, 1856, on the "Bill for the Admission of Kansas into the Union," Mr. Sumner makes a partition, which adds greatly to the clearness and force of the speech, but which, at the same time, has no air of formality and reveals nothing of the character of the argument to follow:—

"Such is the Crime and such the criminal which it is my duty to expose; and, by the blessing of God, this duty shall be done completely to the end. But this will not be enough. The Apologies, which, with strange hardihood are offered for the Crime, must be torn away, so that it shall stand forth without a single rag or fig-leaf to cover its vileness. And, finally, the True Remedy must be shown. The subject is complex in relations, as it is transcendent in importance; and yet, if I am honored by your attention, I hope to present it clearly in all its parts, while I conduct you to the inevitable conclusion that Kansas must be admitted at once, with her present Constitution, as a State of this Union, and give a new star to the blue field of our National Flag. And here I derive satisfaction from the thought that the cause is so strong in itself as to bear even the infirmities of its advocates; nor can it require anything beyond that simplicity of treatment and moderation of manner which I desire to cultivate. Its true character is such that, like Hercules, it will conquer just so soon as it is recognized.

"My task will be divided under three different heads: *first*, THE CRIME AGAINST KANSAS, in its origin and extent; *secondly*, THE APOLOGIES FOR THE CRIME; and, *thirdly*, THE TRUE REMEDY." [1]

III. The Discussion

A. In drawing a brief for use in debate, particular care should be taken in the selection of the main heads. Not only should the question be divided accurately and logically, but also attention should be given to the forms of statement of the headings. These main headings are sure to be the objective points of the attack of the other side, and they must be made strong enough to stand the shock. If an opponent can force you to take back a phrase, or to acknowledge an exaggeration in any of your fundamental propositions, he has scored a point, and the audience will always give him credit for it, often more credit than he really deserves. Carelessness or rhetorical flourish must never be permitted to make a main heading say either more or less than exactly what is meant. Intrenchments are not built because they

[1] Works of Charles Sumner, Vol. IV, pp. 143–144. Lee and Shepard, Boston, 1872.

look well, but because they can be held against attack; main headings are not made because they sound well, but because they offer definite points of resistance to an opponent.

Senator Douglas, in the debates mentioned above, with his habitually bombastic style of oratory, made many wild charges and assertions. Often the point he aimed to establish was valid, but, through carelessness or over-excitement, he exaggerated. He had an able opponent, and every blunder and every exaggeration was laid bare, much to his discomfiture and humiliation. Lincoln, on the other hand, as he himself admitted in the discussion, prepared with sedulous care the statement of every important proposition he advanced. His propositions were attacked and his attitude was repeatedly misrepresented by Senator Douglas, but reply was not difficult; Lincoln had only to read the exact words of his former speeches and reiterate his statements, thus at the same time reënforcing his own position and exposing the trickery of his opponent. For example, in the following selection Lincoln replies to such an attack on one of his fundamental propositions : —

"Out of this Judge Douglas builds up his beautiful fabrication — of my purpose to introduce a perfect, social, and political equality between the white and black races. His assertion that I made an 'especial objection' . . . to the decision [the Dred Scott decision] on this account is untrue in point of fact.

"Now, while I am upon this subject, and as Henry

Clay has been alluded to, I desire to place myself in connection with Mr. Clay as nearly right before this people
as may be.   I am quite aware what the Judge's object is
here by all these allusions.   He knows that we are before
an audience, having strong sympathies southward by relationship, place of birth, and so on.   He desires to place
me in an extremely abolition attitude.   He read upon a
former occasion, and alludes without reading to-day, to a
portion of a speech which I delivered in Chicago.   In his
quotations from that speech, as he has made them upon
former occasions, the extracts were taken in such a way
as, I suppose, brings them within the definition of what is
called *garbling* — taking portions of a speech which, when
taken by themselves, do not present the entire sense of
the speaker as expressed at the time.   I propose, therefore, out of that same speech to show how one portion of
it which he skipped over (taking an extract before and an
extract after) will give a different idea, and the true idea
I intended to convey. . . .

   " Allow me . . . briefly to present one extract from a
speech of mine, more than a year ago, at Springfield, in
discussing this very same question, soon after Judge
Douglas took his ground that negroes were not included
in the Declaration of Independence : —

   " ' I think the authors of that notable instrument intended
to include *all* men, but they did not mean to declare all
men equal *in all respects*.   They did not mean to say all
men were equal in color, size, intellect, moral development,
or social capacity.   They defined with tolerable distinctness in what they did consider all men created equal —
equal in certain inalienable rights, among which are life,
liberty, and the pursuit of happiness.   This they said, and
this they meant.   They did not mean to assert the obvious untruth, that all men were actually enjoying that

equality, or yet, that they were about to confer it immediately upon them. In fact they had no power to confer such a boon. They meant simply to declare the *right*, so that the *enforcement* of it might follow as fast as circumstances should permit.

" 'They meant to set up a standard maxim for free society which should be familiar to all : constantly looked to, constantly labored for, and even, though never perfectly attained, constantly approximated, and thereby constantly spreading and deepening its influence, and augmenting the happiness and value of life to all people, of all colors, everywhere.'

" There again are the sentiments I have expressed in regard to the Declaration of Independence upon a former occasion — sentiments which have been put in print and read wherever anybody cared to know what so humble an individual as myself chose to say in regard to it." [1]

B. Another evidence of the skill of these two debaters is found in the constant repetition by both, of sentences and phrases containing their main propositions. In speech after speech, and many times over in each speech, Senator Douglas repeated his cry of " popular sovereignty, the right of the people of a State to settle the question of slavery for themselves," and his demand for " obedience to the decision of the highest tribunal in the land, the Supreme Court." Lincoln we find reiterating with equal persistence his statements that "a house divided against itself cannot stand ; this government cannot endure permanently half slave and half free " ; that "slavery is

[1] Lincoln-Douglas Debates, p. 224. Follett, Foster and Co., Columbus, 1860.

wrong "; that "slavery must be put where it was put at the foundation of the government, in the course of ultimate extinction."

It is well, in preparing a case, to bear in mind the desirability of this repetition. Every main heading should, as far as possible, be stated in such rhetorical form that it can be easily and forcibly repeated; it should be stated briefly and in clear and simple language. Sometimes it is effective to compress the idea into a single word or phrase; as, for illustration, Charles Sumner did in his speech in the Senate on the "Crime against Kansas," a speech referred to above: —

"And with this exposure I take my leave of the Crime against Kansas. Emerging from all the blackness of this Crime, where we seem to have been lost, as in a savage wood, and turning our backs upon it, as upon desolation and death, from which, while others have suffered, we have escaped, I come now to THE APOLOGIES which the Crime has found. . . .

"They are four in number, and fourfold in character. The first is the *Apology tyrannical;* the second, the *Apology imbecile;* the third, the *Apology absurd;* and the fourth, the *Apology infamous.* That is all. Tyranny, imbecility, absurdity, and infamy all unite to dance, like the weird sisters, about this Crime.

"The *Apology tyrannical* is founded on the mistaken act of Governor Reeder, in authenticating the Usurping Legislature," etc.

Again, later in his speech, he said: —

"As the Apologies were fourfold, so are the proposed Remedies fourfold; and they range themselves in natural order, under designations which so truly disclose their character as even to supersede argument. First, we have *the Remedy of Tyranny;* next, *the Remedy of Folly;* next, *the Remedy of Injustice and Civil War;* and, fourthly, *the Remedy of Justice and Peace.* There are four caskets; and you are to determine which shall be opened by Senatorial votes.

"There is *the Remedy of Tyranny,* which, like its complement, the Apology of Tyranny, — though espoused on this floor, especially by the Senator from Illinois, — proceeds from the President, and is embodied in a special message," etc.[1]

This method has the virtue of vividness. Each of the phrases chosen is striking and likely to stick in the memory; it can be readily repeated and almost turned into a sort of war-cry. But care must be taken in choosing the phrase, to see that it is appropriate and that it expresses the full meaning of the speaker. Furthermore, the audience must always be made to understand just what the phrase implies; the word "heading" is always a name rather than a proposition, and is liable to be vague or ambiguous if left unexplained. Mr. Sumner, in the speech quoted above, was careful, in every case, to state in fair and full language the exact proposition he intended to attack or support; for example, after stating, as quoted above, the four apologies made by his opponents, naming them, respectively, "the apology tyrannical, the apology imbecile, the apology absurd, and the

[1] Works of Charles Sumner, Vol. VI, pp. 184 and 185. Lee and Shepard, Boston, 1872.

apology infamous," he goes on to explain the meaning of each name as follows : —

"Next comes the *Apology imbecile*, which is founded on
the alleged want of power in the President to arrest this
Crime. It is openly asserted, that, under existing laws,
the Chief Magistrate has no authority to interfere in
Kansas for this purpose. . . .

"Next comes the *Apology absurd*, which is, indeed, in
the nature of pretext. It is alleged that a small printed
pamphlet, containing the 'Constitution and Ritual of the
Grand Encampment and Regiments of the Kansas Legion,'
was taken from the person of one George F. Warren, who
attempted to avoid detection by chewing it. The oaths
and grandiose titles of the pretended Legion are also set
forth, and this poor mummery of a secret society, which
existed only on paper, is gravely introduced on this floor,
in order to extenuate the Crime against Kansas. It has
been paraded in more than one speech, and even stuffed
into the report of the Committee," etc. [1]

C. The desirability and proper use of summaries
and partitions in the discussion, has been sufficiently
treated in the chapters on Presentation. But it
should be said here, in addition, that the best opportunity for using these artifices is found in debate.
Something of this kind is necessary to bring order
out of chaos. In the confusion of argument, answer,
and rejoinder, of evidence and counter evidence, of
big things and little things, crowded together and following one another in rapid succession, the effect on
the audience easily becomes kaleidoscopic; they see

[1] Works of Charles Sumner, Vol. IV, pp. 187 and 192. Lee and
Shepard, Boston, 1872.

the combinations of shapes and colors tossing about before their eyes, but there is nothing in particular to be impressed by, or to remember. These defects can be avoided in large measure by the use of internal summaries, *i.e.* summaries at various points within the proof, which serve to pick out the really important things in the question and impress them clearly upon the attention and memory.

Furthermore, used in conjunction with partitions, they keep the audience always informed just where they are and where they are to be led next. At every turn in the course of the debate there are many roads branching out in various directions. A summary or a partition, or the two in combination, makes clear to the listener that he has reached the end of one road and put it behind him, and that he is now to turn in a certain new direction for a time. Particularly when, in debate, some point has been discussed back and forth for a time between the opposing sides, it is almost necessary to summarize what has been said on each side, to compare the opposing proofs, and make clear what you would have the audience believe is the result of it all. It is only in this way that matters can be brought to some conclusion, and the audience made ready to turn their attention elsewhere.

The personal tone to be cultivated in debate is a serious matter, and a matter concerning which many flagrant mistakes are made. The personal element in debate is large. There the speaker

usually stands as the immediate sponsor for all that
he says and does; he is an advocate, personally
responsible for every opinion he advances: the man
and the cause are inextricably bound together. This
condition of affairs has two results: the first is, that
the audience will be greatly influenced by the personality of the speaker; the second, that there is
a temptation to attack an opponent for his personality as well as for the principles he advocates.
It follows that two of the main purposes of a debater
must be to win sympathy for himself and to dis-
countenance his opponent.

But unfortunately these two purposes may conflict
with each other. Sarcasm, ridicule, and even personalities are undoubtedly admissible and helpful,
when properly handled, in discrediting an opponent;
but, improperly handled, they are as harmful in
discrediting the man who uses them. These are
dangerous weapons, treacherously two-edged: a
blow well delivered will cut and maim an enemy,
but a slip or a blunder will surely turn the blow
against its author. With respect to personalities, *i.e.*
attacks on the character or actions of a man, Shakespeare offers a good motto : —

> ". . . Beware
> Of entrance to a quarrel; but, being in,
> Bear't that the opposer may beware of thee."

An audience always sympathizes with the man that
sticks to the question and treats his "friends of the
other side" with courtesy and good humor; if a case

cannot be won on its merits, rarely can it be won by resort to personalities. On the other hand, an audience invariably respects a man who can defend himself, and who has in him the spirit of fight that resents a foul blow. A debater must never give ground, even if his opponent resorts to weapons that he himself scorns to use.

In repelling such a personal attack there is one temptation, — the temptation to answer abuse with abuse. The man who has the quarrel forced on him has the sympathy of the audience at the start, and, if he is wise, he will take care to retain that sympathy by keeping his dignity and self-control. If he descends to the level chosen by his assailant, and combats poison with poison, he has thrown away his advantage and must fight on even terms.

A model of personal tone may be found in Lincoln's conduct of his debate with Douglas, mentioned above. Fully to appreciate his good-humored self-control and his simple, but resolute, dignity, requires the reading of the speeches of Senator Douglas, filled as they are with misrepresentation and personal abuse. In his speech at Springfield, July 17, Mr. Lincoln said : —

" Having made that speech with the most kindly feeling toward Judge Douglas, as manifested therein, I was gratified when I found that he had carefully examined it and had detected no error of fact, nor any inference against him, nor any misrepresentations, of which he thought fit to complain. In neither of the two speeches I have mentioned did he make any such complaint. I will thank

x

any one who will inform me that he, in his speech to-day,
pointed out anything I had stated, respecting him, as being
erroneous. I presume there is no such thing. I have
reason to be gratified that the care and caution used in
that speech left it so that he, most of all others interested
in discovering error, has not been able to point out one
thing against him which he could say was wrong. He
seizes upon the doctrines he supposes to be included in
that speech, and declares that upon them will turn the
issue of this campaign. He then quotes, or attempts to
quote, from my speech. I will not say that he wilfully
misquotes, but he does fail to quote accurately. His
attempt at quoting is from a passage which I believe
I can quote accurately from memory. I shall make the
quotation now, with some comments upon it, as I have
already said, in order that the judge shall be left entirely
without excuse for misrepresenting me. I do so now, as
I hope, for the last time. I do this in great caution, in
order that if he repeats his misrepresentation, it shall be
plain to all that he does so wilfully. If, after all, he still
persists, I shall be compelled to reconstruct the course I
have marked out for myself, and draw upon such humble
resources as I have for a new course, better suited to
the real exigencies of the case. I set out, in this campaign, with the intention of conducting it strictly as
a gentleman, in substance at least, if not in the outside
polish. The latter I shall never be, but that which constitutes the inside of a gentleman I hope I understand, and
am not less inclined to practise than others. It was my
purpose and expectation that this canvass would be
conducted upon principle, and with fairness upon both
sides, and it shall not be my fault if this purpose and
expectation shall be given up." [1]

[1] Lincoln-Douglas Debates, p. 58. Follett, Foster and Co., Columbus, 1860.

Later, in his opening speech in the sixth joint debate, at Quincy, October 13, he said : —

" He reminds me of the fact that he entered upon this canvass with the purpose to treat me courteously ; that touched me somewhat. It sets me thinking. I was aware, when it was first agreed that Judge Douglas and I were to have these seven joint discussions, that they were the successive acts of a drama — perhaps I should say, to be enacted not merely in the face of audiences like this, but in the face of the nation, and to some extent, by my relation to him, and not from anything in myself, in the face of the world ; and I am anxious that they should be conducted with dignity and in the good temper which should be befitting the vast audience before which it was conducted. But when Judge Douglas got home from Washington and made his first speech in Chicago, the evening afterward I made some sort of reply to it. His second speech was made at Bloomington, in which he commented upon my speech at Chicago, and said that I had used language ingeniously contrived to conceal my intentions, or words to that effect. Now, I understand that this is an imputation upon my veracity and candor. I do not know what the Judge understood by it ; but in our first discussion at Ottawa he led off by charging a bargain, somewhat corrupt in character, upon Trumbull and myself — that we had entered into a bargain, one of the terms of which was that Trumbull was to abolitionize the old Democratic party, and I (Lincoln) was to abolitionize the old Whig party — I pretending to be as good an old-line Whig as ever. Judge Douglas may not understand that he implicated my truthfulness and my honor when he said I was doing one thing and pretending another ; and I misunderstood him if he thought he was treating me in a dignified way, as a man of honor and truth, as he now claims he

was disposed to treat me. Even after that time, at Galesburgh, when he brings forward an extract from a speech
made at Chicago, and an extract from a speech made at
Charleston, to prove that I was trying to play a double
part — that I was trying to cheat the public, and get votes
upon one set of principles at one place and upon another
set of principles at another place — I do not understand
but that he impeached my honor, my veracity, and my
candor, and because *he* does this, I do not understand
that I am bound, if I see a truthful ground for it, to keep
my hands off him. As soon as I learned that Judge
Douglas was disposed to treat me in this way, I signified
in one of my speeches that I should be driven to draw
upon whatever of humble resources I might have to adopt
a new course with him. I was not entirely sure that I
should be able to hold my own with him, but I at least
had the purpose made to do as well as I could upon him;
and now I say that I will not be the first to cry 'hold.'
I think it originated with the Judge, and when he quits, I
probably will. But I shall not ask any favors at all. He
asks me, or he asks the audience, if I wish to push this
matter to the point of personal difficulty. I tell him, no.
He did not make a mistake, in one of his early speeches,
when he called me an 'amiable' man, though perhaps he
did when he called me an 'intelligent' man. It really
hurts me very much to suppose that I have wronged anybody on earth. I again tell him, no! I very much prefer,
when this canvass shall be over, however it may result,
that we at least part without any bitter recollections of
personal difficulties.

"The Judge, in his concluding speech at Galesburgh, says
that I was pushing this matter to a personal difficulty, to
avoid the responsibility for the enormity of my principles.
I say to the Judge and this audience now, that I will again

state our principles as well as I hastily can in all their enormity, and if the Judge hereafter chooses to confine himself to a war upon these principles, he will probably not find me departing from the same course."[1]

With these models of personal dignity contrast the following extract from the speech by Senator Pettit in the debate in the Senate on the Fugitive Slave Law, June 26, 1854: —

"Now, sir, to give this clause of the Declaration of Independence any other construction than that which I have given it, is an evident, a self-evident, a palpable lie. What is the language? That 'all men are created equal.' Are they created equally tall, equally broad, equally long, equally short? Are they created politically equal? Are they created physically equal? Are they created mentally equal? Are they created morally equal? . . . I ask the chair, then, whether the Senator from Massachusetts (Mr. Sumner), with his odium on his lips, is the equal of his revolutionary sires? Is he the equal of Adams, of Hancock, of Warren, who was the first martyr in the great cause of liberty, of freedom, and of union? Is he the equal of these men? I had rather ask you, Mr. President, for I think you would answer 'no,' and he might answer 'yes.' . . . I ask that Senator, then, or I ask you, sir, whether that Senator is the equal of the late lamented Daniel Webster, who preceded him here long years ago? . . . I believe as a mere mental man — and I speak of him in no other capacity — Webster had not his equal on this continent, if he had in Europe or on any other continent. Is that Senator his equal? He might as well say that the

[1] Lincoln-Douglas Debates, p. 196. Follett, Foster and Co., Columbus, 1860.

jackal is the equal of the lion, or that the buzzard is the equal of the eagle.

"When you, sir (addressing Mr. Sumner), find no man beneath you; when those who are near you — your own class of men — can find no man beneath you; when you shall claim as your equal the man who rolls in the gutter, whom God has deprived in his own organization and creation of all mental power and capacity; when you shall claim that he who wallows in the gutter with the vilest and most worthless is your equal, then your interpretation of the doctrine is true. Let me go farther. If the Almighty ever intended to create the Senator the equal with the mighty and lamented Webster, I must say that he made a gross blunder and a most egregious mistake. . . . Sir, I am inclined to believe that, in a moral point of view, that Senator cannot find one beneath himself, taking his own declaration to-day. He who will swear here in this body, appealing to God for the truth of what he says, to support the Constitution of the Union, and then boldly proclaim that he will not do it, has sunk, in my estimation, to a depth of humiliation and degradation which it would not be enviable for the veriest serf or the lowest of God's creatures to occupy. It may be in that point of view the Senator regards all others as his equals; but there are some who are not willing to regard that Senator as their equal, and who will never be coerced into any such admission." [1]

The difference between these two speeches is the difference between gentlemanly self-control and coarse vituperation. A debater must never allow himself, no matter how great the provocation, to be carried over the bounds that confine the gentleman;

[1] Congressional Debates, Vol. 28, Part II, p. 1518.

coarseness, even though it appear but for a moment, is always reactionary. Coarseness in debate is most often a matter of loss of temper. A man of low character may be expected to show forth his nature at any time; but for any high-minded man, the thing that usually brings him to grief is the loss of his temper. When he is involved in personal conflict, a debater must always have a smile — a good-humored smile — ready on his lips.

Good humor is even more necessary if one is to use sarcasm or ridicule. The line must not be drawn so strictly against these weapons as against personalities pure and simple. Sarcasm in a skilful hand is formidable, and ridicule can often win a point where nothing else would avail. But it must always be remembered that these are light arms. They are fine-wrought, flexible foils, and they must be wielded with a light hand. They are not suited for the slashing and cutting of broad-sword play. To fence with them a man must be quick, light of hand, and, above all, cool and self-controlled. Some men cannot use sarcasm and ridicule at all, and no man can afford to use them carelessly. Ill temper is both careless and clumsy. It always results in a wild aim and looks like foul play.

Sarcasm and ridicule are most effective when directed against conceit and affectation. A speaker who allows his conceit to rise to the surface, or who assumes a tone of grandiloquence or bombast, has exposed a weak spot in his armor. And there is no weapon that will so readily find the spot and strike through it as one of these light side-arms of oratory. The following is one of the best illustrations of the use of ridicule that can be found in American oratory. It is so interesting and so worthy of study with respect to its general tone, its vivid rhetoric, and its telling choice of figures of speech as to justify the giving of the passage nearly in full. A certain General Crary, on February 14, 1840, in the debate in the House on the Cumberland Road Bill, attacked General William Henry Harrison for alleged deficiencies as a military commander, severely criticising his conduct of the battle of Tippecanoe and of various other campaigns. Thomas Corwin of Ohio replied in a speech of which the following is a part. Mr. Crary was so overwhelmed that John Quincy Adams, a few days after, referred to him as "the late Mr. Crary."

"In all other countries, and in all former times, a gentleman who would either speak or be listened to on the subject of war, involving subtle criticisms and strategy, and careful reviews of marches, sieges, battles, regular and casual, and irregular onslaughts, would be required to show, first, that he had studied much, investigated fully, and digested the science and history of his subject. But here, sir, no such painful preparation is required; witness the gentleman from Michigan! He has announced to the House that he is a militia general on the peace establishment! That he is a lawyer we know, tolerably well read in Tidd's 'Practice' and Espinasse's 'Nisi Prius.' These studies, so happily adapted to the subject of war, with an appointment in the militia in time of peace, furnish him at once with all the knowledge necessary to discourse to us, as from high authority, upon all the mysteries of the 'trade of death.' Again, Mr. Speaker, it must occur to every one, that we, to whom these questions are submitted and these military criticisms are addressed, being all colonels at least, and most of us, like the gentleman himself, brigadiers, are, of all conceivable tribunals, best qualified to decide any nice points connected with military science. I hope the House will not be alarmed with the impression that I am about to discuss one or the other of the military questions now before us at length, but I wish to submit a remark or two, by way of preparing us for a proper appreciation of the merits of the discourse we have heard. I trust we are all brother-officers, that the gentleman from Michigan, and the two hundred and forty colonels or generals of this honorable House, will receive what I have to say as coming from an old brother in arms, and addressed to them in a spirit of candor,

> " ' Such as becometh comrades free,
>   Reposing after victory.'

" Sir, we all know the military studies of the military gentleman from Michigan before he was promoted. I take it to be beyond a reasonable doubt that he had perused with great care the title-page of ' Baron Steuben.' Nay, I go further; as the gentleman has incidentally assured us that he is prone to look into musty and neglected volumes, I venture to assert, without vouching in the least from personal knowledge, that he has prosecuted his researches so far as to be able to know that the rear rank stands right behind the front. This, I think, is fairly inferable from what I understood him to say of the two lines of encampment at Tippecanoe. Thus we see, Mr. Speaker, that the gentleman from Michigan, being a militia general, as he has told us, his brother officers, in that simple statement has revealed the glorious history of toils, privations, sacrifices, and bloody scenes, through which, we know from experience and observation, a militia officer, in time of peace, is sure to pass. We all in fancy now see the gentleman from Michigan in that most dangerous and glorious event in the life of a militia general on the peace establishment — a parade day ! That day, for which all the other days of his life seem to have been made. We can see the troops in motion — umbrellas, hoes, and axe-handles, and other like deadly implements of war, overshadowing all the fields, when lo ! the leader of the host approaches !

" ' Far off his coming shines !'

His plume, which, after the fashion of the great Bourbon, is of awful length, and reads its doleful history in the bereaved necks and bosoms of forty neighboring hen-roosts. Like the great Suwaroff, he seems somewhat careless in forms or points of dress ; hence his epaulettes may be on his shoulders, back, or sides, but still gleaming, gloriously gleaming, in the sun. Mounted he is, too, let it not be forgotten. Need I describe to the colonels and generals of this honorable House the steeds which heroes bestride on these occasions ? No ! I see the memory of other days is with you. You see before you the gentleman from Michigan, mounted on his crop-eared, bushy-tailed mare, the singular obliquity of whose hinder limbs is best described by that most expressive phrase, ' sickle hams ' — for height just fourteen hands, ' all told ' ; yes, sir; there you see his ' steed that laughs at the shaking of the spear '; that is his war horse, ' whose neck is clothed in thunder.' Mr. Speaker, we have glowing descriptions in history of Alexander the Great and his

war horse Bucephalus, at the head of the invincible Mace-
donian phalanx; but, sir, such are the improvements of
modern times, that every one must see that our militia
general, with his crop-eared mare with bushy tail and
sickle hams, would totally frighten off a battle-field a hundred Alexanders. But, sir, to the history of the parade
day. The general, thus mounted and equipped, is in the
field and ready for action. On the eve of some desperate
enterprise, such as giving order to shoulder arms, it may
be, there occurs a crisis, one of those accidents of war,
which no sagacity could foresee nor prevent. A cloud
rises and passes over the sun! Here is an occasion for
the display of that greatest of all traits in the history of a
commander — the tact which enables him to seize upon
and turn to good account unlooked-for events as they arise.
Now for the caution wherewith the Roman Fabius foiled
the skill and courage of Hannibal! A retreat is ordered,
and troops and general, in a twinkling, are found safely
bivouacked in a neighboring grocery." [1]

With respect to all three of the methods mentioned
above, viz., personalities, sarcasm, and ridicule, it is
to be remarked that they are only occasional weapons. They are not substitutes for proof or for the
substance of argument. They are merely auxiliaries.
It is often easier to malign or laugh at an opponent
than to answer him, but it does not accomplish the
same end.

D. The *argumentum ad hominem* belongs in debate more truly than elsewhere. As we have already
seen, in debate the speakers generally stand as per-

[1] Hardwicke, "History of Oratory and Orators," pp. 368–371.
G. P. Putnam's Sons, 1896.

sonally responsible advocates of the opinions they espouse. Consequently, if it can be shown that a speaker is inconsistent in his opinions, the shot often strikes home. If it is proved that a speaker upholds views that he formerly condemned, or that his actions belie his words, his motives are clearly impeached and his sincerity or veracity is opened to suspicion.

The argument may be used as a means of ridicule, making light of the pretended earnestness of an opponent, or it may be used as the foundation of a serious charge of fraud or hypocrisy. Lincoln used it in his speech at Chicago, July 10, to ridicule an excess of oratorical enthusiasm on the part of Senator Douglas. Speaking of the Dred Scott Decision, he said : —

"The sacredness that Judge Douglas throws around this decision, is a degree of sacredness that has never been before thrown around any other decision. I have never heard of such a thing. . . . But Judge Douglas will have it that all hands must take this extraordinary decision, made under these extraordinary circumstances, and give their vote in Congress in accordance with it, yield to it, and obey it in every possible sense. Circumstances alter cases. Do not gentlemen here remember the case of that same Supreme Court, some twenty-five or thirty years ago, deciding that a National Bank was constitutional? I ask if somebody does not remember that a National Bank was declared to be constitutional? Such is the truth, whether it be remembered or not. The Bank charter ran out, and a recharter was granted by Congress. That recharter was laid before General Jackson. It was urged upon him, when he denied the constitutionality of the Bank, that the Supreme Court had decided that it was constitutional; and that General Jackson then said that the Supreme Court had no right to lay down a rule to govern a coördinate branch of the Government, the members of which had sworn to support the Constitution — that each member had sworn to support that Constitution as he understood it. I will venture here to say, that I have heard Judge Douglas say that he approved of General Jackson for that act. What has now become of all his tirade about 'resistance to the Supreme Court'?"[1]

Senator Hayne, in his second speech on the Foote Resolution, used the argument differently, rather making it the foundation of a serious charge of inconsistency and apostasy: —

"I am not at all surprised, however, at the aversion of the gentleman to the very name of tariff. I doubt not that it must always bring up some very unpleasant recollections to his mind. If I am not greatly mistaken, the Senator from Massachusetts was a leading actor at a great meeting got up in Boston in 1820 against the tariff. It has generally been supposed that he drew up the resolutions adopted by that meeting, denouncing the tariff system as unequal, oppressive, and unjust, and, if I am not much mistaken, denying its constitutionality. Certain it is that the gentleman made a speech on that occasion in support of those resolutions, denouncing the system in no very measured terms; and, if my memory serves me, calling its constitutionality in question. I regret that I have not been able to lay my hands on those proceedings, but

[1] Lincoln-Douglas Debates, pp. 20–21. Follett, Foster and Co., Columbus, 1860.

I have seen them, and I cannot be mistaken in their character.   At that time, sir, the Senator from Massachusetts
entertained the very sentiments in relation to the tariff
which the South now entertains.   We next find the Senator from Massachusetts expressing his opinion on the
tariff as a member of the House of Representatives from
the city of Boston in 1824.   On that occasion, sir, the
gentleman assumed a position which commanded the respect and admiration of his country.   He stood forth the
powerful and fearless champion of free trade.   He met,
in that conflict, the advocates of restriction and monop-
oly, and they ' fled from before his face.'   With a profound
sagacity, a fulness of knowledge, and a richness of illustration that has never been surpassed, he maintained and
established the principles of commercial freedom on a
foundation never to be shaken. . . .   Then it was that
he erected to free trade a beautiful and enduring monument, and 'inscribed the marble with his name.'   It is
with pain and regret that I now go forward to the next
great era in the political life of that gentleman, when he
was found upon the floor supporting, advocating, and
finally voting for the tariff of 1828 — that ' bill of abomi-
nations.'   By that act, sir, the Senator from Massachusetts
has destroyed the labors of his whole life, and given a
wound to the cause of free trade, never to be healed.
Sir, when I recollect the position which that gentleman
once occupied, and that which he now holds in public
estimation, in relation to this subject, it is not at all sur-
prising that the tariff should be hateful to his ears.   Sir,
if I had erected to my own fame so proud a monument as
that which the gentleman built in 1824, and I could have
been tempted to destroy it with my own hands, I should
hate the voice that should ring ' the accursed tariff ' in my
ears,   I doubt not the gentleman feels very much in rela-

tion to the tariff as a certain knight did to 'instinct,' and with him would be disposed to exclaim —

"'Ah, no more of that, Hal, an' thou lov'st me.'"[1]

It is evident that in some kinds of debate the *argumentum ad hominem* finds no place. In intercollegiate debate, or before a jury, it is rarely opportune, because the speakers in these situations do not stand as sponsors for what they say. They are merely instruments of competition or of justice, and so are not open to personal attacks.

E. A common stratagem of debate is the asking of questions. By this is not meant the figure of speech known as the "rhetorical question." The stratagem consists rather in directly asking questions that really call for an answer. The purposes of resorting to this stratagem are three : (1) to compel an opponent to take a definite position on some issue, (2) to tempt him to waste time on trivial matters, or (3) to force him into a dilemma, where he may be caught whichever way he answers.

(1) To accomplish the first of these aims, the value of a question is obvious. A debater often encounters an opponent whose power lies less in his ability to prove an issue than in his ability to evade it. Such an opponent is facile in shifting ground and can readily becloud the point in dispute. He is like a cuttlefish that squirts the water full of a black excretion and escapes in the darkness. In exposing

[1] Debates in Congress, Vol. VI, Part I, p. 49. Gales and Seaton, Washington, 1830.

and cornering such a man, there is hardly a better way to "pin him down" than to compress the point in issue into a single, clear, direct question and demand an answer. The question, of course, needs to be framed in such a way that it cannot be readily evaded or distorted from its intended meaning ; also, in asking the question, it should be presented in such a forcible and imperative manner that a failure to answer will be unsafe. But, with these precautions, in the face of a question clearly worded and strongly put, an opponent will find it difficult to evade the issue.

(2) To propound questions for an opponent to waste time upon is good tactics under some circumstances. A question put with an air of taunt or challenge is a great temptation ; an inexperienced or impulsive debater may often be drawn into the trap of answering at any cost. The audience must, however, be made to believe the question is really important, and that a failure to answer must be a sign of weakness. This trick is sometimes tried in intercollegiate debate, where the time is limited and a waste of even a minute is a serious matter. A debater should realize the nature of this stratagem, not only in order to be able to try it himself, but in order to be able to appreciate it when he is the intended victim. There is one rule that is truly a golden rule for an inexperienced debater, " Stick to the point."

There are three ways of evading such questions. One way is to ignore them, a method which is some-

times not safe if the questions have been well presented, and if the audience seems to be impressed
with them.   Another is to avoid them by false or
ambiguous answers, a method which calls for much
tact and shrewdness.   The third, is to expose the
motives of the propounder of the questions, to show
that the questions are not important, but merely intended as snares.

(3) The third purpose that may be served by the
asking of a question is that of forcing an opponent
into a dilemma, where he may be caught, however
he may answer.   Lincoln, with great shrewdness,
drove Senator Douglas into such a situation in the
joint debates of 1858.   Briefly, the circumstances
were these : Lincoln assumed at the start a position
of hostility to the Dred Scott Decision, which declared,
in substance, that Congress had no power to exclude
slavery from any of the territories.   Senator Douglas
attacked Mr. Lincoln bitterly for his position in the
matter, declaring that any decision of the Supreme
Court was final and sacred, and that any man who
rejected or denounced such a decision was " unpatriotic, disloyal, revolutionary," etc.   It also happened
that Mr. Lincoln had charged Senator Douglas with
being concerned with certain other Democrats in a
conspiracy to " nationalize slavery."   He gave evidence tending to expose such a conspiracy, and
showed that but one thing was wanted to make it
complete, viz., a decision of the Supreme Court,
declaring that a state of the Union could not exclude

Y

slavery from its limits ; and he furthermore charged
Senator Douglas with planning and working to pro-
cure such a decision.

Under these circumstances, Mr. Lincoln pro-
pounded the following question : " If the Supreme
Court of the United States shall decide that States
cannot exclude slavery from their limits, are you in
favor of acquiescing in it, adopting it, and following
it as a rule of political action ? " Senator Douglas
was caught. If he answered in the affirmative, he
seemed to substantiate the charge of conspiracy to
get such a decision, and gave Mr. Lincoln an opportunity to drive home his attack ; on the other hand,
if he answered in the negative, he was committing the
very act which he had denounced in Mr. Lincoln as
unpatriotic, revolutionary, and heretical, viz., opposing a decision of the Supreme Court. But one course
was open, and the wily debater adopted it : he evaded
the question. In his speech at Freeport, August 27,
he said : —

" The third question which Mr. Lincoln presented is, if
the Supreme Court of the United States shall decide that
a State of this Union cannot exclude slavery from its own
limits, will I submit to it? I am amazed that Lincoln
should ask such a question. [" A schoolboy knows better."] Yes, a schoolboy does know better. Mr. Lincoln's
object is to cast an imputation upon the Supreme Court.
He knows that there never was but one man in America,
claiming any degree of intelligence or decency, who ever
for a moment pretended such a thing. It is true that the
Washington *Union*, in an article published on the 17th

of last December, did put forth that doctrine, and I denounced the article on the floor of the Senate in a speech which Mr. Lincoln now pretends was against the President. The *Union* had claimed that slavery had a right to go into the free States, and that any provision in the constitution or laws of the free States to the contrary were null and void. I denounced it in the Senate, as I said before, and I was the first man who did. Lincoln's friends, Trumbull, and Seward, and Hale, and Wilson, and the whole black Republican side of the Senate, were silent. They left it to me to denounce it. And what was the reply made to me on that occasion? Mr. Toombs of Georgia got up and undertook to lecture me on the ground that I ought not to have deemed the article worthy of notice, and ought not to have replied to it; that there was not one man, woman, or child south of the Potomac, in any slave State, who did not repudiate any such pretension. Mr. Lincoln knows that that reply was made on the spot, and yet now he asks this question. He might as well ask me, suppose Mr. Lincoln should steal a horse, would I sanction it; and it would be as genteel in me to ask him, in the event he stole a horse, what ought to be done with him. He casts an imputation upon the Supreme Court of the United States by supposing that they would violate the Constitution of the United States. I tell him that such a thing is not possible. It would be an act of moral treason that no man on the bench could ever descend to. Mr. Lincoln himself would never in his partisan feelings so far forget what was right as to be guilty of such an act." [1]

[1] Lincoln-Douglas Debates, p. 96. Follett, Foster and Co., Columbus, 1860.

IV. The Conclusion

With respect to the conclusion, little needs to be
said more than has already been said in the book on
Presentation.

A. The importance of the conclusion in debate is
obvious. It is undoubtedly an advantage to be so
placed as to be able to direct the course of things to
come ; but it is a greater advantage to be so placed as
to be able to review and sum up the things that are
past. To the last speaker is given the opportunity
of leaving his interpretation of the facts, and his summary of the important points, fresh in the minds of
his audience. So that a closing speaker is even better
situated than an opening speaker, to obtain the acceptance of his method of dividing the question and his
statement of the issues ; that is, he is in such a position that he can finally persuade the audience to look
at the question through his eyes. Moreover, on any
contested point he has the privilege of the last word.

Oftentimes a speaker, if he knows beforehand that
he is to have the privilege of the final reply, can with
good effect hold his fire till the end and surprise his
enemy with new arguments, to which reply is thus
impossible. This is a bit of strategy that can be
practised in many situations. For example, in intercollegiate or interscholastic debate, or any similar
prearranged contest where the number and order of
speakers is fixed, it is not unusual that one side keeps
silence on some point in the discussion till its last

rebuttal. By this means the opposing side may perhaps be led to think that the point has been conceded and so be tempted to keep silence themselves. Again, it is a wise stratagem when a speaker feels that he has the weaker end of the proof on a point: if he reveals his answer too early, his opponents may make a rejoinder and lay bare the weakness; but by waiting till later he deprives his opponent of any chance to reply, and so may hope to conceal his deficiency and make his own proof seem plausible. It will, however, be kept clearly in mind that what is said in this paragraph refers only to answers that are to be made to opponents' arguments; for it is generally conceded that a debater ought not to introduce new positive arguments in his rebuttal.

B. From the viewpoint of conviction, the first duty of a speaker who closes the argument for his side of the case, is to summarize the whole proof. We have already spoken several times of the confusion natural to debate, a confusion arising from the rapid succession of arguments and evidence, and from the conflicts, crossings, and interminglings of the proofs and ideas of both sides. We refer to it again only to emphasize the value of concluding summaries. After an audience have listened, for any considerable time, to the presentation of a mass of heterogeneous facts and ideas, they need to have their conceptions of the case as a whole straightened out again, and to have their memories refreshed with a new understanding of the points that are important. An audience cannot be relied on to carry in mind to the end the things that are vital; their vision is sure to become clouded by details, and they turn with relief to a man who will clear up matters and set them right. For this reason the audience can be counted on to give careful attention to a concluding summary, and so they are more likely to remember it than almost anything else in the debate. The desirability of the summary is made greater by the fact that, in the debate, the proof of either side is scattered along through the discussion; it consequently becomes necessary, if the proof is to be properly unified, that these broken threads be woven together at the end by a summary.

In some circumstances a mere recapitulation by the last speaker is not enough. In debates where there is "team-work," it is often desirable that each speaker in his conclusion should summarize what has preceded. This keeps the audience always in close touch with the proof, and gives them an understanding of just what is being accomplished at each forward step; then when the end is finally reached, the case, as a whole, is embedded in their minds, and the final summary is much more intelligible and effective.

The mistake may easily be made of making a summary too long or too detailed. To be effective it needs always to be direct, incisive, and as brief as is consistent with clearness. To be diffuse or tediously technical destroys the aggressive force that is indispensable. Any kind of a recapitulation must be as sharp, as firm, and as bold as the blows of the hammer on white-hot iron. Such a conclusion is exemplified in the following peroration of a speech by Sir Robert Peel, in the debate in the House of Commons on the bill relieving the disabilities of the Jews. It is especially to be noticed for its skilful repetition and emphasis of the central idea of the whole speech, viz., forgiveness and reparation for past wrongs :—

" It is for these reasons — because I believe it to be in conformity with the enlarged and comprehensive spirit of the British Constitution — that these disqualifications should no longer exist; because I rejoice in the opportunity of making reparation for the injuries and persecutions of former times ; because I think the Jew has fairly earned the privileges which it is proposed to extend to him, by patience and forbearance, by tried fidelity and loyalty; but above all, because I am a member of a Christian people, because I am a member of a Christian legislature, I will perform an act which I believe to be in strict conformity with the spirit and precepts of the Christian religion. We are commanded by that religion, as the condition of our own forgiveness, to forgive those who have trespassed against us. That duty is not in this case imposed upon us ; but there is another duty as sacred in point of moral obligation, and more trying to human pride, namely, that we should forgive those against whom we have trespassed. Sir, I shall give my cordial support to the bill before the House." [1]

C. Of all the forms of summaries that may be used, the most effective in debate is that which in an earlier part we have called " to amplify and diminish."

[1] " World's Orators " (England), Part III, p. 211. G. P. Putnam's Sons, 1900.

The distinguishing characteristic of debate is the directness of conflict between the opposing sides. The audience is kept constantly balancing one argument against another and swaying back and forth with the struggle of the contending factions. Consequently in the end their judgment is always relative. It is not that one side is strong or weak, but that it is on the whole stronger or weaker than the other. So it is clearly wiser to assist the audience in this comparison, and try to make them see the relative strength of the two sides as you wish them to see it, than to take the chance of leaving them to make the comparison by themselves, according to whatever standards may happen to be uppermost in their minds.

Sometimes, if a speaker feels that he has the weaker side of the proof, it is more politic for him to leave his hearers in uncertainty, and to cover up the logical conclusion that would result from such a comparison. This is good tactics, for example, when a man adopts a policy of obstruction, *i.e.* when he finds that he has not a strong positive case, and so resorts to the trick of lying in wait and throwing up objections against his opponent. If all his objections were carefully analyzed and logically summed up, they would not really amount to much; so his only hope lies in the general discredit he may throw upon the proof against him. In such a situation he would suffer by a contrast of point with point, and he would gain by leaving matters in confusion. But, presum-

ing that a speaker has a fair side of the argument,
to amplify and diminish is advisable. It makes the
proof complete and presents definitely a statement of
the conclusion that must be drawn. It is a final
charge, where all the forces of your own side are
gathered together and thrown directly against the
enemy. A good illustration of its effectiveness is
found in the conclusion of Senator Douglas's speech
at Chicago, July 9, 1858 : —

"Thus you see, my fellow-citizens, that the issues between Mr. Lincoln and myself, as respective candidates
for the U. S. Senate, as made up, are direct, unequivocal,
and irreconcilable. He goes for uniformity in our domestic institutions, for a war of sections, until one or the other
shall be subdued. I go for the great principle of the
Kansas-Nebraska bill, the right of the people to decide for
themselves.

"On the other point, Mr. Lincoln goes for a warfare on
the Supreme Court of the United States, because of their
judicial decision in the Dred Scott case. I yield obedience
to the decision of that court — to the final determination
of the highest judicial tribunal known to our constitution.
He objects to the Dred Scott decision because it does not
put the negro in the possession of the rights of citizenship
on an equality with the white man. I am opposed to
negro equality. I repeat that this nation is a white people
— a people composed of European descendants — a people
that have established this government for themselves and
their posterity, and I am in favor of preserving not only
the purity of the blood, but the purity of the government
from any mixture or amalgamation with inferior races. I
have seen the effects of this mixture of superior and inferior races — this amalgamation of white men and Indians

and negroes; we have seen it in Mexico, in Central America, in South America, and in all the Spanish-American States, and its result has been degeneration, demoralization, and degradation below the capacity for self-government.

"I am opposed to taking any step that recognizes the negro man or the Indian as the equal of the white man. I am opposed to giving him a voice in the administration of the government. I would extend to the negro, and the Indian, and to all dependent races every right, every privilege, and every immunity consistent with the safety and welfare of the white races; but equality they never should have, either political or social, or in any other respect whatever.

"My friends, you see that the issues are distinctly drawn. I stand by the same platform that I have so often proclaimed to you and to the people of Illinois heretofore. I stand by the Democratic organization, yield obedience to its usages, and support its regular nominations. I indorse and approve the Cincinnati platform, and I adhere to and intend to carry out, as part of that platform, the great principle of self-government, which recognizes the right of the people in each State and Territory to decide for themselves their domestic institutions. In other words, if the Lecompton issue shall arise again, you have only to turn back and see where you have found me during the last six months, and then rest assured that you will find me in the same position, battling for the same principle, and vindicating it from assault from whatever quarter it may come, so long as I have the power to do it."[1]

In this summary the speaker has stated with fair accuracy the points of difference between him and

[1] Lincoln-Douglas Debates, pp. 12–13. Follett, Foster and Co., Columbus, 1860.

his opponent, but he has so stated them as to present his own side always in the better light. He places the arguments side by side, but he states the points in a manner favorable to himself; and at the close he drives home the fact and the idea that lies at the foundation of his own case, thus leaving in the minds of his hearers an impression that, on the whole, their votes and their support should be given to his cause.

V. Presentation

A. Every public speaker, at the very beginning of his career, is confronted with the questions : " How much shall I write ? How far shall I put my preparation into written form?" This is an important question : habits ill-formed in this particular have been responsible for the failures of many preachers, lecturers, and advocates; on the other hand, correct habits are equally potent for success. Moreover, every beginner should realize that strength or weakness in this respect is truly a matter of habit, for practices adopted early grow fast and soon become difficult to abandon. Even at the cost of hard work and discouraging failures, a young debater should begin right.

When we come to consider this question, we find there are two extremes : the first consists in writing everything and reading from the manuscript; the other consists in writing nothing and speaking wholly without notes. For a beginner, neither of these extremes merits serious consideration; they are both to be condemned.   Any one who has ever heard a preacher read his sermons, sentence by sentence, from a manuscript, need not be told that in the scrimmage of a debate such a practice would be fatal. This method lacks all the spontaneity, all the power of adaptation to circumstances, all the aggressiveness that is essential.   The opposite plan is hardly less objectionable.   The power of extemporaneous speech is not to be disparaged, and it is undoubtedly true that many veteran speakers can debate a proposition with very brief preparation and from a very few notes ; but such powers are begotten of long practice and self-cultivation ; for a beginner to make such men the models for his own early efforts is foolhardy, and always has unfortunate results.   To make such a venture at the start, would be like attempting to learn to swim by jumping into mid-ocean at the first lesson ; the well-nigh certain result is to be lost in a flood of bad habits.   From such beginnings are produced the rambling, incoherent, inconclusive speakers that are always inferior or mediocre in debate.   The weakness of such arguers is that they are wholly lacking in the element of form : they never learn how to conserve their strength to spend it to some purpose ; they waste their forces because they have never learned how to marshal and direct them.

The practice of writing is a great benefit to any speaker.   Especially to a debater, in the early stages of his career, the writing of briefs and finished speeches is of the greatest value.   Enough has already been said in the preceding parts of this book to make it evident that argumentation is a distinct art with rules and methods peculiar to itself. Upon the understanding of these methods and the observation of these rules success depends, and in bringing one's self to comprehend these various principles, and to create habits in conformity with them, there is no practice so good as constant writing. In preparing a careful and detailed brief, which shall present all of his proof in its full strength to a reader, a student must at every step, from the statement of the proposition to the final summary, be conscious of the principles he is following and of his reasons for doing so; he has time and opportunity to realize just why he introduces his proof in a certain way, why he selects certain evidence, why he arranges his material in accordance with a certain plan.

Furthermore, what is written can be subsequently examined for defects and virtues. In this way a student can detect his weaknesses and set himself to remedy them.

Finally, a person who is writing thinks more closely and concisely, and uses more exact language than one who is speaking, and so develops the qualities of straightforward, logical reasoning, and of clear, accurate use of words. It does not follow that a debater should write all he says, or that he should always keep up the practice of writing as a means of self-training. Study and experience gradually turn these qualities mentioned above into habits of mind, and the habits once formed are a permanent asset. But, for the debater in the formative period of his career, the regular writing of briefs and speeches is invaluable.

Lying between the two extreme methods mentioned above are two other possible methods of presentation that deserve consideration. Both are more rational than either of the other two. The first consists in writing down and memorizing speeches; the second consists in speaking from a brief or a short outline.

Considered as a method to be adopted permanently and for regular use, memorizing must undoubtedly be condemned. The most obvious defect of such a practice is the lack of adaptability to circumstances. We have already seen that a large element of debating power lies in the ability to appreciate and grapple with situations; but a speaker who has learned the sentences he is to deliver is powerless if anything unexpected arises, or if his written speech does not happen to fit the occasion. He is liable to find himself delivering a demonstrative oration instead of an argument. Again, the memoriter method involves a great physical strain. It demands the most severe mental and nervous exertion in committing the speech, in worrying over the chances of forgetting, and in delivery. So serious a strain does it require, that a continuance of such practices tends to diminish spontaneity and quickness of thought, which gradually impairs the fineness and clearness of the whole mind.

Memorizing also prevents, in a great degree, the necessary closeness of contact between speaker and audience. It demands a remarkable degree of elocutionary skill, to infuse into committed passages the variety and the spontaneity of extempore speaking. The memoriter speaker all too easily becomes an actor, posing and soliloquizing — an attitude fatal to power in debate, for it destroys the leadership which we have seen is indispensable in the work of persuasion. Then, too, all the inspiration that should come from the reflex action of the audience is lost. The declaimer, instead of being stirred and directed by any manifestations of thought or emotion on the part of his hearers, is liable to be confused by such influences, and is constantly fearful of their appearance.

It is possible to combine the memorizing method with the extemporaneous, and under some conditions the combination may be effective. The peroration of an otherwise extempore speech may often be memorized with good results. A beginner may find this a helpful means of weaning himself from declamation, and taking on the strength of extemporaneous speech. But as a permanent practice, by which the attempt is made to mix the two and deceive an audience into thinking the whole to be extempore, it is a failure. An excellent criticism is given by Dr. James M. Buckley, in his book on " Extemporaneous Oratory for Professional and Amateur Speakers " — a book to be commended to every public speaker or student of oratory : —

"A joint use of the extemporaneous and the recitative has marked advantages, and is to be commended to those who cannot trust themselves wholly to the former. But it is extremely difficult to adjust it gracefully and forcefully. Transitions of style are usually obvious, extemporized portions being spoken more swiftly or more slowly than the recited. Emphasis and accent are different, and gesticulation undergoes a noticeable change. The reciter is prone to proceed more rapidly than when he extemporizes ; at other times, according to the strength of his memory or his excitability when uttering words not previously prepared, he may speak more slowly. A lawyer delivered a Fourth of July oration, in preparation for which he had composed perhaps ten epigrams and half as many paragraphs, some consisting of at least three times that number of sentences, and had committed these to memory, expecting to extemporize the connective tissue. What he had learned he recited perfectly ; what he extemporized he delivered under slight embarrassment, and his course resembled that of a man crossing a bridge, some of the planks of which were weak and others strong. He fairly leaped when he came to one of his committed paragraphs, and it was obvious that he rejoiced in spirit, but more than once his hesitation and awkwardness were pitiable.

"The highest gift of extemporization is usually like a spirited steed, which cannot be driven double, or like a jealous maiden, who will not brook divided attention." [1]

In spite of the criticisms given above, memorizing is not an unmitigated evil for a young debater. Nearly every speaker begins his training by the reciting of declamations. He takes this means to learn

[1] Buckley, "Extemporaneous Oratory," pp. 25-26. Eaton and Mains, 1898.

the principles and form some of the habits of elocution; in this way he helps himself to overcome his diffidence and avert impending stage fright. He may make a similar use of memorizing when he first tempts the fortunes of debate. *But* he must not allow himself to forget that it is a temporary expedient. He will surely be confronted with a temptation. He may find that in these small efforts he is winning full success, and he may fear to leave this seemingly firm ground and venture into the uncertainty of extemporizing. The longer memorizing is continued, the harder it is to break from its bonds, and no ambitious beginner should allow himself to keep up the practice for any considerable length of time.

Extemporaneous oratory should undoubtedly be the ideal of a debater. A distinction should always be made between extemporaneous speaking and impromptu speaking. An impromptu speech is wholly unpremeditated: the speaker rises on the moment and talks off-hand, not having deliberated on the subject at all. But "extemporaneous," as the term is now used, is a name applied to any speech for which the language and details of rhetorical form have not been previously prepared. The speaker is always assumed to have deliberated at length on the question; and he may or may not use notes, provided the notes are not read or recited.

The advantages of this extempore method are many and great. The first advantage — and first in

z

order of importance — is the power of adaptation which it gives to the speaker. The debater who depends upon nothing but his ever present power of making up his words as he goes, can at any time omit any of his ideas or arguments that the circumstances make unnecessary; he can put into his proof anything that an unexpected turn of affairs requires; he can, if expedient, adopt a wholly new line of demonstration. Furthermore, the extemporizer can adapt himself to the mood of his audience : if he sees they do not understand a point, he can stop to explain and enforce it upon them; if they seem personally hostile or inattentive, he can resort to persuasion to remedy the situation. At all times, he can hold his position as leader of the assembly both in thought and in feeling.

Then, too, extemporizing carries with it great physical advantages. " The voice of the speaker is deeper, stronger, and more flexible, and the effort required to produce it much less. The head being held erect, there is no constriction of the throat, the lungs are fully expanded, and the respiratory muscles are free to perform their functions." [1] Again, the inspiration of sympathy from the audience comes with its full power only to the extemporizer. William Pitt truly said that " eloquence is not in the man; it is in the assembly." The response of hearer to speaker may disturb a declaimer, but it gives added strength to the

[1] Buckley, "Extemporaneous Oratory," p. 13. Eaton and Mains, 1898.

extemporizer, helping him to mount to eloquence with a greater boldness and self-confidence.

Extemporaneous speaking, with all the great benefits that flow from it, is attended with dangers. There are two that a young speaker needs particularly to guard against. The first is exaggeration. The youthful orator, to whom word and idea usually come with tantalizing difficulty, when at length he begins to feel the flow of words coming full and free to his lips, is too liable to be caught up in the onward rush and carried much farther than he intends ; swollen by the rising enthusiasm, the tide of eloquence mounts higher and higher till it sweeps over the bounds of accuracy, even of truthfulness, and turns into a flood of hyperbole. Then it is that a speaker makes statements that he is afterward forced to take back, calls his opponent bad names, and in general forgets his self-control. Lord Chatham, with all his long experience and constant practice, said that he did not dare to speak extemporaneously with a state secret lurking in his mind, " for in the Sibylline frenzy of his oratory he knew not what he said." [1] A common form of misrepresentation consists in stating evidence carelessly. If a speaker has in his mind the general nature and effect of certain facts, but has not decided just how to put them into words, he finds himself sorely tempted to color the facts with a little rhetorical flourish, to make a " few " into a " great many," to augment " a score " into " hundreds," or to transform

[1] Matthews, "Orators and Oratory," p. 109.

" often " into " always." Such exaggeration may, with constant practice, become something of a habit, so that the tendency should be repressed at the start.

A second danger is that of awkward repetition. If a speaker permits himself to become indolent in his choice of phrases, he will surely find that certain combinations of words will be constantly coming to his lips till they become tiresome. This often results in a confusion of thoughts : one stock phrase is made to represent several different ideas ; two ideas that are similar but not exactly alike are both expressed in these same hackneyed terms, simply because the speaker is too careless to know the distinction, or has formed the habit of stating things with approximate truth. This danger, of course, threatens particularly a speaker whose range of words is small; and for such a man the fault may be overcome by resorting to the dictionary, to the reading of good literature and good orations, or to any expedient for the increase of the vocabulary. The same fault appears in the awkward repetition of introductory and transitional phrases, such as : " Let us next consider," " My next point is," " In the next place," " Along this same line," etc. A speaker composing as he goes, does not realize how often these phrases are reiterated ; but it is noticeable to the audience.

Another form of the same danger lies in the fault of explaining or reasoning out everything in the same way. It is very easy to adopt a sort of logical formula in accordance with which argument after argument is unfolded. A certain mode of reasoning in his own mind is peculiar to the speaker, and when before an audience it is natural to explain the matter to others just as he explained it to himself. The effect of such repetition is much the same as that which a reader gets, from page after page of syllogisms in a treatise on formal logic. The reasoning is clear and accurate, but uninteresting and tiresome.

Such dangers as these, though they must surely be met with, should not be a source of discouragement. The dangers attendant upon other methods of public speaking are equally great and usually far more formidable. The young extemporizer to whom the beginning seems hard, may well bear in mind an example cited by Dr. Buckley from Mr. Gilchrist's "Life of Richard Cobden" : —

"I saw Richard Cobden sitting beside John Bright in the House of Commons. Perhaps no more persuasive speaker, whose power depended largely upon a clear and earnest statement of facts, has ever sat in the British Parliament. Speaking of the Treaty of Commerce with France in 1860, Mr. Gladstone six years later said, 'I don't believe that the man breathed upon earth at that epoch, or now breathes upon earth, that could have effected that great measure with the single exception of Mr. Cobden.'

"His was the triumph of the pure extemporizer. In 1864 he wrote to Mr. Delane, editor of the *London Times:* —

"'It is known that I am not in the habit of writing a word beforehand of what I speak in public. Like other speakers, practice has given me as perfect self-possession in the presence of an audience as if I were writing in my closet. Now my ever constant and overruling thought while addressing a public meeting — the only necessity which long experience of the arts of the controversialist has impressed upon my mind — is to avoid the possibility of being misrepresented, and prevent my opponents from raising a false issue, a trick as old as ARISTOTLE.'

"Yet this master persuader of hard-headed business men was nervous and confused in his first speech; in fact, he practically broke down, and the chairman had to apologize for him. For some time afterward he was so discouraged by his maiden effort that if he had been allowed to follow the bent of his inclination, he would never again have appeared as a public speaker."[1]

We have said that in extemporaneous oratory a speaker may or may not use notes, provided the notes are neither read nor recited. For a beginner in any kind of oratory it is desirable that some notes be used. It takes a mature mind and much experience, to enable a man to carry the complete outline of a speech, in such a way as to guard against the forgetting of points, on the one hand, and wandering from the subject, on the other. And particularly in debate, where the situation is ever changing and where so much depends upon the circumstances of the moment, it is doubtful if even a veteran can work effectively without notes.

Undoubtedly a brief is the best form of notes in debate. It presents to the speaker's eye, more clearly

[1] Buckley, "Extemporaneous Oratory," pp. 369–370. Eaton and Mains, 1898.

than any other kind of outline, the relation and the sequence of proofs as they should be set forth, and so helps to create a good logical and rhetorical framework. The numbering and lettering of a well-made brief also enable a debater to gather more from a single glance at the paper, than he could from notes made in any other form. He can "find his place" more easily, and see more quickly what point of the proof he has reached.

However, it should be understood that the use of a brief, as that word is used in Chapter IX, is not to be recommended. As the term "brief" is used there, it means an outline into which are put all the details of arguments, evidence, and explanation of the question. To use such an outline is more of the nature of reading than of extemporizing, and is open to many of the serious objections against the reading method. The outline for use in debate should be much shorter, containing little more than, perhaps, the issues, the main headings, a few important subheadings, and notes for refutation. To use a more extended form of notes is to sacrifice the virtues of the extemporaneous method.

VI. Refutation

With respect to refutation, aside from the work of preparation which has already been discussed, the first and foremost of all precepts for the beginner to take to heart, and for every debater, however experienced, always to remember, is : —

A. *Answer the whole case of the other side.* One of the fatal weaknesses in the power of any debater, and a weakness that is almost invariably displayed by a beginner, is the weakness of attacking only a part of an opponent's proof. It is easiest in refutation to pick out the weak points of the opposition and attack them, leaving the more formidable points standing: it demands less careful preparation, and a less accurate analysis of the case of the other side; and it often seems to make the greatest impression on the audience. Consequently there is a temptation to pick up the more obvious errors of an opponent and dramatically expose them, or to seize upon some foolish word or phrase and ridicule it; it creates a laugh or a burst of applause, whereas, in an attempt to refute any of the stronger proofs, success is not so easy, for the audience, feeling that there are two sides to the issue, are not so readily convinced. But in the end, the audience will adhere to the man who has made them believe that his case, as a whole, is the stronger. Consequently, to achieve final success, the debater must make them see, not that he has destroyed an argument here and there, but that he has overwhelmed the proof against him, in its entirety.

In order to make such an attack upon the whole case of the other side, two things are necessary: (1) the speaker must analyze the entire proof of his opponents and pick out the few fundamental points in it, and (2) he must make it clear to the audience that he is thus meeting the whole of the case against him.

It is necessary to determine upon the few fundamental points of an opponent's proof, for the same reason that it is necessary to determine upon those of one's own. It is necessary for the sake of clearness: to give the same attention to the large and the small points of the other side perplexes a hearer in his understanding of the question as a whole. It is necessary for the sake of emphasis: it is only by neglecting or slighting trivial facts and dwelling upon the important ones, that the vital points of the question can be brought out into a clear light. Furthermore, to give attention to the facts of secondary importance is a waste of time. If the main headings of an opponent's brief are destroyed, his subheadings fall with them and so do not need special rebuttal. These main headings must be answered if an opponent is to be defeated at all, and, if they are answered, to do more is superfluous.

But it is not enough merely to pick out in one's own mind the important points of the other side, and proceed to refute them. To give the rebuttal its full effect requires that the audience be made to see that the speaker is attacking the entire proof in opposition, and that, if he is successful, he has won his case. To do this requires that the arguments to be answered shall be stated clearly beforehand, and that they shall be explained in such a way as to make it evident that in them is contained the whole case of the other side.

For example, Webster, in his Reply to Hayne in the debate on the Foote Resolution, devoted the body of his speech to the refutation of Senator Hayne's theory of states' rights under the Constitution. Before entering on this task, he set forth in full the case presented by Senator Hayne, stating all the essential propositions of his doctrine, and making it evident that taken together they embraced everything that demanded refutation : —

" There yet remains to be performed by far the most grave and important duty, which I feel to be devolved on me by this occasion. It is to state, and to defend, what I conceive to be the true principles of the constitution under which we are here assembled. I might well have desired that so weighty a task should have fallen into other and abler hands. I could have wished that it should have been executed by those whose character and experience give weight and influence to their opinions, such as cannot possibly belong to mine. But, sir, I have met the occasion, not sought it ; and I shall proceed to state my own sentiments, without challenging for them any particular regard, with studied plainness, and as much precision as possible.

" I understand the honorable gentleman from South Carolina to maintain, that it is a right of the State Legislatures to interfere, whenever, in their judgment, this Government transcends its constitutional limits, and to arrest the operation of its laws.

" I understand him to maintain this right, as a right existing under the constitution ; not as a right to overthrow it, on the ground of extreme necessity, such as would justify violent revolution.

" I understand him to maintain an authority, on the part of the States, thus to interfere, for the purpose of correcting the exercise of power by the General Government, of checking it, and of compelling it to conform to their opinion of the extent of its powers.

" I understand him to maintain that the ultimate power of judging of the constitutional extent of its own authority is not lodged exclusively in the General Government, or any branch of it; but that, on the contrary, the States may lawfully decide for themselves, and each State for itself, whether, in a given case, the act of the General Government transcends its power.

" I understand him to insist that, if the exigency of the case, in the opinion of any State Government, require it, such State Government may, by its own sovereign authority, annul an act of the General Government, which it deems plainly and palpably unconstitutional."[1]

It is often desirable, as a means of making it evident that the whole case of the other side is being attacked, to analyze openly the proof of an opponent and explain just what his arguments as a whole amount to. For example, a speaker in rebuttal might well begin in some such manner as this : " Everything of any importance that my opponent has tried to prove in this question may be reduced to these three propositions, viz., first, etc., second, etc., third ; " " my opponent's case, as far as it has any bearing on the question we have in hand, can be stated in his own words, as follows," etc. In some such way the audience may be made to have faith in the speaker's

[1] Congressional Debates, Vol. VI, Part I, pp. 72–73. Gales and Seaton, 1830.

sincerity, and in the importance of his efforts in rebuttal, and so be made ready to acknowledge the full
force of his refutation.

B. The natural tendency of young debaters in refutation is toward carelessness of method. It is true,
even of more experienced men, that speakers who
are very careful in arranging and presenting their
original proofs, when they come to the work of refutation, forget themselves and degenerate into a weak
informality, wandering from the point and mixing up
their materials without regard for clearness of statement, the proper arrangement of evidence, or the
natural sequence of the proofs. Refutation is no
more informal than any other kind of demonstration,
and requires just as much care in presentation. The
materials for it must be selected as judiciously,
arranged as logically, and stated as clearly. A
young debater does well to watch himself consciously
till he has formed firm habits of the right kind.

C. It has already been suggested that it is well in
a debate where a man may speak more than once to
hold material in reserve for rebuttal. It is, of course,
possible to repeat or refer to arguments and evidence
already given. But the repetition of old materials is
never quite so strong as the production of new. So
that it is often good strategy, even at the cost of
taking something away from the strength of a first
speech, to hold back some evidence and a few good
arguments as a reserve.

D. Refutation is not treated more fully in this

chapter, not because it is less important, but because
it has been sufficiently discussed in a previous chapter. Refutation is the very essence of debate, and
the power to refute well is one to be sought by a
debater as earnestly as he would seek any single
power that a public speaker may hope to possess.

VII. Practice

"If you want to be a good public speaker, whenever any one is fool enough to ask you to speak, you
be fool enough to do it." Such was the advice of a
friend to Edward Everett Hale at the opening of his
career. There is a wealth of wisdom in the words.
Many of the essential qualities of a good debater can
be acquired in one way only —*practice*. As well might
the athlete hope to become a winner in the race by
poring over athletic treatises, as the student to become a debater by merely studying the principles of
argumentation and practising with the pen. Self-
confidence, the ability to take advantage of peculiar
circumstances, the self-control that is necessary to
the control of others, that indefinable power of fusing
into one the mind of speaker and hearer, — these
come only from the industrious, continued effort on
the public platform which is well summed up in the
one word —*practice*.

APPENDIX A

THE following suggestions are appended in the hope that they may be helpful to teachers, especially to those who are introducing courses in argumentation and debate.

Length of Course.

Two hours per week for one year has been found a very convenient length for a course of this kind. The length, however, may easily be varied according to the inclination of the instructor and the time at his disposal.

Division of the Course.

The first part of the course, preferably one semester, should be given to the study of the principles of argumentation, with the use of text-book, supplemented by lectures and various written exercises (see Appendix B). The second semester may be given entirely to oral debate with the requisite written preparation.

Subjects for Debate.

A method of securing a list of live subjects for use in debate, which has proved practicable, is to have each student bring into class a list of three or four subjects, properly stated in the form of propositions, and from all the lists for the instructor to select and post on the bulletin board those from which the students may choose for their work in brief-drawing, for the writing of forensics, or for debate.

Incidental Suggestions.

The plan of scheduling men for debates, and the arrangements to be followed in presenting briefs for the criticism of the instructor, must be worked out according to the conditions at a given place and time.

It is very desirable that each man on a given debate have an opportunity to speak, not only in positive proof, but also in rebuttal; and also that a chance be offered to the members of the class to discuss the question from the floor.

As to whether the debaters should speak from a completely written forensic or from a brief, there is a great difference of opinion; but, after years of experiment and observation, the writers of this book are fully convinced that, for most men, debating from a brief is the better method. The very nature of debate seems to call for this. There must be spontaneity, a great readiness to take advantage of a peculiar situation, and an assurance of meeting squarely the opponents. But all this seems hardly possible when the debate has been fully written beforehand. It is, however, fully recognized that no absolute method can be suggested that will fit every case, but the instructor can readily modify his method to make it applicable to exceptional men.

A student "critic" of a given debate, or a board of award appointed from the class by the instructor, or a vote of the class as to who are the winners, may be introduced occasionally, with mutual benefit.

The practice of asking the debater questions while he is doing his work, whenever there is any doubt regarding the point he is trying to make, has a most enlivening and invigorating influence on the whole class.

APPENDIX B

BELOW are given a number of suggestions for exercises that may be used in connection with the text, while the class is studying the principles of argumentation.

SUGGESTIONS FOR EXERCISES

The Proposition.

It is by no means an easy task to persuade a class of beginners in argumentation that the statement of the proposition is particularly important. The mere declaration that such is the case will not suffice. One way that has been of great help in emphasizing this fact is as follows: Each man in class is asked to write out a proposition; then he is, in turn, called upon to read aloud his proposition, which is freely criticised by students and instructor. In this way each one receives benefit from the experience of all the rest.

The student may then be asked to bring, at the next session, a written definition of all terms in his proposition that would need to be defined before he could proceed to his argument.

The Issues.

The very best exercise in this connection is the analysis of argumentative masterpieces — preferably legal addresses — and the presenting, in written form, of a careful statement of the issues involved in the discussion. This may be followed by practice for the student in stating the issues

on assigned subjects, and by a careful explanation of the
processes of finding the issues, by the instructor.

Evidence.

Before the student is prepared to decide intelligently
what kinds of evidence he would better use in a given case,
or to test thoroughly either his own evidence or that of
an opponent, he will probably find it necessary to study
the methods of the great arguers and learn what are their
methods. The only practicable way to do this is to take
the speeches themselves and analyze them carefully with
this end in view. In John Churton Collins's " Swift's Relationship to Stella," as found in J. H. Gardiner's " The
Forms of Prose Literature," will be found an excellent
selection, to be used especially in illustrating the various
tests that may be applied to evidence.

Arguments.

The attempt to understand the distinctions between the
different kinds of arguments has often proved to be the
point of discouragement to the student. If each student
is asked to bring into class an example of the argument
from antecedent probability, example, and sign, and he
is there met by open discussion and patient explanation,
there is little danger of his discouragement becoming
permanent.

Brief-drawing.

The whole work in the principles of argumentation finds
its centre in brief-drawing. The importance of study and
practice at this point cannot be overemphasized.

An exercise that has proved most elucidating is this:
After the student has been over the text and secured a
more or less vague idea of what it is to draw a brief, the
instructor will take a simple question and put it on the

blackboard, developing the brief before the class, with full opportunity for questions and suggestions. He will probably find it best to confine his work, — one day to the introduction, and the next to the discussion. The conclusion of the brief presents no serious difficulty.

The drawing of briefs from speeches, and the writing of briefs on assigned subjects, will of course be given in such measure as the length of the course will permit.

In order to show the importance of a brief in argumentative composition, it is sometimes desirable to have the students write a complete argument — forensic — before they take up the subject of brief-drawing; then, after it has been taken up, write another forensic from the brief on the same subject, and make a comparison of the first and second forensics.

When students present briefs in class, it is often advisable to have them exchange papers with each other, and criticise each other's work, marking their suggestions on the manuscript. A man often gets a better idea of what is correct or incorrect by reading another's work than by reading his own.

For practice in drawing briefs, almost any of the better argumentative productions furnish excellent materials, and one selection worthy of particular recommendation for this purpose is " Swift's Relationship to Stella," mentioned above.

Presentation.

In addition to what has been made clear in the text, exercises are necessary to emphasize the importance, in the finished argument, of the introduction and the conclusion. It is a very common fault for students to slight one or both of these parts. The instructor, stating a simple proposition, might say: " Imagine certain conditions under which you are to speak on this question, and write an introduction of three hundred words, more or less, to fit the circumstances." "How would you modify your introduction if the audience were opposed to you?" "What change would you make if you learned that your audience would be composed of working men?" etc. The same procedure might be followed with the conclusion, the method of treatment being decided according to the attitude of the audience, the turn of the discussion, or the special end sought.

On the days when finished arguments are to be brought into class, some such list of questions as the following may be given to the students, according to which each man is to criticise the forensic of his neighbor.

CRITICISM OF FORENSIC

Introduction.

   A. Are the definitions clear and conclusive?

      1. Are there any terms left undefined that call for definition?

   B. Are the processes of finding the issues properly followed?

      1. Are the issues stated clearly?

      2. Could the issues be stated more narrowly?

   C. Is the partition properly made?

   D. Is the introduction phrased so as to arouse interest?

Discussion.

   A. Is the connection between the main points and the proposition made perfectly apparent?

   B. Is the arrangement in any way defective?

   C. Are there well-managed transitions?

   D. Is the English clear and forcible?

   E. In reading the forensic, do you get a clear idea of the whole argument?

Conclusion.

A. Is the conclusion clear, brief, and forcible ?
B. Is the summary sufficient ?
C. Does persuasion play a proper part in the conclusion ?

The above suggestions are considered neither exclusive nor inclusive. They are merely given as *some* of the exercises that have proved useful to students and instructors during six or eight years of experience in college work.

INDEX

Addison's Sir Roger de Coverley. Edited by ZELMA GRAY, East Side High School, Saginaw, Mich.

Browning's Shorter Poems. Edited by FRANKLIN T. BAKER, Teachers' College, New York.

Browning, Mrs., Poems (Selected). By Miss HERSEY, Boston, Mass.

Burke's Speech on Conciliation. Edited by S. C. NEWSOM, Manual Training High School, Indianapolis, Ind.

Byron's Childe Harold. Edited by A. J. GEORGE, High School, Newton, Mass.

Byron's Shorter Poems. Edited by RALPH H. BOWLES, A.M., Instructor in English in the Phillips Exeter Academy, Exeter, N. H.

Carlyle's Essay on Burns, with Selections. Edited by WILLARD C. GORE, Armour Institute, Chicago, Ill.

Chaucer's Prologue to the Book of the Tales of Canterbury, the Knight's Tale, and the Nun's Priest's Tale. Edited by ANDREW INGRAHAM, Late Headmaster of the Swain Free School, New Bedford, Mass.

Coleridge's The Ancient Mariner. Edited by T. F. HUNTINGTON, Leland Stanford University.

Cooper's Last of the Mohicans. Edited by W. K. WICKES, Principal of High School, Syracuse, N. Y.

Cooper's The Deerslayer.

De Quincey's Confessions of an English Opium Eater. Edited by ARTHUR BEATTY, University of Wisconsin.

Dryden's Palamon and Arcite. Edited by PERCIVAL CHUBB, Vice Principal Ethical Culture Schools, New York.

Early American Orations, 1760–1824. Edited by LOUIE R. HELLER, Instructor in English in the De Witt Clinton High School, New York City.

Epoch-making Papers in United States History. Edited by MARSHALL S. BROWN, Professor of History, New York University.

Franklin's Autobiography.

George Eliot's Silas Marner. Edited by E. L. GULICK, Lawrenceville School, Lawrenceville, N. J.

Goldsmith's Vicar of Wakefield. Edited by H. W. BOYNTON, Phillips Academy, Andover, Mass.

Hawthorne's Twice Told Tales. By C. R. GASTON, Richmond Hill High School, Borough of Queens, New York City.

Irving's Alhambra. Edited by ALFRED M. HITCHCOCK, Hartford Public High School, Conn.

Irving's Life of Goldsmith. Edited by GILBERT S. BLAKELY, A.M., Teacher of English in the Morris High School, New York City.

Irving's Sketch Book.

John Woolman's Journal.

Longfellow's Evangeline. Edited by LEWIS B. SEMPLE, Commercial High School, Brooklyn.

Lowell's Vision of Sir Launfal. Edited by HERBERT E. BATES, Manual Training High School, Brooklyn, N. Y.

Macaulay's Essay on Addison. Edited by C. W. FRENCH, Principal of Hyde Park High School, Chicago, Ill.

Macaulay's Essay on Clive. Edited by J. W. PEARCE, Assistant Professor of English in Tulane University.

Macaulay's Essay on Milton. Edited by C. W. FRENCH.

Macaulay's Essay on Warren Hastings. Edited by Mrs. M. J. FRICK, Los Angeles, Cal.

Milton's Comus, Lycidas, and Other Poems. Edited by ANDREW J. GEORGE, Newton, Mass.

Milton's Paradise Lost. Books I and II. Edited by W. I. CRANE, Steele High School, Dayton, O.

Poe's Prose Tales (Selections from).

Pope's Homer's Iliad. Edited by ALBERT SMYTH, Head Professor of English Language and Literature, Central High School, Philadelphia, Pa.

Ruskin's Sesame and Lilies, and King of the Golden River. Edited by HERBERT E. BATES, Manual Training High School, Brooklyn, N. Y.

Scott's Ivanhoe. Edited by ALFRED M. HITCHCOCK, Hartford Public High School, Conn.

Scott's Lady of the Lake. Edited by ELIZABETH A. PACKARD, Oakland, Cal.

Scott's Marmion. Edited by GEORGE B. AITON, State Inspector of High Schools for Minnesota.

Shakespeare's As You Like It. Edited by CHARLES ROBERT GASTON, Teacher of English, Richmond Hill High School, Queens Borough, New York City.

Shakespeare's Hamlet. Edited by L. A. SHERMAN, Professor of English in the University of Nebraska.

Shakespeare's Julius Cæsar. Edited by GEORGE W. HUFFORD and LOIS G. HUFFORD, High School, Indianapolis, Ind.

Shakespeare's Macbeth. Edited by C. W. FRENCH, Hyde Park High School.

Shakespeare's Merchant of Venice. Edited by CHARLOTTE W. UNDERWOOD, Lewis Institute, Chicago, Ill.

Shelley and Keats (Selections from). Edited by S. C. NEWSOM, Manual Training High School, Indianapolis, Ind.

Southern Poets. Edited by W. L. WEBER, Professor of English Literature in Emory College, Oxford, Ga.

Spenser's Faerie Queene. Book I. Edited by GEORGE A. WAUCHOPE, M.A., Professor of English in the South Carolina College.

Stevenson's Treasure Island. Edited by HIRAM ALBERT VANCE, Ph.D. (Jena), Professor of English in the University of Nashville.

Tennyson's The Princess. Edited by WILSON FARRAND, Newark Academy, Newark, N. J.

Tennyson's Idylls of the King. Edited by W. T. VLYMEN, Principal of Eastern District High School, Brooklyn, N. Y.

Tennyson's Shorter Poems. Edited by CHARLES R. NUTTER, A.B., Instructor in English at Harvard University.

Wordsworth's Shorter Poems. Selections. Edited by EDWARD FULTON, Ph.D., Assistant Professor of Rhetoric in the University of Illinois.

THE MACMILLAN COMPANY

66 FIFTH AVENUE, NEW YORK